Creative Beading

VOL. 13

Beading

The best projects from a year of *Bead&Button* magazine

KB
KALMBACH BOOKS

Waukesha, Wisconsin

Kalmbach Books
21027 Crossroads Circle
Waukesha, Wisconsin 53186
www.JewelryAndBeadingStore.com

Published in 2018
22 21 20 19 18   1 2 3 4 5

Manufactured in China

ISBN: 978-1-62700-517-3
EISBN: 978-1-62700-518-0

The material in this book has appeared previously in *Bead&Button* magazine. Bead&Button is registered as a trademark.

Editor: Erica Barse
Book Design: Lisa Bergman
Illustrator: Kellie Jaeger
Photographer: William Zuback

Publisher's Cataloging-In-Publication Data

Creative beading : the best projects from a year of Bead&Button magazine.

v. : ill.

Annual
Vol. [1] (2006)-
Description based on: vol. 7 (2012).
Latest issue consulted: vol. 7 (2012).
Material in each volume appeared in the previous year's issues of Bead&Button magazine.
Includes index.

1. Beadwork—Periodicals. 2. Beads—Periodicals. 3. Jewelry making—Periodicals. I. Kalmbach Publishing Company. II. Title: Bead&Button magazine.

TT860 .C743
745.594/2

Contents

22

36

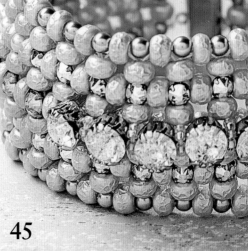

45

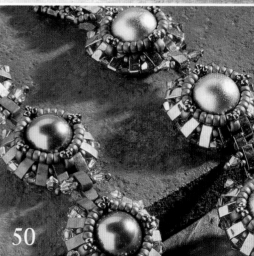

50

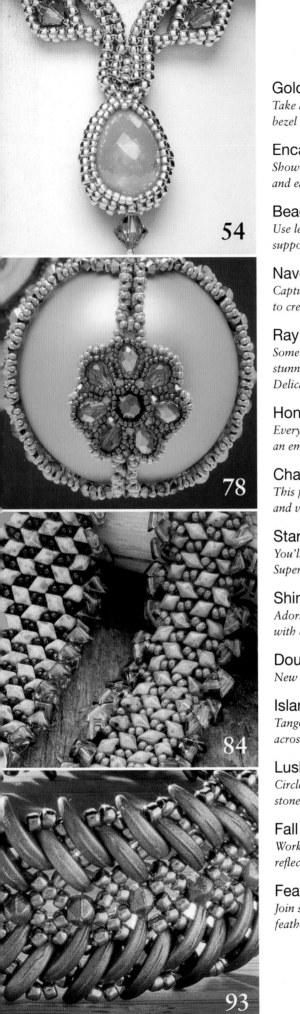

104

113

122

124

MULTI-STITCH PROJECTS

162

166

180

189

OTHER TECHNIQUES

203

206

214

218

Introduction

Welcome to *Creative Beading, Volume 13*. The latest collection of projects from a year of *Bead&Button* magazine, this edition features gorgeous pieces by beaders from around the world. We're proud to present these talented designers and thank them for advancing the art of beading and generously sharing their new ideas and visions with the beading and jewelry-making communities.

Inside you'll find wonderfully creative projects made using your favorite stitches, including herringbone, peyote, and right-angle weave. A wide array of necklaces, pendants, earrings, bracelets, ornaments, and more will bring you endless hours of creativity and relaxation as you enjoy your favorite pastime. With 65+ fresh designs, you'll find something to love in this collection, no matter your taste or skill level. And whether you enjoy working with traditional materials, such as seed beads, crystals, and pearls, or you prefer using the very latest multi-hole shaped beads available on the market today, these designs will inspire and delight as you make, wear, and love them.

Each project within these pages is fully illustrated and tested by our editors to ensure beading success. If you need extra guidance or want to brush up on your skills, visit our website, FacetJewelry.com, for beading basics, helpful tips, sourcing information, how-to videos, and much more.

I hope these projects will inspire your creativity now and in the future.

Happy beading!

Julia Gerlach

Julia Gerlach
Editor, *Bead&Button*

Tools & Materials

Excellent tools and materials for making jewelry are available in bead and craft stores, through catalogs, and on the Internet. Here are the essential supplies you'll need for the projects in this book.

TOOLS

Chainnose pliers have smooth, flat inner jaws, and the tips taper to a point. Use them for gripping, bending wire, and for opening and closing loops and jump rings.

Roundnose pliers have smooth, tapered, conical jaws used to make loops. The closer to the tip you work, the smaller the loop will be.

Use the front of a **wire cutters'** blades to make a pointed cut and the back of the blades to make a flat cut. Do not use your jewelry-grade wire cutters on memory wire, which is extremely hard; use heavy-duty wire cutters, or bend the memory wire back and forth until it breaks.

Crimping pliers have two grooves in their jaws that are used to fold and roll a crimp tube into a compact shape.

Make it easier to open split rings by inserting the curved jaw of **split-ring pliers** between the wires.

Beading needles are coded by size. The higher the number, the finer the beading needle. Unlike sewing needles, the eye of a beading needle is almost as narrow as its shaft. In addition to the size of the bead, the number of times you will pass through the bead also affects the needle size that you will use; if you will pass through a bead multiple times, you need to use a thinner needle.

A **hammer** is used to harden wire or texture metal. Any hammer with a flat face will work, as long as the face is free of nicks that could mar your metal. The light ball-peen hammer shown here is one of the most commonly used hammers for jewelry making.

A **bench block** provides a hard, smooth surface on which to hammer wire and metal pieces. An anvil is similarly hard but has different surfaces, such as a tapered horn, to help form different shapes.

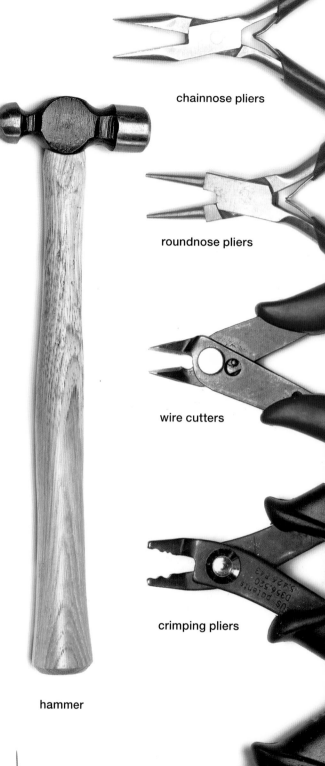

chainnose pliers

roundnose pliers

wire cutters

crimping pliers

hammer

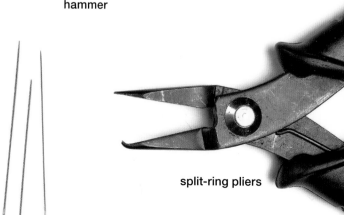

split-ring pliers

beading needles

bench block

Tools & Materials

head pin

eye pin

jump rings

split ring

crimp beads and tubes

clasps

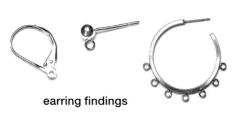

earring findings

FINDINGS

A **head pin** looks like a long, blunt, thick sewing pin. It has a flat or decorative head on one end to keep beads on. Head pins come in different diameters (gauges) and lengths.

Eye pins are just like head pins except they have a round loop on one end instead of a head. You can make your own eye pins from wire.

A **jump ring** is used to connect components. It is a small wire circle or oval that is either soldered closed or comes with a cut so it can be opened and closed.

Split rings are used like jump rings but are much more secure. They look like tiny key rings and are made of springy wire.

Crimp beads and tubes are small, large-holed, thin-walled metal beads designed to be flattened or crimped into a tight roll. Use them when stringing jewelry on flexible beading wire.

Clasps come in many sizes and shapes. Some of the most common (clockwise from the top left) are the toggle, consisting of a ring and a bar; slide, consisting of one tube that slides inside another; lobster claw, which opens when you pull on a tiny lever; S-hook, which links two soldered jump rings or split rings; and box, with a tab and a slot.

Earring findings come in a huge variety of metals and styles, including (from left to right) lever back, post, hoop, and French hook. You will almost always want a loop (or loops) on earring findings so you can attach beads.

WIRE

Wire is available in a number of materials and finishes, including brass, gold, gold-filled, gold-plated, fine silver, sterling silver, anodized niobium (chemically colored wire), and copper. Brass, copper, and craft wire are packaged in 10- to 40-yd. (9.1–37 m) spools, while gold, silver, and niobium are sold by the foot or ounce. Wire thickness is measured by gauge—the higher the gauge number, the thinner the wire. It is available in varying hardnesses (dead-soft, half-hard, and hard) and shapes (round, half-round, square, and others).

STITCHING & STRINGING MATERIALS

Selecting beading thread and cord is one of the most important decisions you'll make when planning a project. Review the descriptions below to evaluate which material is best for your design.

Threads come in many sizes and strengths. Size (diameter or thickness) is designated by a letter or number. OO and A/O are the thinnest; B, D, E, F, and FF are subsequently thicker. **Cord** is measured on a number scale; 0 corresponds in thickness to D-size thread, 1 equals E, 2 equals F, and 3 equals FF.

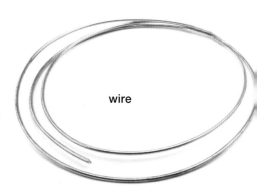

wire

Parallel filament nylon, such as Nymo or C-Lon, is made from many thin nylon fibers that are extruded and heat-set to form a single-ply thread. Parallel filament nylon is durable and easy to thread, but it can be prone to fraying and stretching. It is best used in beadweaving and bead embroidery.

Plied nylon thread, such as Silamide, is made from two or more nylon threads that are extruded, twisted together, and coated or bonded for further strength, making them strong and durable. It is more resistant to fraying than parallel filament nylon, and some brands do not stretch. It's a good material to use for twisted fringe, bead crochet, and beadwork that needs a lot of body.

Plied gel-spun polyethylene (GSP), such as Power Pro or DandyLine, is made from polyethylene fibers that have been spun into two or more threads that are braided together. It is almost unbreakable, it doesn't stretch, and it resists fraying. The thickness can make it difficult to make multiple passes through a bead. It is ideal for stitching with larger beads, such as pressed glass and crystals.

Parallel filament GSP, such as Fireline, is a single-ply thread made from spun and bonded polyethylene fibers. It's extremely strong, it doesn't stretch, and it resists fraying. However, crystals may cut through parallel filament GSP, and smoke-colored varieties can leave a black residue on hands and beads. It's most appropriate for bead stitching.

Polyester thread, such as Gutermann, is made from polyester fibers that are spun into single yarns and then twisted into plied thread. It doesn't stretch and comes in many colors, but it can become fuzzy with use. It is best for bead crochet or bead embroidery when the thread must match the fabric.

Flexible beading wire is composed of wires twisted together and covered with nylon. This wire is stronger than thread and does not stretch. The higher the number of inner strands (between 3 and 49), the more flexible and kink-resistant the wire. It is available in a variety of sizes. Use .014 and .015 for stringing most gemstones, crystals, and glass beads. Use thicker varieties, .018, .019, and .024, for heavy beads or nuggets. Use thinner wire, .010 and .012, for lightweight pieces and beads with very small holes, such as pearls. The thinnest wires can also be used for some bead-stitching projects.

flexible beading wire

nylon threads

parallel filament GSP

Tools & Materials

seed beads

SEED BEADS

A huge variety of beads is available, but the beads most commonly used in the projects in this book are **seed beads**. Seed beads come in packages, tubes, and hanks. A standard hank (a looped bundle of beads strung on thread) contains 12 20-in. (51 cm) strands, but vintage hanks are often much smaller. Tubes and packages are usually measured in grams and vary in size.

Seed beads have been manufactured in many sizes ranging from the largest, 5º (also called "E beads"), which are about 5 mm wide, to tiny size 20º or 22º, which aren't much larger than grains of sand. (The symbol º stands for "aught" or "zero." The greater the number of aughts, e.g., 22º, the smaller the bead.) Beads smaller than Japanese 15ºs have not been produced for the past 100 years, but vintage beads can be found in limited sizes and colors. The most commonly available size in the widest range of colors is 11º.

Most round seed beads are made in Japan and the Czech Republic. **Czech seed beads** are slightly irregular and rounder than **Japanese seed beads**, which are uniform in size and a bit squared off. Czech beads give a bumpier surface when woven, but they reflect light at a wider range of angles. Japanese seed beads produce a uniform surface

and texture. Japanese and Czech seed beads can be used together, but a Japanese seed bead is slightly larger than the same size Czech seed bead.

Seed beads also come in sparkly cut versions. Japanese **hex-cut** or hex beads are formed with six sides. **2-** or **3-cut** Czech beads are less regular. **Charlottes** have an irregular facet cut on one side of the bead.

Japanese **cylinder beads**, otherwise known as Delicas (the Miyuki brand name), Toho Treasures (the brand name of Toho), and Toho Aikos, are extremely popular for peyote stitch projects. These beads are very regular and have large holes, which are useful for stitches requiring multiple thread passes. The beads fit together almost seamlessly, producing a smooth, fabric-like surface.

Bugle beads are thin glass tubes. They can be sized by number or length, depending on where they are made. Japanese size 1 bugles are about 2 mm long, but bugles can be made even longer than 30 mm. They can be hex-cut, straight, or twisted, but the selection of colors, sizes, shapes, and finishes is limited. Seed beads also come in a variety of other shapes, including **triangles, cubes,** and **drops**.

In stitches where the beads meet each other end to end or side by side — peyote stitch, brick stitch, and square stitch — try using Japanese cylinder beads to achieve a smooth, flat surface. For a more textured surface, use Czech or round Japanese seed beads. For right-angle weave, in which groups of four or more beads form circular stitches, the rounder the seed bead, the better; otherwise you risk having gaps. Round seed beads also are better for netting and strung jewelry.

cube beads

triangle beads

drop beads

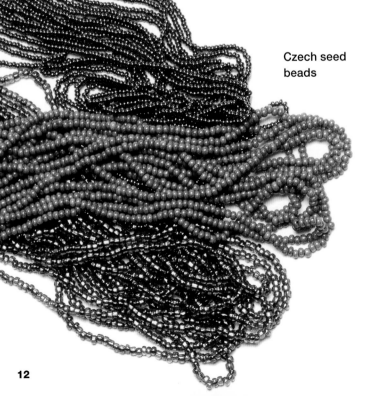

Czech seed beads

twisted bugle beads

hex-cut beads

Basics

THREAD AND KNOTS

Adding thread

To add a thread, sew into the beadwork several rows or rounds prior to the point where the last bead was added, leaving a short tail. Follow the thread path of the stitch, tying a few half-hitch knots (see "Half-hitch knot") between beads as you go, and exit where the last stitch ended. Trim the short tail.

Conditioning thread

Use beeswax or microcrystalline wax (not candle wax or paraffin) or Thread Heaven to condition nylon beading thread and Fireline. Wax smooths nylon fibers and adds tackiness that will stiffen your beadwork slightly. Thread Heaven adds a static charge that causes the thread to repel itself, so don't use it with doubled thread. Both conditioners help thread resist wear. To condition, stretch nylon thread to remove the curl (Fireline doesn't stretch). Lay the thread or Fireline on top of the conditioner, hold it in place with your thumb or finger, and pull the thread through the conditioner.

Ending thread

To end a thread, sew back through the last few rows or rounds of beadwork, following the thread path of the stitch and tying two or three half-hitch knots (see "Half-hitch knot") between beads as you go. Sew through a few beads after the last knot, and trim the thread.

Half-hitch knot

Pass the needle under the thread bridge between two beads, and pull gently until a loop forms. Cross back over the thread between the beads, sew through the loop, and pull gently to draw the knot into the beadwork.

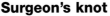

Overhand knot

Make a loop with the thread. Pull the tail through the loop, and tighten.

Square knot

[1] Cross one end of the thread over and under the other end. Pull both ends to tighten the first half of the knot.
[2] Cross the first end of the thread over and under the other end. Pull both ends to tighten the knot.

Stop bead

Use a stop bead to secure beads temporarily when you begin stitching. Choose a bead that is different from the beads in your project. Pick up the stop bead, leaving the desired-length tail. Sew through the stop bead again in the same direction, making sure you don't split the thread. If desired, sew through it one more time for added security.

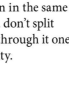

Surgeon's knot

[1] Cross one end of the thread over and under the other twice. Pull both ends to tighten the first half of the knot.
[2] Cross the first end of the thread over and under the other end. Pull both ends to tighten the knot.

Crochet

Slip knot and chain stitch

[1] Make a slip knot: Leaving the desired length tail, make a loop in the cord, crossing the spool end over the tail. Insert the hook in the loop, yarn over, and pull the cord through the loop.
[2] Yarn over the hook, and draw through the loop. Repeat this step for the desired number of chain stitches.

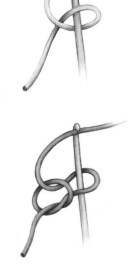

Beaded backstitch

To stitch a line of beads, come up through the fabric from the wrong side, and pick up three beads. Place the thread where the beads will go, and sew through the fabric right after the third bead. Come up between the second and third beads, and go through the third bead again. Pick up three more beads, and repeat. For a tighter stitch, pick up only one or two beads at a time.

Basics

Brick stitch

[1] To work the typical method, which results in progressively decreasing rows, work the first row in ladder stitch (see "Ladder stitch") to the desired length, exiting the top of the last bead added.

[2] Pick up two beads, sew under the thread bridge between the second and third beads in the previous

row, and sew back up through the second bead added. To secure this first stitch, sew down through the first bead and back up through the second bead.

[3] For the remaining stitches in the row, pick up one bead per stitch, sew under the thread bridge between the next

two beads in the previous row, and sew back up through the new bead. The last stitch in the new row will be centered above the last two beads in the previous row, and the new row will be one bead shorter than the previous row.

Increasing

To increase at the start of the row, repeat step 1 above, then repeat step 2, but sew

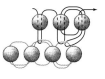

under the thread bridge between the first and second beads in the previous row. To increase at the end of the row, work two stitches off of the thread bridge between the last two beads in the previous row.

Tubular

[1] Begin with a ladder of beads, and join the ends to form a ring (see "Ladder stitch: Forming a ring"). Position the thread to exit the top of a bead.

[2] Following the instructions for flat brick stitch, pick up two beads to begin the row. Stitch around the ring in brick stitch.

[3] Join the first and last beads of the round by sewing down through the first bead and up through the last bead.

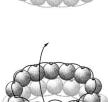

Herringbone stitch
Flat

[1] Work the first row in ladder stitch (see "Ladder stitch") to the desired length, exiting the top of an end bead in the ladder.

[2] Pick up two beads, and sew down through the next bead in the previous row (a–b). Sew up through the following bead in the previous row, pick up two beads, and sew down through the next bead (b–c). Repeat across the first row.

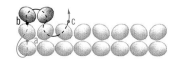

[3] To turn to start the next row, sew down through the end bead in the previous row and back through the last bead of the pair just added (a–b). Pick up two beads, sew down through the next bead in the previous row, and sew up through the following bead (b–c). Continue adding pairs of beads across the row.

Tubular

[1] Work a row of ladder stitch (see "Ladder stitch") to the desired length using an even number of beads. Form it into a ring to create the first round (see "Ladder stitch: Forming a ring"). Your thread should exit the top of a bead.

[2] Pick up two beads, sew down through the next bead in the previous round (a–b), and sew up through the following bead. Repeat to complete the round (b–c).

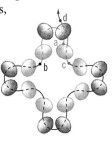

[3] You will need to step up to start the next round. Sew up through two beads — the next bead in the previous round and the first bead added in the new round (c–d).

[4] Continue adding two beads per stitch. As you work, snug up the beads to form a tube, and step up at the end of each round until your rope is the desired length.

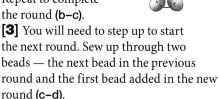

Twisted tubular

[1] Work a ladder and two rounds of tubular herringbone as explained above.

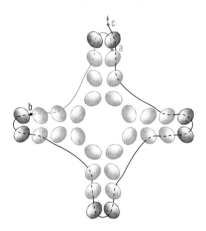

[2] To create a twist in the tube, pick up two beads, sew down through one bead in the next stack, then sew up through two beads in the following stack (a–b). Repeat around, adding two beads per stitch. Step up to the next round through three beads (b–c). Snug up the beads. The twist will begin to appear after the sixth round. Continue until your rope is the desired length.

Ladder stitch
Making a ladder

[1] Pick up two beads, and sew through them both again, positioning the beads side by

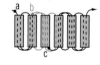

side so that their holes are parallel (a–b).
[2] Add subsequent beads by picking up one bead, sewing through the previous bead, then sewing through the new bead (b–c). Continue for the desired length.

This technique produces uneven tension, which you can correct by zigzag-ging back through the beads in the opposite direction or by choosing the "Crossweave method" or "Alternative method."

Crossweave technique

[1] Thread a needle on each end of a length of thread, and center a bead.
[2] Working in crossweave technique, pick up a bead with one needle, and cross the other needle through it (a–b and c–d). Add all subsequent beads in the same manner.

Alternative method

[1] Pick up all the beads you need to reach the length your project requires. Fold the last two beads so they are parallel, and sew through the second-to-last bead again in the same direction (a–b).

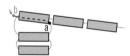

[2] Fold the next loose bead so it sits parallel to the previous bead in the ladder, and sew through the loose bead in the same direction (a–b). Continue sewing back through each bead until you exit the last bead of the ladder.

Forming a ring

With your thread exiting the last bead in the ladder, sew through the first bead and then through the last bead again. If using the "Crossweave method" or "Alternative method" of ladder stitch, cross the threads from the last bead in the ladder through the first bead in the ladder.

Basics

Peyote stitch

Flat even-count

[1] Pick up an even number of beads, leaving the desired length tail **(a–b)**. These beads will shift to form the first two rows as the third row is added.

[2] To begin row 3, pick up a bead, skip the last bead  added in the previous step, and sew back through the next bead, working toward the tail **(b–c)**. For each stitch, pick up a bead, skip a bead in the previous row, and sew through the next bead until you reach the first bead picked up in step 1 **(c–d)**. The beads added in this row are higher than the previous rows and are referred to as "up-beads."

[3] For each stitch in subsequent rows, pick up a bead, and sew through the next up-bead in the previous row **(d–e)**. To count peyote stitch rows, count the total number of beads along both straight edges.

Flat odd-count

Odd-count peyote is the same as even-count peyote, except for the turn on odd-numbered rows, where the last bead of the row can't be attached in the usual way because there is no up-bead to sew through.

Work the traditional odd-row turn as follows:

[1] Begin as for flat even-count peyote, but pick up an odd number of beads. Work row 3 as in even-count, stopping before adding the last bead.

[2] Work a figure-8 turn at the end of row 3: Pick up the next-to-last bead (#7), and sew 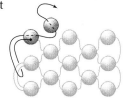 through #2, then #1 **(a–b)**. Pick up the last bead of the row (#8), and sew through #2, #3, #7, #2, #1, and #8 **(b–c)**.

[3] In subsequent odd-numbered rows, pick up the last bead of the row, sew under the thread bridge between the last two edge beads, and sew back through the last bead added to begin the next row.

Tubular even-count

Tubular peyote stitch follows the same stitching pattern as flat peyote, but instead of sewing back and forth, you work in rounds.

[1] Start with an even number of beads tied into a ring (see "Square knot").

[2] Sew through the first bead in the ring. Pick up a bead, skip a bead in the ring, and sew through the next bead. Repeat to complete the round.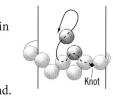

[3] To step up to start the next round, sew through the first bead added in round 3 **(a–b)**. Pick up a bead, and sew through the next bead in round 3 **(b–c)**. Repeat to complete the round.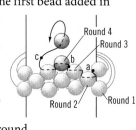

[4] Repeat step 3 to achieve the desired length, stepping up after each round.

Tubular odd-count

[1] Start with an odd number of bead tied into a ring (see "Square knot").

[2] Sew through the first bead into the ring. Pick up a bead, skip a bead in the ring, and sew though the next bead. Repeat to complete the round. At the end of the round, you will sew through the last bead in the original ring. Do not step up. Pick up a bead, and sew through the first bead in the previous round. You will be stitching in a continuous spiral.

Two-drop

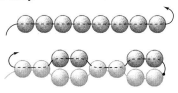

[1] Work two-drop peyote stitch the same as basic peyote, but treat pairs of beads as if they were single beads.

[2] Start with an even number of beads divisible by four. Pick up two beads (stitch 1 of row 3), skip two beads, and go through the next two beads. Repeat across the row.

Bezels

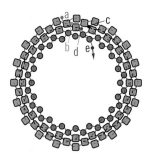

[1] Pick up enough seed beads to fit around the circumference of a rivoli or stone, and sew through the first bead again to form a ring **(a–b)**.

[2] Pick up a bead, skip the next bead in the ring, and sew through the following bead **(b–c)**. Continue working in tubular peyote stitch to complete the round, and step up through the first bead added **(c–d)**.

[3] Work the next two rounds in tubular peyote using beads one size smaller than those used in the previous rounds **(d–e)**. Keep the tension tight to decrease the size of the ring.

[4] Position the rivoli or stone in the bezel cup. Using the tail thread, repeat steps 2 and 3 to work three more rounds on the other side of the stone.

Increasing

[1] At the point of increase, pick up two beads instead of one, and sew through the next bead.

[2] When you reach the pair of beads in the next row, sew through the first bead, pick up a bead, and sew through the second bead.

Decreasing

[1] At the point of decrease, sew through two up-beads in the previous row.

[2] In the next row, when you reach the two-bead space, pick up one bead.

Zipping up or joining

To join two sections of a flat peyote piece invisibly, match up the two pieces so the end rows fit together. "Zip up" the pieces by zigzagging through the up-beads on both ends.

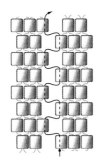

Right-angle weave
Flat strip

[1] To start the first row of right-angle weave, pick up four beads, and tie them into a ring (see "Square knot"). Sew through the first three beads again.

[2] Pick up three beads. Sew through the last bead in the previous stitch (a–b), and continue through the first two beads picked up in this stitch (b–c).

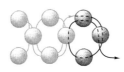

[3] Continue adding three beads per stitch until the first row is the desired length. You are stitching in a figure-8 pattern, alternating the direction of the thread path for each stitch.

Adding rows

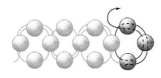

[1] To add a row, sew through the last stitch of row 1, exiting an edge bead along one side.

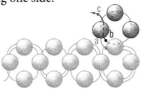

[2] Pick up three beads, and sew through the edge bead your thread exited in the previous step (a–b). Continue through the first new bead (b–c).

[3] Pick up two beads, and sew back through the next edge bead in the previous row and the bead your thread exited at the start of this step (a–b). Continue through the two new beads and the following edge bead in the previous row (b–c).

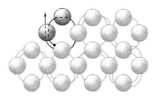

[4] Pick up two beads, and sew through the last two beads your thread exited in the previous stitch and the first new bead. Continue working a figure-8 thread path, picking up two beads per stitch for the rest of the row.

Square stitch

[1] String all the beads needed for the first row, then pick up the first bead of the second row. Sew through the last bead of the first row and the first bead of the second row again. Position the two beads side by side so that their holes are parallel.

[2] Pick up the next bead of row 2, and sew through the corresponding bead in row 1 and the new bead in row 2. Repeat across the row.

Basics

Cubic Right-Angle Weave
Working the first CRAW unit

[1] On the specified length of thread, pick up four beads. Tie the beads into a ring with a square knot, leaving the specified length tail, and continue through the first two beads in the ring. This ring of beads will count as the first stitch of the unit.

[2] Work two right-angle weave stitches off of the bead your thread is exiting to create a flat strip of right-angle weave.

[3] To join the first and last stitches: Pick up a bead, sew through the end bead in the first stitch (**CRAW 1, a–b**), pick up a bead, and sew through the end bead in the last stitch (**b–c**). CRAW 2 shows a three-dimensional view of the resulting cube-shaped unit.

[4] To make the unit more stable, sew through the four beads at the top of the unit (**CRAW 3**). Sew through the beadwork to the bottom of the unit, and sew through the four remaining beads. This completes the first CRAW unit.

Working more CRAW units

[1] Each new CRAW unit is worked off of the top four beads of the previous unit. These beads are identified in CRAW 4. Sew through the beadwork to exit one of these top beads.

[2] For the first stitch of the new unit: Pick up three beads, and sew through the top bead your thread exited at the start of this step. Continue through the three beads just picked up (**CRAW 5**). Sew through the next top bead in the previous unit.

[3] For the second stitch of the new unit: Pick up two beads, and sew through the side bead in the previous stitch, the top bead your thread exited at the start of this stitch (**CRAW 6**), and the next top bead in the previous unit.

[4] For the third stitch of the new unit: Repeat step 3 (**CRAW 7**), and continue through the side bead in the first stitch of the new unit.

[5] For the fourth stitch of the new unit: Pick up a bead, and sew through the side bead in the previous stitch and the top bead in the previous unit (**CRAW 8**).

[6] To make the unit more stable, sew through the beadwork to exit a top bead in the new unit, and sew through all four top beads (**CRAW 9**). This completes the new CRAW unit.

[7] Repeat steps 2–6 for the desired number of CRAW units.

Crimping

Use crimp beads to secure flexible beading wire. Slide the crimp bead into place over two strands of wire, and squeeze it firmly with chainnose pliers to flatten it. For a more finished look, use crimping pliers:

[1] Position the crimp bead in the hole that is closest to the handle of the crimping pliers.

[2] Holding the wires apart, squeeze the pliers to compress the crimp bead, making sure one wire is on each side of the dent.

[3] Place the crimp bead in the front hole of the pliers, and position it so the dent is facing the tips of the pliers. Squeeze the pliers to fold the crimp in half.

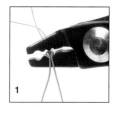

1

2

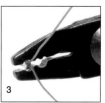

3

Opening and closing loops and jump rings

[1] Hold a loop or a jump ring with two pairs of pliers, such as chainnose, flatnose, or bentnose pliers.

[2] To open the loop or jump ring, bring the tips of one pair of pliers toward you, and push the tips of the other pair away from you.

[3] The open jump ring. Reverse the steps to close.

1

2

3

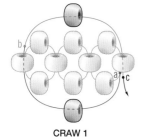

CRAW 1

CRAW 2

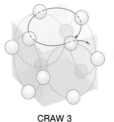

CRAW 3

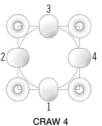

CRAW 4

CRAW 5

CRAW 6

CRAW 7

CRAW 8

CRAW 9

Plain loop

[1] Using chainnose pliers, make a right-angle bend in the wire directly above a bead or other component or at least ¼ in. (6 mm) from the end of a naked piece of wire. For a larger loop, bend the wire further in.

[2] Grip the end of the wire with roundnose pliers so that the wire is flush with the jaws of the pliers where they meet. The closer to the tip of the pliers that you work, the smaller the loop will be. Press downward slightly, and rotate the wire toward the bend made in step 1.

[3] Reposition the pliers in the loop to continue rotating the wire until the end of the wire touches the bend.

[4] The plain loop.

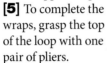

Wrapped loop

[1] Using chainnose pliers, make a right-angle bend in the wire about 2 mm above a bead or other component or at least 1¼ in. (3.2 cm) from the end of a naked piece of wire.

[2] Position the jaws of the roundnose pliers in the bend. The closer to the tip of the pliers that you work, the smaller the loop will be.

[3] Curve the short end of the wire over the top jaw of the roundnose pliers.

[4] Reposition the pliers so the lower jaw fits snugly in the loop. Curve the wire downward around the bottom jaw of the pliers. This is the first half of a wrapped loop.

[5] To complete the wraps, grasp the top of the loop with one pair of pliers.

[6] With another pair of pliers, wrap the wire around your stem two or three times. Trim the excess wire, and gently press the cut end close to the wraps with chainnose pliers.

Loops, wrapped above a top-drilled bead

[1] Center a top-drilled bead on a 3-in. (7.6 cm) piece of wire. Bend each wire end upward, crossing them into an X above the bead.

[2] Using chainnose pliers, make a small bend in each wire end so they form a right angle.

[3] Wrap the horizontal wire around the vertical wire as in a wrapped loop. Trim the excess wrapping wire.

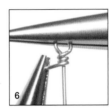

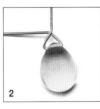

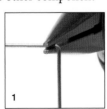

Loomwork
Set up the warp

[1] Tie the end of the spool of thread to a screw or hook at the end of the loom.

[2] Bring the thread over one spring and across to the spring at the other end of the loom. Wrap the thread around the back of the rod behind the bottom spring and back to the spring at the top of the loom.

[3] Continue wrapping the thread between springs, keeping the threads a bead's width apart until you have one more warp thread than the number of beads in the width of the pattern. Keep the tension even, but not too tight. Secure the last warp thread to a hook or screw on the loom, then cut the thread from the spool.

Weave the pattern

[1] Tie the end of a 1-yd. (.9m) length of thread to the first warp thread just below the spring at the top of the loom. Bring the needle under the warp threads. String the first row of beads as shown on the pattern and slide them to the knot.

[2] Push the beads up between the warp threads with your finger.

[3] Sew back through the beads, keeping the needle above the warp threads. Repeat, following the pattern row by row. Once you complete the last row, weave the working thread into the beadwork.

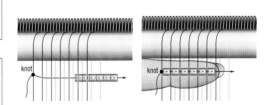

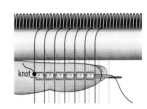

Single-Stitch
Projects

Crescent rosettes
NECKLACE

This unique stitch using crescent
and seed beads creates a
necklace of tiny rosette shapes.

designed by **Cassandra Spicer**

How to hold the crescent beads when adding them: Hold the bead with the tips of the crescent facing down, and sew through the left hole (LH) or right hole (RH), going in the direction indicated in the instructions.

Rosettes

1 On a comfortable length of thread, pick up eight 8º seed beads, and tie the beads into a ring with a square knot, leaving a 12-in. (30 cm) tail. Sew through all the beads again, and continue through the next 8º.
2 Working in a clockwise direction, pick up a 15º seed bead, an 11º seed bead, a crescent (RH) going from back to front, an 11º, and a 15º. Skip the next 8º in the ring, and sew through the following 8º **(figure 1, a–b)**. Repeat this stitch three times to complete the round **(b–c)**. Continue through the first 15º, 11º, crescent (through the same hole), and 11º added **(c–d)**. The open holes of the crescents should be positioned toward the center of the ring.
3 Sew through the open hole of the next crescent **(figure 2, a–b)**. Pick up a 15º, an 11º, and a 15º, and sew through the 11º adjacent to the crescent your thread is exiting **(b–c)**. Repeat these stitches three times to complete the round **(c–d)**. Sew through the adjacent 15º and next three 8ºs in the ring **(figure 3, a–b)**.
4 Pick up two 8ºs and a 3 mm round bead, and sew through the 8º your thread exited at the start of this step **(b–c)**. Retrace the thread path (not shown in the figure for clarity), and continue through the two new 8ºs **(c–d)**.

5 Pick up seven 8ºs, and sew through the 8º your thread exited at the start of this step **(d–e)**. Retrace the thread path to form a ring for the next rosette.
6 Repeat steps 2–5 for the desired length, ending with step 3 for the last rosette. Our 17-in. (43 cm) necklace has 31 rosettes. End and add thread as needed.

Clasp

With the working thread, pick up three 11ºs, the loop of the toggle ring, and three 11ºs, and sew through the 8º your thread exited at the start of this step **(figure 4)**. Retrace the thread path several times, and end the working thread.

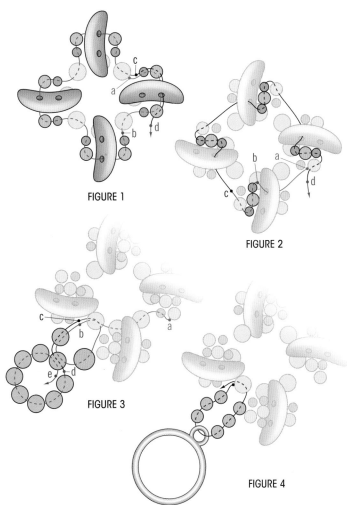

FIGURE 1

FIGURE 2

FIGURE 3

FIGURE 4

⬭	8º seed bead
•	15º seed bead
●	11º seed bead
⌒	2 x 10 mm crescent bead
●	3 mm round bead

Using the tail, add the toggle bar as before, but add five or more 11ºs to each side instead of three 11ºs so the toggle pivots properly. End the thread. ●

Difficulty rating

    ○ ○ ○

Materials

necklace 17 in. (43 cm)
- **124** 2 x 10 mm two-hole CzechMates crescent beads (blue iris)
- **30** 3 mm melon beads or round beads (luster iris cobalt)
- **7 g** 8º seed beads (Toho 377, teal-lined aqua)
- **4 g** 11º seed beads (Toho 221, bronze)
- **3 g** 15º seed beads (Toho 504, higher metallic violet iris)
- **1** toggle clasp
- Fireline, 6 lb. test, or OneG thread
- beading needles, #11 or #12

Basics, p.13
- ending and adding thread

bracelet option

To make a bracelet, in step 4, replace the 3 mm round bead with an 8º.

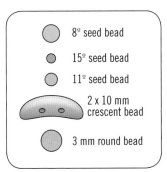

Adoring arch
bracelet and pendant

Detailed components dome in the center for a beautiful bracelet and matching pendant.

designed by
Zsuzsanna Veres

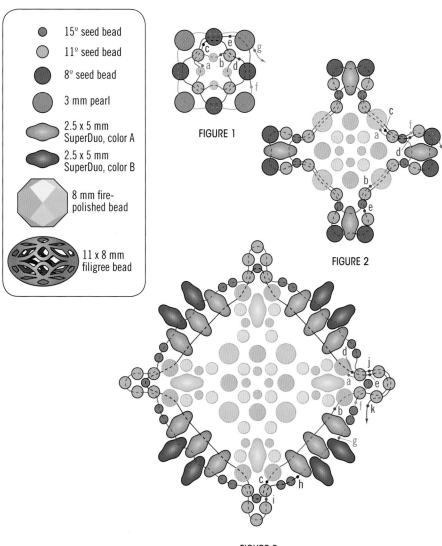

Legend (key)

- 15º seed bead
- 11º seed bead
- 8º seed bead
- 3 mm pearl
- 2.5 x 5 mm SuperDuo, color A
- 2.5 x 5 mm SuperDuo, color B
- 8 mm fire-polished bead
- 11 x 8 mm filigree bead

FIGURE 1

FIGURE 2

FIGURE 3

Difficulty rating

   ◯ ◯

Materials

bracelet 1¼ x 6½ in. (3.2 x 16.5 cm)
- 2.5 x 5 mm SuperDuo beads
  - **6 g** color A (metallic suede gold)
  - **4 g** color B (pastel Montana blue)
- **40** 3 mm glass pearls (blue gray)
- **2 g** 8º seed beads (Toho 1701, gilded marble blue)
- **4 g** 11º seed beads (Toho 223, antique bronze)
- **2 g** 15º seed beads (Toho PF567F, permanent finish purple matte metallic)
- **2** magnetic clasps (bronze)
- Fireline, 6 lb. test
- beading needles, #11 or #12

pendant 1⁷⁄₈ in. (4.8 cm)
- **1** 11 x 8 mm filigree bead (bronze)
- **6** 8 mm fire-polished beads (glittery matte amber)
- 2.5 x 5 mm SuperDuo beads
  - **21** color A (metallic suede gold)
  - **25** color B (pastel Montana blue)
- **8** 3 mm glass pearls (blue gray)
- **1 g** 8º seed beads (Toho 1701, gilded marble blue)
- **2 g** 11º seed beads (Toho 223, antique bronze)
- **1 g** 15º seed beads (Toho PF567F, permanent finish purple matte metallic)
- Fireline, 6 lb. test
- beading needles, #11 or #12

Basics, p. 13
- ending and adding thread

Component

1 On 4 ft. (1.2 m) of thread, pick up four 15º seed beads, sew through the beads again to form a ring, and continue through the next 15º, leaving a 6-in. (15 cm) tail.

2 Pick up an 11º seed bead, and sew through the next 15º **(figure 1, a-b)**. Repeat this stitch three times to complete the round, and step up through the first 11º added in this round **(b-c)**.

3 Pick up an 8º seed bead, and sew through the next 11º **(c-d)**. Repeat this stitch three times to complete the round, and step up through the first 8º added in this round **(d-e)**.

4 Pick up a 3 mm pearl, and sew through the next 8º **(e-f)**. Repeat this stitch three times to complete the round, and step up through the first pearl added in this round **(f-g)**. Retrace the thread path, pulling tight

to dome the beadwork slightly. End the tail.

5 Pick up an 11º, a 15º, a color A SuperDuo bead, a 15º, and an 11º, and sew through the next pearl **(figure 2, a-b)**. Repeat this stitch three times to complete the round **(b-c)**. Retrace the thread path (not shown in the figure for clarity), and continue through the first 11º and 15º added in this round **(c-d)**.

6 Pick up an 11º and an 8º, and sew through the open hole of the next A. Pick up an 8º and an 11º, and sew through the following 15º, 11º, pearl, 11º, and 15º **(d-e)**. Repeat this stitch three times to complete the round **(e-f)**. Retrace the thread path (not shown in the figure for clarity), and continue through the first 11º and 8º added in this round **(f-g)**.

7 Pick up an 11º, a 15º, and an 11º, and sew through the next 8º **(figure 3, a-b)**.

25

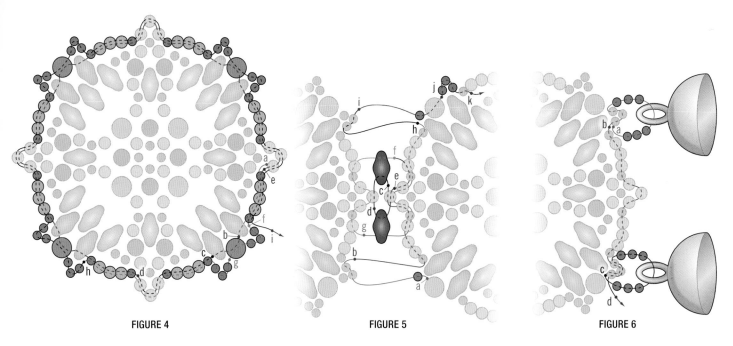

FIGURE 4

FIGURE 5

FIGURE 6

Pick up three As, and sew through the following 8º **(b–c)**. Repeat these two stitches three times to complete the round **(c–d)**. Retrace the thread path (not shown in the figure for clarity) using an even tension so this round lies flat when the open holes of the As are positioned to the outside. Continue through the first 11º added in this round **(d–e)**.

8 Pick up three 11ºs, skip the next 15º, and sew through the following 11º **(e–f)**. Pick up two 15ºs, and sew through the open hole of the following A **(f–g)**. Pick up a color B SuperDuo, and sew through the open hole of the next A. Work another stitch with a B **(g–h)**. Pick up two 15ºs, and sew through the following 11º **(h–i)**. Repeat these stitches three times to complete the round **(i–j)**, and continue through the first three 11ºs added in this round **(j–k)**. Pull the thread just tight enough so the center of the beadwork domes slightly but does not twist.

9 Pick up a 15º, three 11ºs, and a 15º, and sew through the open hole of the next B **(figure 4, a–b)**. Pick up a pearl, and sew through the open hole of the following B **(b–c)**. Pick up a 15º, three 11ºs, and a 15º, and sew through the next three 11ºs **(c–d)**. Repeat these stitches three times to complete the round **(d–e)**, and continue through the first 15º, three 11ºs, and 15º added in this round **(e–f)**.

10 Pick up three 15ºs, and sew through the next pearl to add a picot **(f–g)**. Pick

up three 15ºs, and continue through the next 13 beads as shown to add another picot **(g–h)**. Repeat these stitches three times to complete the round **(h–i)**, and end the working thread.

11 Repeat steps 1–9 to make another component, and continue through the beadwork to exit the next pearl. The 15ºs in the outer round will be added when joining the components together.

Joining

1 Position the two components next to each other with the first component on the left and the new component on the right, and the domed areas facing up. Your thread on the new component should be exiting a pearl near the other component, with the needle pointing toward the opposite edge of the beadwork **(figure 5, point a)**.

2 Pick up a 15º, skip the first 15º in the adjacent picot on the first component, and sew through the next two 15ºs **(a–b)**. Continue through the adjacent

15º, three 11ºs, 15º, and two 11ºs on the new component **(b–c)**.

3 Pick up a B, and sew through the corresponding 11º on the first component **(c–d)**. Pick up a B, and sew through the 11º your thread exited at the start of this step **(d–e)**. Retrace the thread path (not shown in the figure for clarity), and continue through the next 11º, 15º, and 11º in the new component **(e–f)**. Sew through the open hole of the adjacent B, and continue through the next seven beads in the first component as shown **(f–g)**. Sew through the open hole of the adjacent B, and continue through the following 10 beads in the new component to exit a 15º **(g–h)**.

4 Sew through the first two 15ºs in the adjacent picot on the first component **(h–i)**, pick up a 15º, and sew through the next pearl **(i–j)**. Pick up three 15ºs, and sew through the following 15º **(j–k)** and the next 12 beads to exit a 15º on the new component. Work as in step 10 of "Component" to complete

check your stash
Any style of oblong or drop bead can be used in the pendant dangle.

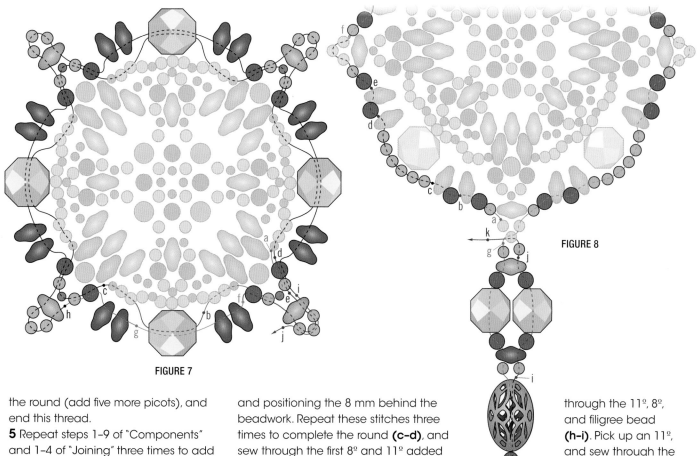

FIGURE 7

FIGURE 8

the round (add five more picots), and end this thread.

5 Repeat steps 1–9 of "Components" and 1–4 of "Joining" three times to add three more components for a 6½-in. (16.5 cm) length bracelet.

Clasp

Add 12 in. (30 cm) of thread to an end component, exiting at **figure 6, point a**. Pick up three 15ºs, half of the clasp, and three 15ºs, and sew through the three 15ºs in the picot your thread exited at the start of this step, going in the same direction **(a–b)**. Retrace the thread path (not shown in the figure for clarity), and sew through the next 16 beads on the end **(b–c)**. Work as before to add another clasp **(c–d)**, and end the thread. If needed, add more 15ºs to each loop to lengthen the bracelet. Repeat this step at the other end of the bracelet.

Pendant

1 Using 2 yd. (1.8 m) of thread, repeat steps 1–9 of "Component."

2 Pick up an 8º, an 11º, a 15º, an 11º, and an 8º, skip the next B, pearl, and B, and sew through the following 15º and two 11ºs **(figure 7 a–b)**. Pick up an 8 mm fire-polished bead, skip the next seven beads, and sew through the next two 11ºs and 15º **(b–c)**, pulling tight

and positioning the 8 mm behind the beadwork. Repeat these stitches three times to complete the round **(c–d)**, and sew through the first 8º and 11º added in this round **(d–e)**.

3 Pick up an A and three 11ºs, sew through the open hole of the same A, and continue through the next 11º and 8º **(e–f)**. Pick up two Bs, and sew through the next 8 mm **(f–g)**. Pick up two Bs, and sew through the next 8º and 11º added in the previous round **(g–h)**. Repeat these stitches three times to complete the round **(h–i)**, and sew through the first A and three 11ºs added **(i–j)**.

4 Pick up an 11º and an 8º, and sew through the open hole of the next B **(figure 8, a–b)**. Pick up an 8º, and sew through the open hole of the following B **(b–c)**. Pick up six 11ºs, and sew through the open hole of the next B **(c–d)**. Pick up an 8º, and continue through the open hole of the following B **(d–e)**. Pick up an 8º and an 11º, and sew through the next three 11ºs **(e–f)**. Repeat these stitches three times to complete the round, but after the final stitch, sew through only two 11ºs instead of three **(f–g)**.

Dangle

Pick up an 11º, an A, an 8º, an 8 mm, an 8º, a B, an 11º, a filigree bead, an 8º, an 11º, and a 15º **(g–h)**. Sew back

through the 11º, 8º, and filigree bead **(h–i)**. Pick up an 11º, and sew through the open hole of the next B, pick up an 8º, an 8 mm, and an 8º, and sew through the open hole of the following A **(i–j)**. Pick up an 11º, and sew through the 11º your thread exited at the start of this step, going in the same direction **(j–k)**. Retrace the thread path, and end the thread.

Bail

With the back of the pendant facing up, add 2 ft. (61 cm) of thread to the beadwork, exiting one of the 8 mms on the top of the pendant, with the needle pointing toward the top. Pick up eight 11ºs, sew through the top A, and continue through the other hole of the same A. Pick up eight 11ºs, and sew through the corresponding top 8 mm **(photo)**. Retrace the thread path, and end the thread. ◗

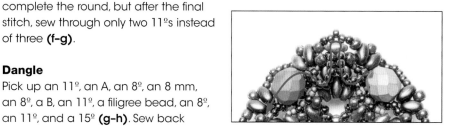

Arco deco
necklace

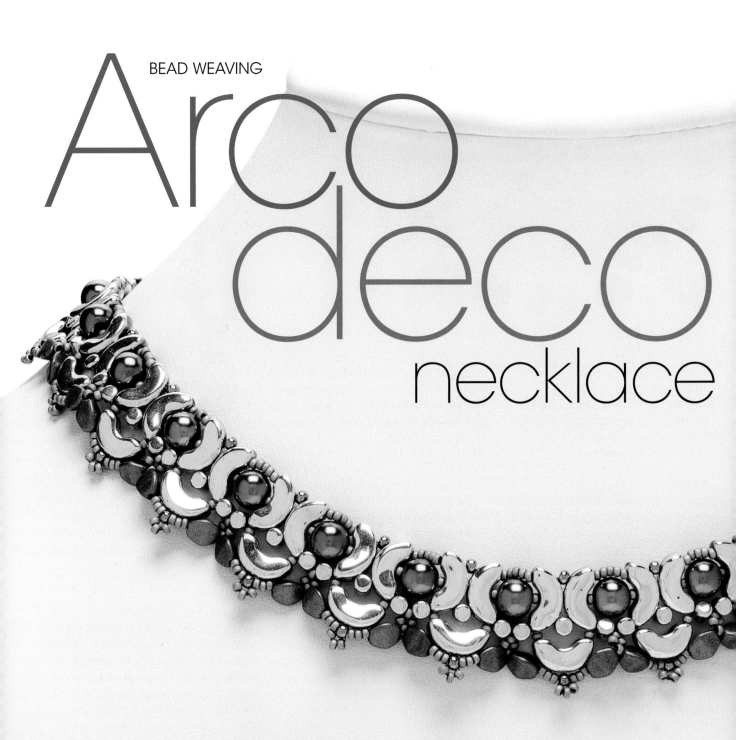

See how easy it is
to use the new Arcos
par Puca and Minos
par Puca beads in
this stunning yet easy
to stitch necklace.

designed by **Puca**

Difficulty rating

Materials

necklace 17 in. (43 cm)

- **27** 6 mm pearls (Swarovski, gray)
- **80** 5 x 10 mm Arcos par Puca beads (argentees)
- **80** 2.5 x 3 mm Minos par Puca beads (argentees)
- **52** 3 x 5 mm pinch beads (metallic suede light green)
- **1 g** 11º seed beads (Toho 512, galvanized blue haze)
- **2 g** 15º seed beads (Miyuki 2030, Duracoat steel blue matte)
- **1** magnetic clasp
- Fireline, 6 lb. test
- beading needles, #11 or #12

Basics, p. 13

- attaching a stop bead
- ending and adding thread

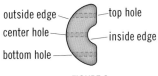

FIGURE 1

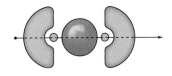

FIGURE 2

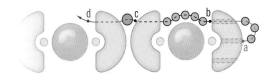

FIGURE 3

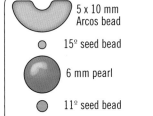

- 5 x 10 mm Arcos bead
- 15º seed bead
- 6 mm pearl
- 11º seed bead
- 2.5 x 3 mm Minos bead
- 3 x 5 mm pinch bead

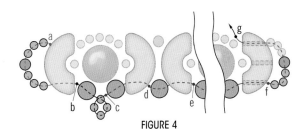

FIGURE 4

Necklace

The Arcos beads have an outside edge and an inside edge, and the instructions will state which edge to sew through. When sewing through the Arcos, the holes will be referred to as the top hole (TH), the center hole (CH), and the bottom hole (BH) **(figure 1)**.

1 On 2 yd. (1.8 m) of thread, attach a stop bead, leaving a 6-in. (15 cm) tail. Pick up an Arcos bead through the outside edge (CH), a 15º seed bead, a 6 mm pearl, a 15º, and an Arcos through the inside edge (CH) **(figure 2)**. Repeat this pattern 26 times for a 17-in. (43 cm) necklace.

2 Pick up three 15ºs, and sew through the outside edge (TH) of the same Arcos bead **(figure 3, a–b)**.
3 Pick up five 15ºs, skip the next 15º, pearl, and 15º, and sew through the inside edge (TH) of the following Arcos bead **(b–c)**.
4 Pick up an 11º seed bead, and sew through the outside edge (TH) of the next Arcos bead **(c–d)**.
5 Repeat steps 3–4 for the remainder of the necklace, ending with step 3.
6 Pick up three 15ºs, an 11º, and three 15ºs, and sew through outside edge (BH) of the same Arcos **(figure 4, a–b)**.
7 Pick up a Minos bead

and four 15ºs, and sew through the first 15º just picked up, going in the same direction to form a picot **(b–c)**. Tighten the beads. Pick up a Minos, and sew through the inside edge (BH) of the next Arcos **(c–d)**.
8 Pick up a Minos, and sew through the outside edge (BH) of the next Arcos **(d–e)**.
9 Repeat steps 7–8 for the remainder of the necklace, ending with step 7 **(e–f)**. The beadwork will curve as you work these stitches.
10 Pick up three 15ºs and an 11º, and sew through the next three 15ºs and the outside edge (TH) of the same Arcos **(f–g)**. End the working thread, but not the tail.

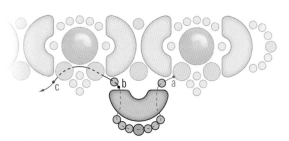

FIGURE 5

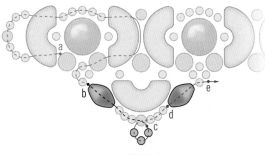

FIGURE 6

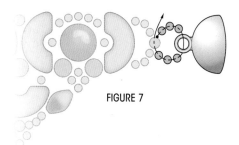

FIGURE 7

11 Attach 2 yd. (1.8 m) of thread to the end of the necklace opposite the tail, exiting the second-to-last Minos bead, with the needle pointing toward the opposite end of the necklace **(figure 5, point a)**. Pick up a 15º, an Arcos (inside edge, TH), three 15ºs, an 11º, and three 15ºs, and sew through the outside edge (BH) of the same Arcos **(a–b)**. Pick up a 15º, skip the next Arcos, Minos, and Arcos, and sew through the following two Minos **(b–c)**. Repeat these stitches for the remainder of the necklace.

12 Sew through the beadwork as shown to exit the tip of the end picot with the needle pointing toward the other end of the necklace **(figure 6, a–b)**.

13 Pick up a pinch bead, and sew through the next three 15ºs and 11º **(b–c)**. Pick up three 15ºs, and sew through the 11º your thread is exiting, going in the same direction, and the following three 15ºs **(c–d)**. Pick up a pinch bead, and sew through the tip of the next picot **(d–e)**. Repeat these stitches for the remainder of the necklace. Sew through the beadwork to exit the 11º at the end of the necklace.

14 Pick up three 15ºs, the loop of a clasp, and three 15ºs, and sew through the 11º your thread is exiting, going in the same direction **(figure 7)**. Retrace the thread path several times, and end the thread. Repeat this stitch at the tail end of the necklace, and end the thread. ●

FLIRTATIOUS DAGGER EARRINGS

designed by
Thomasin Alyxander

DIFFICULTY ●●●○○

bead weaving

materials

gold earrings 1½ x 2 in. (3.8 x 5 cm)

- **2** SS47 (10.5 mm) rivolis (Swarovski, medium vitrail)
- **14** 5 x 16 mm CzechMates two-hole dagger beads (matte metallic flax)
- **24** 3 x 10 mm CzechMates two-hole crescent beads (matte metallic bronze iris)
- **42** 2 mm fire-polished beads (matte metallic bronze iris)
- **1 g** 11º seed beads (Toho 221, bronze)
- **1 g** 15º seed beads (Toho 994, gold-lined rainbow crystal)
- **2** 4–5 mm soldered jump rings
- **1** pair of earring findings
- Fireline, 6 lb. test or nylon thread, size D
- beading needles, #11 or #12 (#13 optional)
- thread bobbin or piece of cardboard (optional)

Basics, p. 13

- ending and adding thread
- attaching a stop bead
- opening and closing loops and jump rings

Dagger beads add a little fun and flair to these earrings bezeled with crescent beads.

BEFORE YOU BEGIN

How to pick up the crescent beads: With the tips of the crescent pointing toward you, pick up the crescent through the left hole (LH) or the right hole (RH).

How to pick up the two-hole dagger beads: The hole closest to the narrow end will be referred to as the inside hole and the hole closest to the wide end will be the outside hole.

LEFT EARRING BEZEL

1) On 4 ft. (1.2 m) of thread, pick up 24 11º seed beads, and sew through the beads again to form a ring, leaving an 18-in. (46 cm) tail. Do not continue through the first 11º again. Wrap the tail onto a thread bobbin or piece of cardboard if desired. If needed, pull on the tail to keep the tension in the ring during the next couple of steps.

2) Pick up a crescent (RH) and a 15º seed bead, and sew back through the same hole of the crescent (**figure 1, a–b**) and the next two 11ºs in the ring (**b–c**). The first 11º you sew through in the ring should be the 11º with the tail exiting it. Position the crescent so the open hole of the crescent is to the outside of the ring and the tip is pointing clockwise. Repeat this stitch 11 times to complete the round (**c–d**), and continue through the first crescent and 15º added (**d–e**).

3) Pick up a 2 mm fire-polished bead, and sew through the next 15º (**figure 2, a–b**). Repeat this stitch 11 times to complete the round (**b–c**), retrace the thread path (not shown in the figure for clarity), and continue through the first 2 mm added (**c–d**).

4) Pick up an 11º and a 15º, and sew through the open hole of the next crescent (**d–e**). Pick up an 11º, and sew back through the same hole of the crescent (**e–f**). Continue back through the 15º and 11º just added, the 15º on top of the crescent your thread is exiting, and the following 2 mm (**f–g**). Repeat these stitches 11 times to complete the round, and end the working thread.

5) Flip the beadwork over so the back is facing up. With the tail thread, pick up five 15ºs, skip the next three 11ºs in the ring, and sew through the following 11º to form a loop (**figure 3, a–b**). For clarity, the bottom view of the beadwork is shown in the remaining figures and the beads from the front of the beadwork are not shown. Repeat this stitch five times to complete the round, and sew through the first three 15ºs added (**b–c**).

6) Place the 10.5 mm rivoli face-down in the beadwork by sliding the rivoli under the ring of 11ºs and loops of 15ºs. It may be a tight fit, so start by sliding one edge of the rivoli under the 11ºs, and slowly work your way around. The edge of the rivoli will sit between the ring of 11ºs and the tips of the crescents on the top surface.

7) Pick up a 15º, and sew through the center 15º in the next loop (**c–d**). Repeat this stitch five times to complete the round (**d–e**). Retrace the thread path through the final round.

8) Sew through the next two 15ºs in the same loop (**figure 4, a–b**). Continue through the first two 15ºs in the next loop, skip the center 15º in this loop, and sew through the last two 15ºs in this loop (**b–c**). Repeat this last stitch five times to complete the round (**c–d**), and end this thread.

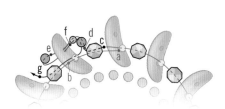

FIGURE 2

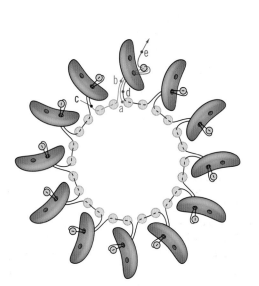

FIGURE 1

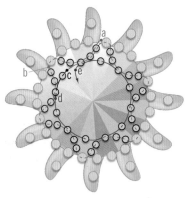

FIGURE 3

FIGURE 4

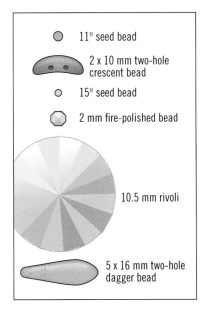

- ● 11º seed bead
- ◗ 2 x 10 mm two-hole crescent bead
- ○ 15º seed bead
- ⬡ 2 mm fire-polished bead
- ◯ 10.5 mm rivoli
- ◗ 5 x 16 mm two-hole dagger bead

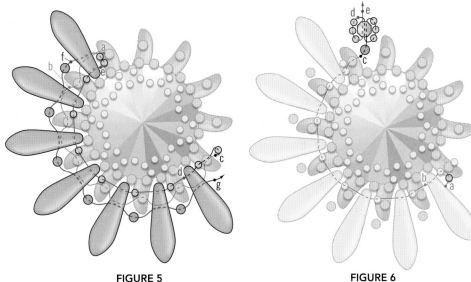

FIGURE 5

FIGURE 6

EMBELLISHMENT

1) On 1 yd. (.9 m) of thread, attach a stop bead, leaving a 12-in. (30 cm) tail. Sew through an 11º near the tip of a crescent on the back of the bezel, going in a counter-clockwise direction **(figure 5, point a)**. Pick up a dagger through the outside hole, and sew through the 11º on the tip of the next crescent **(a–b)**, making sure the wide part of the dagger is pointing outward. Repeat this stitch six times **(b–c)**.

2) Pick up a 15º, and sew back through the 11º your thread is exiting. Pick up a 15º, and sew through the open hole of the next dagger **(c–d)**. Repeat this last stitch six times **(d–e)**. Pick up two 15ºs, and sew through the other hole of the same dagger **(e–f)**.

3) Pick up an 11º, and sew through the outside hole of the next dagger. Repeat this stitch five times **(f–g)**.

4) Pick up a 15º, and sew through the adjacent 15º and other hole of the same dagger **(figure 6, a–b)**. Sew through the next 15º and dagger six times, and continue through the adjacent 15º and the 11º on the tip of the following crescent **(b–c)**. Remove the stop bead. Your working thread and tail should be exiting the same side of this 11º.

EARRING CONNECTOR

If you have trouble getting through the beads in this section, switch to a #13 beading needle.

1) Pick up an 11º, a 2 mm, and three 15ºs, skip the 11º just added, and sew through the 2 mm, going in the same direction to form a loop on one side of the 2 mm **(c–d)**. Snug up the beads. Pick up three 15ºs, and sew through the 2 mm again, going in the same direction, to form a loop on the other side of the 2 mm **(d–e)**. Repeat these stitches three times using a tight tension to form a strap.

2) Pick up two 11ºs, a 2 mm, and a soldered jump ring, and sew back through the 2 mm **(figure 7, a–b)**. Pick up two 11ºs **(b–c)**.

3) Work as in step 1 to add four 2 mm units to form another strap.

4) Pick up two 11ºs, skip the next crescent, and sew through the 11º on the tip of the following crescent **(d–e)**. Pick up a 15º, and sew back through the same 11º on the tip and the two 11ºs just added **(e–f)**.

5) Sew back through the 2 mms and 11ºs in this strap and the soldered jump ring. Continue back through the last few beads in this strap, and end this thread.

6) Using the tail, repeat step 5 for this strap.

7) Open the loop on an ear wire, and attach it to the soldered jump ring.

RIGHT EARRING BEZEL

1) Work as in "Left earring bezel" except for the following changes:
- In step 2, pick up a crescent

through the left hole instead of the right hole.
- At the end of step 3, sew through the first 2 mm added and the next 15º.
- In step 4, work as before, but when sewing back through the crescent, 15º, and 11º, skip the next 15º on top of the crescent your thread is exiting, and continue through the following 2 mm and 15º.

2) Work as in "Embellishment" except for the following changes:
- In step 1, sew through an 11º going in a clockwise direction, and work the remainder of steps 1–3 and step 4 in the opposite direction from the left earring.

3) Work as in "Earring connector" to complete. **B·B**

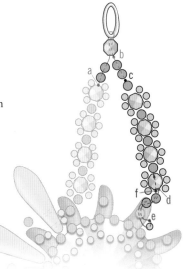

FIGURE 7

materials
bracelet 7 in. (18 cm)

- **8** 4 mm fire-polished beads (lime opal)
- 11º Miyuki Delica cylinder beads
  - **1 g** color A (DB0733, opaque chartreuse)
  - **2 g** color C (DB1345, silver-lined bright violet)
  - **5 g** color D (DB0310, matte black)
  - **1 g** color E (DB0724, opaque pea green)
  - **1 g** color F (DB1379, opaque red-violet)
  - **1 g** color G (DB1840F, galvanized baby pink)
  - **1 g** color H (DB0651, opaque squash)
  - **1 g** color I (DB0727, opaque light Siam)
  - **1 g** color J (DB0164, opaque light blue AB)
  - **1 g** color K (DB0760, matte opaque light sapphire)
  - **1 g** color L (DB0721, opaque yellow)
  - **1 g** color M (DB0681, semi-matte silver-lined squash)
  - **1 g** color N (DB0150, silver-lined bronze)
  - **1 g** color O (DB1340, silver-lined bright fuchsia)
  - **1 g** color P (DB1511, matte opaque pale yellow)
  - **1 g** color Q (DB1523, matte opaque light salmon AB)
  - **1 g** color R (DB1517, matte opaque light sky blue)
  - **1 g** color S (DB1363, opaque peach)
  - **1 g** color T (DB0200, opaque chalk white)
- **1** four-strand slide clasp (purple, metaldesinz.com)
- beading needles, #10
- Fireline, 6 lb. test, or nylon beading thread, size D

Get a Word chart for this pattern at
FacetJewelry.com/resourceguide

basics, p. 13
- peyote stitch: flat, even-count
- attaching a stop bead
- ending and adding thread

Stitch up this bracelet featuring a lively school of fish in a bright array of colors.

PEYOTE BAND

1) On a comfortable length of thread, attach a stop bead, leaving a 6-in. (15 cm) tail. Starting at the upper-right corner of the pattern, pick up 11º cylinder beads for rows 1 and 2: one A, one C, 18 Ds, one C, and one A.

2) Following the **pattern** or the Word chart (get it at FacetJewelry.com/resourceguide), work in flat even-count peyote stitch using the appropriate color cylinders. End and add thread as needed while you stitch, and end the working thread and tail when you complete the band.

CLASP

Add a new 1-ft. (30 cm) thread to one end of the beadwork, and exit the third up-bead from the edge that ends with an up-bead **(figure, point a)**. Pick up a 4 mm fire-polished bead and the end loop of a slide clasp. Sew back through the 4 mm, and continue through the next three end beads in the band **(a–b)**. Repeat this stitch three times to attach each clasp loop to the band **(b–c)**. Retrace the thread path through the clasp connections at least once, and end the thread. Repeat at the other end to attach the other clasp half. **B&B**

11º cylinder beads	
▨	color A
◙	color B
◘	color C
■	color D
▦	color E
▩	color F
▨	color G
░	color H
▓	color I
▫	color J
▨	color K
▢	color L
▨	color M
▨	color N
▥	color O
▢	color P
▨	color Q
▢	color R
▨	color S
▢	color T

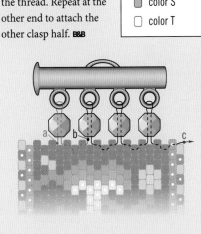

FIGURE

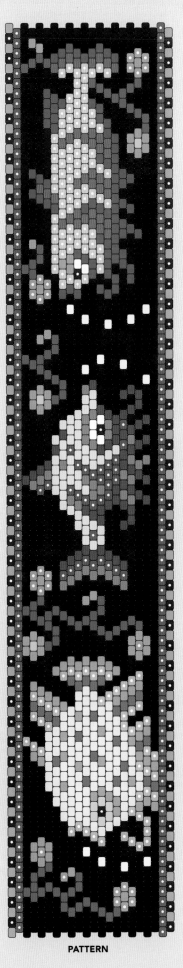

PATTERN

CRYSTAL BRILLIANCE NECKLACE

Create a delightful,
wintery pendant
with seed beads
and sparkling crystals.

designed by **Alicia Campos**

Bezel

1 On a comfortable length of thread,
pick up 40 11º cylinder beads, and sew
through the first three beads again to
form a ring, leaving a 6-in. (15 cm) tail.
These beads will shift to form rounds 1
and 2 as the next round is added. End
and add thread throughout the project
as needed.

2 Work rounds of tubular peyote stitch
for the front of the bezel as follows,
and step up at the end of each round:

Round 3–5: Work rounds using cylinders.

Rounds 6–7: Work both rounds using
15º seed beads.

Round 8: Pick up a 15º, and sew
through the next two 15ºs in the previous
round using a tight tension. Repeat this
stitch nine times to complete the round.
Sew through the beadwork to exit a
cylinder in round 1, and flip the beadwork over. Place the rivoil facedown
in the beadwork.

3 Stitching off the cylinders in round 1,
work a round using 15ºs.

4 Pick up a 15º, and sew through
the next two 15ºs in the previous
round using a tight tension. Repeat
this stitch nine times to complete

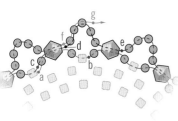

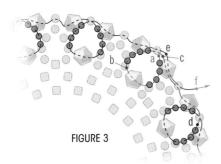

FIGURE 1

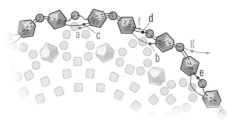

FIGURE 2

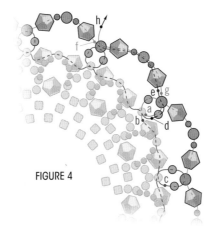

FIGURE 3

FIGURE 4

Difficulty rating

   ◇ ◇

Materials

**opal pendant 2¼ in. (5.7 cm)
on a 21-in. (53 cm) necklace**
- **1** 16 mm Swarovski rivoli (light vitrail)
- **90** Swarovski bicone crystals (white opal AB2X)
- **2 g** 8º seed beads (Miyuki 4220, Duracoat eggplant)
- **2 g** 11º seed beads (Toho 565F, permanent finish frosted galvanized blue slate)
- **1 g** 11º Delica cylinder beads (Miyuki DB1850, Duracoat eggplant)
- **1 g** 15º seed beads (Japanese P487, silver sage permanent galvanized)
- **42 in. (1.06 m)** chain (silver)
- **1** 13 mm spring ring clasp (silver)
- **1** 6 mm jump ring
- Fireline, 6 lb. test
- beading needles, #11 or #12
- **2** pairs of chainnose, bentnose, and/or flatnose pliers

Basics, p.13
- tubular peyote
- ending and adding thread

the round.

5 Sew through the beadwork to exit a cylinder in round 3 (center round of cylinders in the bezel). Work a round of stitch-in-the-ditch, adding a cylinder in every other stitch: Pick up a cylinder, and sew through the next cylinder in this round, the following cylinder in an adjacent round, and the next cylinder in the center round. Repeat this stitch nine times to complete the round, and step up through the first cylinder added in this round.

Embellishment

1 Pick up an 11º seed bead, a 4 mm bicone crystal, and an 11º, and sew through the next cylinder in the previous round **(figure 1, a–b)**. Repeat this stitch nine times to complete the round **(b–c)**, and sew through the first 11º and crystal added in this round **(c–d)**.

2 Pick up five 11ºs, and sew through the next crystal to add a picot **(d–e)**. Repeat this stitch nine times to complete the round **(e–f)**, and sew through the first three 11ºs in the first picot **(f–g)**.

3 Pick up a crystal, an 11º, and a crystal, and sew through the center 11º in the next picot **(figure 2, a–b)**. Repeat this stitch nine times to complete the round **(b–c)**, retrace the thread path (not shown in the figure for clarity), and sew through the first crystal, 11º, and crystal added in this round **(c–d)**.

4 Pick up an 11º, and sew through the next crystal, 11º, and crystal **(d–e)**. Repeat this stitch nine times to complete the round **(e–f)**, and sew through the following 11º, crystal, and 11º **(f–g)**.

5 Pick up four 15ºs, and sew through the adjacent crystal on the inner ring of crystals **(figure 3, a–b)**. Pick up four 15ºs, and sew through the 11º your thread exited at the start of this step, going in the same direction **(b–c)**. Continue through the next crystal, 11º, crystal, and 11º **(c–d)**. Repeat these stitches nine times to complete the round **(d–e)**, and continue through the following crystal and 11º **(e–f)**.

6 Pick up an 11º, an 8º seed bead, and an 11º, and sew through the 11º your thread exited at the start of this step, going in the same direction **(figure 4, a–b)**. Retrace the thread path

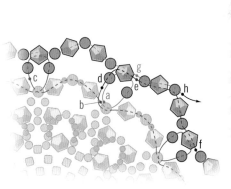

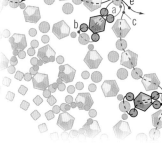

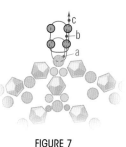

FIGURE 5

FIGURE 6

FIGURE 7

(not shown in the figure for clarity), and continue through the next crystal, 11º, crystal, and 11º **(b–c)**. Repeat these stitches nine times to complete the round **(c–d)**, and continue through the first 11º and 8º added **(d–e)**.

7 Pick up a crystal, a 15º, an 8º, a 15º, and a crystal, and sew through the next 8º **(e–f)**. Repeat this stitch nine times to complete the round **(f–g)**, retrace the thread path (not shown in the figure for clarity), and continue through the next six beads **(g–h)**.

8 Pick up an 8º, a crystal, and an 8º, and sew through the 8º your thread exited at the start of this step **(figure 5, a–b)**. Retrace the thread path (not shown in the figure for clarity), and continue through the next crystal, 15º, 8º, 15º, crystal, and 8º **(b–c)**. Repeat these stitches nine times to complete the round **(c–d)**, and continue through the first 8º and crystal added in this round **(d–e)**.

9 Pick up an 8º, a crystal, an 8º, a crystal, and an 8º, and sew through the next crystal added in the previous round **(e–f)**. Repeat this stitch nine times to complete the round **(f–g)**, retrace the thread path (not shown in the figure for clarity), and continue through the first 8º, crystal, and 8º added in this round **(g–h)**.

10 Pick up an 11º, a crystal, and an 11º, and sew through the 8º between the 15ºs in the adjacent inner round **(figure 6, a–b)**. Pick up an 11º, sew back through the crystal just added, pick up an 11º, and sew through the 8º your thread exited at the start of this step **(b–c)**. Continue through the next six beads **(c–d)**. Repeat these stitches nine

times to complete the round **(d–e)**.

Bail

Pick up two 11ºs, and sew through the 8º your thread is exiting, going in the same direction. Retrace the thread path (not shown in the illustration for clarity), and continue through the first 11º picked up **(figure 7, a–b)**. Pick up two 11ºs, sew through the previous two 11ºs, and continue through the first 11º just picked up **(b–c)**. Repeat this stitch 12 times using 11ºs to form a strip. Curve the strip to the back of the pendant, sew through the 8º your thread exited

at the start of this step, and continue through the last two 11ºs added. Retrace the thread path several times and end the thread.

Chain attachment

Attach a 6 mm jump ring to both ends of a 42-in. (1.06 m) piece of chain and to the connector loop of the spring ring clasp. Attach the clasp to the pendant loop. Place the doubled chain around your neck, and slide the pendant through the loop of chain to wear like a lariat. ●

CHANGE IT UP

This pendant can be worn several different ways:
- As a lariat (p. 36)
- Remove it from the spring clasp, and hang it from a ribbon.
- Suspend it from a chain.

materials
bracelet 7 in. (18 cm)

- **3 g** 2.5 x 5 mm SuperDuo beads
  (turquoise Picasso)
- **32** 4 mm crystal pearls (Swarovski, white)
- **60** 2 mm fire-polished beads (gold-
  plated AB)
- **1 g** 11º seed beads (Miyuki 199, gold iris)
- **2 g** 15º seed beads (Toho 223,
  antique bronze)
- **1** box clasp
- Fireline, 6 lb. test
- beading needles, #11 or #12

earrings 1¹/₂ in. (3.8 cm)

- **16** 2.5 x 5 mm SuperDuo beads
- **16** 4 mm crystal pearls
- **20** 2 mm fire-polished beads
- **1 g** 11º seed beads
- **1 g** 15º seed beads
- **1** pair of ear wires

basics, p. 13

- ending thread
- square knot

Join fun and easy-to-make components together to create a dainty bracelet and earring set that is perfect for everyday or an evening out.

Bracelet
Components

1) On 1 yd. (.9 m) of thread, pick up a repeating pattern of a SuperDuo and an 11º seed bead four times, leaving a 6-in. (15 cm) tail. Tie a square knot, and sew through the next SuperDuo and the open hole of the same SuperDuo **(figure 1, a–b)**.

2) Pick up a 15º seed bead, a 4 mm pearl, and a 15º, and sew through the open hole of the next SuperDuo **(b–c)**. Repeat this stitch three times to complete the round, and continue through the first 15º added **(c–d)**.

3) Pick up three 15ºs, and sew through the next 11º **(figure 2, a–b)**. Pick up three 15ºs, and sew through the next 15º,

SuperDuo, and 15º **(b–c)**. Repeat these stitches three times to complete the round **(c–d)**.

4) Sew through the adjacent set of three 15ºs and the next 11º in the inner ring **(figure 3, a–b)**. Pick up a 2 mm fire-polished bead, and sew through the following 11º **(b–c)**. Repeat this last stitch three times to complete the round, and continue through the first 2 mm added **(c–d)**. Retrace the thread path through the 2 mms, and sew through the bead-work to exit a pearl. End the tail, but not the working thread.

5) Work as in steps 1–4 to make a total of eight components for a 7-in. (18 cm) bracelet, but leave the tail on one of the components to use for attaching the clasp.

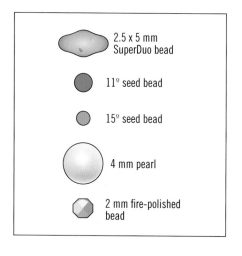

	2.5 x 5 mm SuperDuo bead
	11º seed bead
	15º seed bead
	4 mm pearl
	2 mm fire-polished bead

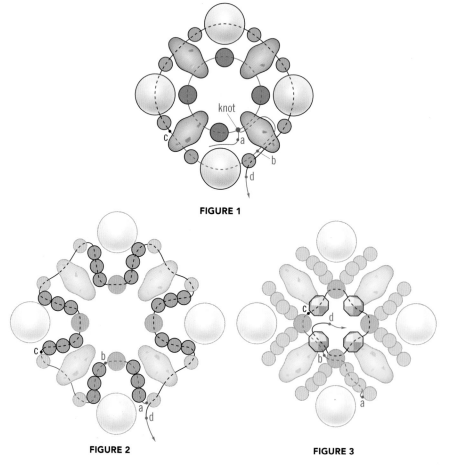

FIGURE 1

FIGURE 2

FIGURE 3

Assembly

1) Align two components side-by-side on your work surface, making sure one still has the tail thread attached. With the working thread from the component without the tail, pick up a 15º, a 2 mm, a SuperDuo, a 2 mm, and a 15º, and sew through the corresponding pearl on the other component **(figure 4, a–b)**. Pick up a 15º and a 2 mm, and sew through the open hole of the SuperDuo just added. Pick up a 2 mm and a 15º, and sew through the pearl your thread exited at the start of this step, going in the same direction **(b–c)**. Retrace the thread path of the connection, and end the working thread.

2) Work as in step 1 to connect the remaining components, leaving the component with the tail at the end. Do not end the working thread on the last component.

Clasp

1) With the working thread on the end component exiting the end pearl, pick up three 15ºs, an 11º, and the loop of the clasp, and sew back through the 11º just added **(figure 5, a–b)**. Pick up three 15ºs, and sew through the pearl your thread exited at the start of this step, going in the same direction **(b–c)**. Retrace the thread path several times, and end the working thread.

2) Using the tail on the other end, sew through the beadwork to exit the end pearl. Work as in step 1 to attach the other half of the clasp.

Earrings

1) Work as in steps 1–4 of "Components" to make two components.

2) With the working thread of one component exiting a pearl, pick up three 15ºs, a 2 mm, six 15ºs, and the loop of an ear wire, and sew back through the 2 mm just added. Pick up

three 15ºs, and sew through the pearl your thread exited at the start of this step, going in the same direction. Retrace the thread path, and end the thread.

3) Position the second component below the first component on your work surface. Using the working thread from the second component, pick up three 15ºs, a 2 mm, and three 15ºs, and sew through the pearl your thread is exiting, going in the same direction to form a loop. Continue through the first three 15ºs and 2 mm just added **(figure 6, a–b)**.

4) Pick up three 15ºs, and sew through the corresponding pearl on the other component. Pick up three 15ºs, and sew through the 2 mm your thread exited at the start of this step, going in the same direction **(b–c)**. Retrace the thread path of the connection, and end the thread.

5) Repeat steps 1–4 to make another earring. B·B

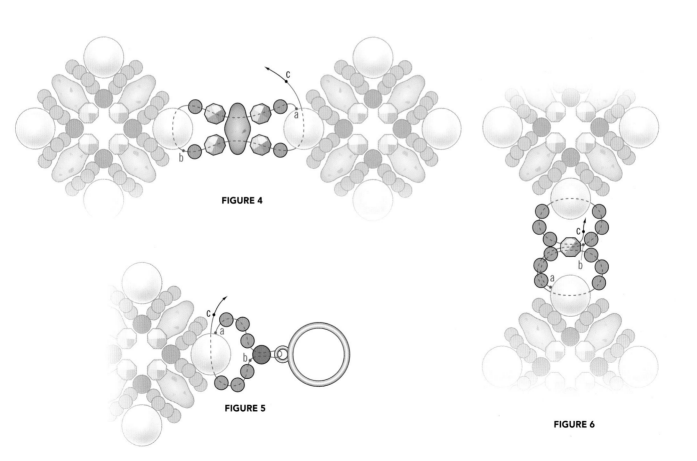

FIGURE 4

FIGURE 5

FIGURE 6

DIAGONAL PEYOTE

Autumn
leaves
collection

Work in diagonal
peyote to make
adorable leaf
components for
earrings, a bracelet,
and a pendant.

designed by
Lane Landry

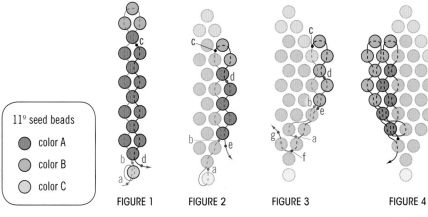

11º seed beads
- color A
- color B
- color C

FIGURE 1   FIGURE 2   FIGURE 3   FIGURE 4

Earrings

1 On 2 ft. (61 cm) of thread, pick up a color C 11º seed bead. Leaving a 3-in. (7.6 cm) tail, sew through the bead again to use it as a stop bead temporarily **(figure 1, a–b)**. This bead will be part of the design. Pick up nine color A 11º seed beads and three color B 11º seed beads. Sew back through the last A picked up **(b–c)**. The three Bs will form a picot at the end. Working back toward the tail, work four peyote stitches with As **(c–d)**. Pull the thread tight so the beadwork is straight. If needed, pull on the tail as well to even out the tension. Sew through the end C, and then sew back through the last two As your thread exited **(figure 2, a–b)**.
2 Work three peyote stitches with As **(b–c)**. To turn, pick up two Bs, and sew back through the last A added **(c–d)**. Work two stitches with As **(d–e)**.
3 Sew up through the adjacent A, turn, and sew back through the last A added **(figure 3, a–b)**. Make sure the thread gets tucked between the rows of As. Work two stitches with Bs **(b–c)**. To turn, pick up two Bs, and sew back through the last B added **(c–d)**. Work one stitch with a B **(d–e)**, and then sew down through the next three As **(e–f)**.
4 Sew up through the adjacent A **(f–g)**, and then work as in steps 2–3 to complete the center lobe **(figure 4)**.
5 To begin a side lobe, sew down through the next A **(figure 5, a–b)**. Pick up seven As and three Bs, and sew back through the last A just added **(b–c)**. Work three stitches with As **(c–d)**.
6 Sew through the adjacent C and back through the last two As your thread exited **(figure 6, a–b)**. Work two

FIGURE 5

FIGURE 6

FIGURE 7

stitches with As **(b–c)**, turn with two Bs, and work a stitch with a B **(c–d)**.
7 Join the side lobe to the center lobe: Sew up through the adjacent A on the center lobe **(figure 7, a–b)** and the next B on the side lobe **(b–c)**. Sew down through the two adjacent As on the center lobe **(c–d)** and the next A on the side lobe **(d–e)**, and sew through the adjacent A **(e–f)**. Complete this lobe with two As and three Bs **(f–g)**.
8 To finish this side of the leaf, add a tiny

Difficulty rating

    ⬡ ⬡

Materials

all projects
- beading needles, #12
- Fireline, 6 lb. test

earrings 1 x 1¼ in. (2.5 x 3.2 cm)
- 11º seed beads
  - **1 g** color A (Toho 25C, silver-lined ruby)
  - **1 g** color B (Toho 2208, silver-lined burnt orange)
  - **2** color C (Toho 557, permanent-finish gold)
- **1** pair of earwires
- **2** 4 mm outside-diameter soldered jump rings
- **2** pairs of chainnose, bentnose, and/or flatnose pliers

bracelet 6¾ in. (17.1 cm)
- 11º seed beads
  - **3 g** color A (Toho 25C, silver-lined ruby)
  - **2 g** color B (Toho 2208, silver-lined burnt orange)
  - **7** color C (Toho 557, permanent-finish gold)
  - **2 g** color D (Toho 30B, silver-lined light orange)
- **1** 6 mm outside-diameter soldered jump ring
- **1** lobster-claw clasp

pendant 1¼ x 1½ in. (3.2 x 3.8 cm)
- 8º seed beads
  - **2 g** color A (Toho 25C, silver-lined ruby)
  - **1 g** color B (Toho 2208, silver-lined burnt orange)
  - **1 g** color D (Toho 22, silver-lined light topaz)
- **1** 11º seed bead, color C (Toho 557, permanent-finish gold)
- **1** 8 mm outside-diameter soldered jump ring

Basics, p. 13

- peyote stitch: flat even-count
- attaching a stop bead
- square knot
- ending thread
- opening and closing loops and jump rings

lobe: Sew through the next two As **(figure 8, a–b)**. Pick up an A and four Bs, and sew back through the first B just added **(b–c)**. Join the tiny lobe to the side lobe by sewing through the adjacent A on the side lobe and the last B added on the tiny lobe **(c–d)**. Sew back through the adjacent A on the side lobe and the bottom B and A on the tiny lobe before sewing through the C **(figure 9)**.

9 Work as in steps 5–8 to add another side lobe and tiny lobe on the other side of the center lobe. At the end of step 8, do not sew through the final A and C.

10 To attach a jump ring, pick up a jump ring, and sew through the next A and then continue through the adjacent A on the opposite lobe. Sew through the jump ring again, and sew back through the A your thread just exited **(figure 10)**. Retrace the thread path through the As and jump ring. After retracing the thread path, your working thread and tail should be exiting at the same point. If they aren't, sew through the beadwork so the working thread is exiting next to the tail. Tie the working thread and tail together with a square knot, and end both threads.

11 Open the loop on an earwire, and attach it to the jump ring.

12 Repeat steps 1–11 to make another earring.

Bracelet

1 Work as in steps 1–9 of "Earrings" to make a total of seven leaf components, with the following changes:
• Start with 3 ft. (.9 m) of thread for each component, and leave a 6-in. (15 cm) tail.
• Make four components with colors A and B as in the earrings and three components substituting Bs for the As and Ds for the Bs.
• After each component is complete, sew through the beadwork to exit the tip of one side lobe, with the thread facing down toward the base of the leaf. With the tail, sew through the beadwork to exit the tip of the other side lobe, but exit with the thread facing up toward the tip of the leaf.

2 Arrange two components as shown in **figure 11**. Using the corresponding thread from each component, follow the existing thread paths to stitch the components together **(a–b and c–d)**. End each thread when the connection is secure.

3 When all the components are connected, thread a needle on the remaining thread that is facing down on an end component. Following the existing thread path, sew a lobster claw clasp to this spot **(e–f)**. Retrace the thread path, and end the thread.

4 With the remaining thread at the other end, sew through the beadwork to exit between the side and center lobes on the end component. Following the existing thread paths, stitch a 6 mm jump ring to this spot, attaching it to the four adjacent Bs of the two lobes **(g–h)**. End the thread.

Pendant

Following **figure 12** as a guide, work as in steps 1–9 of "Earrings" using three colors of 8º seed beads and one color C 11º. When the pendant is complete, attach a jump ring at the base of the leaf as in **figure 12**. ●

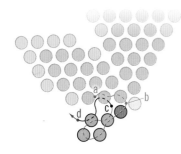

FIGURE 8

FIGURE 9

FIGURE 10

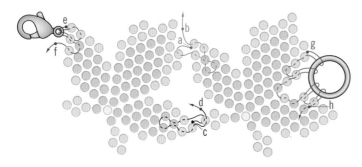

FIGURE 11

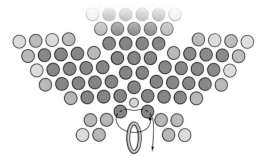

FIGURE 12

materials

golden bracelet 7¼ in. (18.4 cm)

- **6 cups** SS29 Swarovski Tiffany cup chain (white patina, mybeadgallery.com)
- **6** SS16 (4 mm) rose montées (Swarovski 53102, blue shade)
- **32** SS12 (3 mm) rose montées (Swarovski 53100, crystal AB)
- 3 mm Swarovski crystal pearls
  - **64** color A (bronze)
  - **36** color B (gold)
- **268** 6º Baroque seed beads (Miyuki 3953, gold)
- **1 g** 11º seed beads (Toho 279, color-lined antique gold/crystal)
- **1 g** 15º seed beads (Toho 989, gold-lined crystal)
- **1** 5-strand box clasp (Elegant Elements)
- Fireline, 10 lb. test
- beeswax or thread conditioner
- beading needle, #11
- flexible twisted wire needle – medium

Find info for the alternate colorway at FacetJewelry.com/resourceguide

basics, p. 13

- conditioning thread
- square knot
- right-angle weave: flat strip, adding rows
- ending and adding thread

	6º Baroque seed bead
	3 mm pearl, color A
	3 mm pearl, color B
	SS12 rose montée
	SS16 rose montée
	7 x 5 mm cup chain
	cup chain side view
	15º seed bead
	11º seed bead

Rose montées and pearls add shine and interest to this right-angle weave base made with Baroque seed beads. Top the cuff with Tiffany cups for an elegant focal piece.

Base

1) On a comfortable length of conditioned thread, pick up four 6º Baroque seed beads. Tie a square knot, and sew through the first three beads again to form a ring **(figure 1, a–b)**.

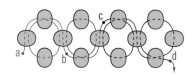

FIGURE 1

2) Working in right-angle weave **(RAW)**, pick up three 6ºs, and sew through the 6º your thread exited at the start of this step. Continue through the first two 6ºs just added **(b–c)**. Continue working in RAW to add two more stitches using a tight tension, but sew through only one bead instead of two for the last stitch **(c–d)**.

3) To add more rows, pick up three 6ºs, and sew through the 6º your thread is exiting in the previous row. Sew through the three 6ºs just added and next edge 6º **(figure 2, a–b)**. Working in a figure-eight pattern pick up two 6 ºs per stitch to complete the second row **(b–c)**. Continue working in RAW for a total of 28 rows, or to your desired length, ending and adding thread as needed.

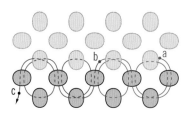

FIGURE 2

AIN'T BAROQUE

Baroque seed beads have a special coating, resembling a pearl. The crepey ruggedness adds texture and reflects light.

Embellishment

1) Sew through the beadwork to exit the end 6º on the edge as shown **(figure 3, point a)**. Pick up a color A pearl, and sew through the next edge 6º **(a–b)**. Repeat this stitch for the remainder of the base **(b–c)**. Sew through the next two 6ºs as shown to start the next row **(c–d)**.

2) Pick up a color B pearl, and sew through the next 6º in the row **(d–e)**. Repeat this stitch eight times **(e–f)**.

3) Pick up a SS12 rose montée, and sew through the next 6º **(f–g)**. Repeat this stitch eight times **(g–h)**.

4) Work as before to add nine B pearls **(h–i)**. Sew through the next two 6ºs as shown to start the next row **(i–j)**.

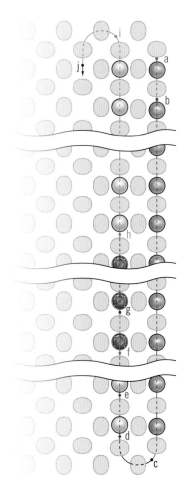

FIGURE 3

5) Work as before to add seven SS12 rose montées, and then add three SS16 rose montées. Remove the beading needle, and attach the flexible needle.

6) Pick up the end cup of the cup chain, and carefully sew under the chaton. Continue through the remaining cups, skipping the next six 6ºs below, and sew through the following 6º **(figure 4)**. Remove the flexible needle, and attach the beading needle to the working thread.

FIGURE 4

7) Work as before to add three SS16 rose montées and seven SS12 rose montées. Sew through the next two 6ºs to start the next row.

8) Repeat steps 2–4 to complete the fourth row.

9) Work as in step 1 to add As along this edge.

Clasp and Finishing

1) Pick up an A pearl and a 15º seed bead, and sew through the end loop of the clasp. Pick up a 15º, and sew back through the pearl and the 6º your thread exited at the start of this step **(figure 5, a–b)**. Sew through the next two 6ºs as shown **(b–c)**. Repeat these stitches four times to attach each clasp loop, but exit the second edge 6º **(c–d)**.

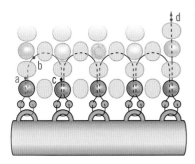

FIGURE 5

2) Reinforce the 10 rose montées on this end by sewing through the beadwork in a zigzag **(figure 6, a–b)**. When reaching the cup chain **(point b)**, pick up an 11º seed bead, three 15ºs, and an 11º, sew over the cup chain tab, and continue through the corresponding 6º **(b–c)**. Continue through the next rose montée, three 6ºs, rose montée, and 6º as shown **(c–d)**. Repeat these stitches to secure all the remaining cups and rose montées.

3) Repeat step 1 to attach the other half of the clasp, and end the thread. **B&B**

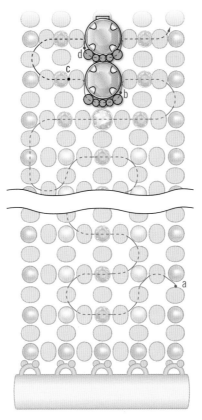

FIGURE 6

TIP This bracelet is designed for a 6¼ in. (15.9 cm) wrist. Each row adds ⅜ in. (1 cm) to the length of the cuff. Add or omit rows as needed for the desired length.

BEAD-CAPPED PEARL EARRINGS

**designed by
Gianna Zimmerman**

DIFFICULTY ●●●○○

bead weaving

materials
**turquoise / red earrings
1½ in. (3.8 cm)**

- **2** 8 x 11 mm crystal pearl drops (Swarovski 5821, white) *or* **2** 8 mm round crystal pearls and **2** each of size 6º and 8º seed beads
- **18** 3 mm crystal pearls (Swarovski, gold)
- **8** 11º seed beads (Miyuki 2029, sea foam blue)
- **15º** seed beads (Miyuki)
  - **1 g** color A (2428, silver-lined dark topaz)
  - **1 g** color B (182, galvanized gold)
  - **1 g** color C (1464, dyed opaque maroon)
  - **1 g** color D (413, opaque light blue)
- **2** 2-in. (5 cm) head pins
- **1** pair of earring findings
- Fireline, 6 lb. test
- beading needles, #11
- **2** pairs of chainnose, flatnose, and/or bentnose pliers
- roundnose pliers
- wire cutters

basics, p. 13
- square knot
- ending thread
- plain loops
- opening and closing loops and jump rings

Key
- 3 mm pearl
- 15º seed bead, color A
- 15º seed bead, color B
- 15º seed bead, color C
- 15º seed bead, color D
- 11º seed bead

FIGURE 1

FIGURE 2

Turn plain pearls into a stunning pair of earrings with sweet beaded bead caps made of tiny seed beads and more pearls.

Beaded bead cap

1) For each earring, work as follows: On 1 yd. (.9 m) of thread, pick up a repeating pattern of a 4 mm pearl and a color A 15º seed bead eight times. Tie the beads into a ring with a square knot, and sew through the first pearl again. This is round 1.

2) Pick up a color B 15º seed bead, two color C 15º seed beads, and a B, and sew through the same pearl and the first B and C just added **(figure 1)** to form a loop around the pearl.

3) Pick up a C, sew through the next C and B, and continue through the same pearl and the following A and pearl **(figure 2, a–b)**.

4) Pick up a B and two Cs, sew through the adjacent B in the previous loop, and continue through the same pearl and the first B and C added in this step **(b–c)**.

5) Pick up a C, sew through the next C and B, and continue through the same pearl and the following A and pearl **(figure 3)**.

6) Repeat steps 4–5 five times. Sew through the adjacent B in the first loop, and then work as in step 4 but pick up only two Cs, and sew through the adjacent B in the previous stitch **(figure 4)**. Repeat step 5 to add a C between the previous two Cs, and then sew through the beadwork to exit a center C **(figure 5, point a)**.

7) Continue working in rounds:

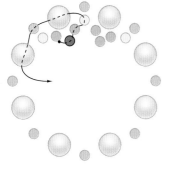

FIGURE 3

FIGURE 4

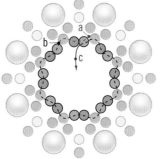

FIGURE 5

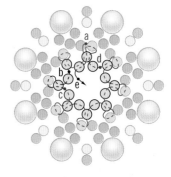

FIGURE 6

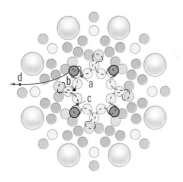

FIGURE 7

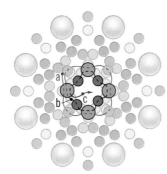

FIGURE 8

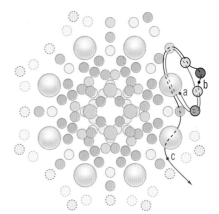

FIGURE 9

T I P With all the thread passes through the 3 mm pearls in round 1, you may find it difficult to get your needle through them in the final steps. If this is the case, either switch to a thinner needle or sew through the adjacent beads to avoid sewing through the pearls again.

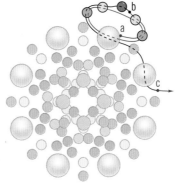

FIGURE 10

Round 3: Pick up a color D 15º and an A, and sew through the center C in the next stitch of the previous round (**a–b**). Repeat this stitch seven times to complete the round, retrace the thread path (not shown in the figure for clarity), and sew through the first D added in this step (**b–c**).

Round 4: Pick up three Bs, sew through the next D in the previous round, and sew back through the third B just picked up (**figure 6, a–b**). Pick up two Bs, sew through the next D in the previous round, and sew back through the last B just added (**b–c**). Repeat this last stitch five times (**c–d**). For the final stitch in the round, pick up a B, sew down through the first B added in this round, sew through the D below it, and sew back through the same B and the next B (**d–e**).

Round 5: Pick up an A, and sew through the center B in the next stitch of the previous round (**figure 7, a–b**). Without adding a bead, retrace the thread path of the next stitch in the previous round (**b–c**). Repeat these two stitches

three times, and step up through the first A added in this step (**c–d**).

Round 6: Sewing through the As in the previous round, work four stitches with one 11º seed bead per stitch. Retrace the thread path through this round twice (not shown in the figure for clarity), and step up through the first 11º added (**figure 8, a–b**).

Round 7: Sewing through the 11ºs in the previous round, work four stitches with one C per stitch (**b–c**), and then sew through the bead-work to exit a pearl in round 1.

8) End the tail but not the working thread.

Finishing

1) On a head pin, string an 8 x 11 mm pearl drop and an 8º seed bead. Alternatively, string an 8 mm round pearl, a 6º seed bead, and an 8º.

2) String the bead cap over the pearl. Add or remove beads under the bead cap as desired to achieve the desired fit. String a 3 mm pearl and a 15º after the bead cap.

3) Make a plain loop above the beads just strung.

4) With the working thread, pick up a D, two Bs, and a D, and sew through the same pearl and the first D and B added in this step (**figure 9, a–b**). Pick up a C, and sew through the next B and D, the same pearl, and the next A and pearl in round 1 (**b–c**).

5) Pick up a D and two Bs, and sew through the adjacent D in the previous step, the same pearl, and the first D and B added in this step (**figure 10, a–b**). Pick up a C, and

sew through the next B and D, the same pearl, and the next A and pearl in round 1 (**b–c**).

6) Repeat step 5 five times. For the final stitch, sew through the adjacent D. Pick up two Bs, and sew down through the D in the previous stitch, the pearl below, and the first D and B. Pick up a C, and sew through the next B and D, the same pearl, and the next A and pearl in round 1. End the working thread.

7) Open the loop of an ear wire, and attach the dangle. **B&B**

CONE FLOWERS BRACELET

designed by
SZIDONIA PETKI

DIFFICULTY ●●●○○

bead weaving

materials

green bracelet 7½ in. (19.1 cm)

- **5** 10 mm crystal pearls (Swarovski, iridescent green)
- **5 g** 5 x 2.3 mm Half Tila beads (Miyuki, metallic bronze)
- **66** 3 mm bicone crystals (Swarovski, olivine AB)
- **1 g** 8º seed beads (Miyuki 2006, matte metallic dark bronze)
- **2 g** 11º seed beads (Miyuki 2006, matte metallic dark bronze)
- 15º seed beads (Miyuki)
  - **2 g** color A (2006, matte metallic dark bronze)
  - **1 g** color B (457, metallic dark bronze)
- **1** ball and socket clasp
- **2** 5 mm jump rings
- Fireline, 6 lb. test
- beading needles, #11 or #12

basics, p. 13

- ending thread
- opening and closing loops and jump rings

Nestle large pearls within stylized flower settings to create a stunning, dimensional bracelet.

The front of the Half Tila is the side that is smooth and flat. With the holes running horizontally, you will pick up the Half Tila through the top hole (TH) or the bottom hole (BH) per the instructions.

BRACELET

End components

1) On 4 ft. (1.2 m) of thread and leaving a 10-in. (25 cm) tail, pick up a 10 mm pearl and an 8º seed bead, and sew back through the pearl (**figure 1, a–b**). Pick up an 8º, and sew back through the pearl and the first 8º added (**b–c**). Sew back through the pearl and the last 8º added (**figure 2, a–b**). These two 8ºs will be used as anchor points.

2) Pick up a repeating pattern of a Half Tila (TH) and a color A 15º seed bead twice, and then pick up a Half Tila (TH) once more. Pick up an 8º and the same pattern of beads added before the 8º, and sew through the opposite anchor 8º to form a loop on one side of the pearl (**b–c**). Repeat to form a loop on the other side of the pearl (**c–d**). Retrace the thread path of the ring (not shown in the figure for clarity), and sew through the open hole of the first Half Tila (**d–e**). For now, the ring will sit loosely around the pearl.

3) Pick up a Half Tila (BH), and sew through the open hole of the next Half Tila to form a tab for joining the components (**e–f**). Pick up a 3 mm bicone crystal, and sew through the open hole of the following Half Tila (**f–g**). Repeat this last stitch four times (**g–h**).

4) Work as in step 3 to complete the round (**h–i**), retrace the thread path of the round (not shown in the figure for clarity), and continue through the first Half Tila added and the open hole of the same Half Tila (**i–j**). Set the working thread aside.

5) Using the tail, sew through the adjacent anchor 8º bead (**figure 3, a–b**). Pick up five 11º seed beads, and sew through the next 8º in the ring (**b–c**). Repeat this stitch three times to complete the round (**c–d**), and continue through the first five 11ºs added (**d–e**).

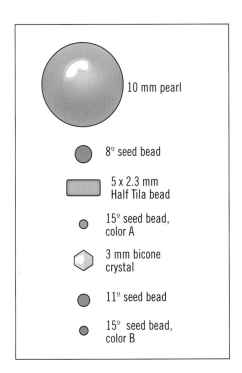

⬤	10 mm pearl
●	8º seed bead
▭	5 x 2.3 mm Half Tila bead
•	15º seed bead, color A
⬡	3 mm bicone crystal
●	11º seed bead
●	15º seed bead, color B

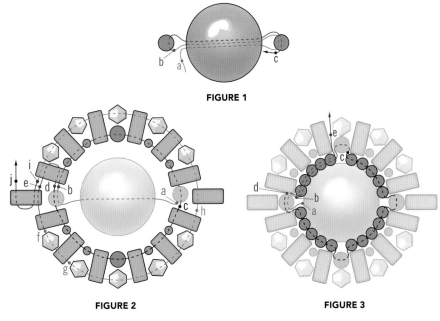

FIGURE 1

FIGURE 2

FIGURE 3

6) Pick up three color B 15º seed beads, skip the next 8º in the ring, and sew through the following set of five 11ºs to form a picot (**figure 4, a–b**). Repeat this stitch three times to complete the round (**b–c**). Retrace the thread path, skipping the center B in each picot, and end the tail. The front of the component should be slightly domed.

7) With the working thread, pick up a Half Tila (BH), sew through the Half Tila your thread is exiting, going in the same direction, and continue through the Half Tila (BH) just added (**figure 5**). Pull the thread snug but not so tight that the beads overlap.

8) Pick up a Half Tila (BH), and sew through the Half Tila your thread is exiting, going in the same direction. Position it so it sits on top and between the previous two Half Tilas to create a double layer (**figure 6**).

9) Sew through the nearest hole of the Half Tila on the top layer, and continue through the other hold of the same Half Tila (**figure 7, a–b**). Sew through the nearest hole of the adjacent Half Tila on the bottom layer (**b–c**) and then se throught the nearest hole of the Half Tila on the top layer again (**c–d**).

10) Sew through the beadwork as shown to exit the open hole of the end Half Tila on the bottom layer (**figure 8**).

11) Repeat steps 7–10 twice.

12) Pick up five As, and sew through the other hole of the Half Tila your thread is exiting to form a picot (**figure 9, a–b**). Repeat this stitch to add a picot on the opposite side of this Half Tila (**b–c**). Retrace the thread path, skipping the center As, and exit the end A on the bottom-edge picot (**c–d**).

13) Pick up five As, and sew through the picot on the top edge (**figure 10, a–b**). Sew through the beadwork to retrace the thread path of the picots, skipping the center A of the picot added in this step, and continue through the Half Tila on the top layer (**b–c**).

14) Work as in step 12 to add a picot on each edge of each of the Half Tila, sewing through the bottom layer beads as needed. Exit the center A in the top edge picot (**figure 11**).

15) Pick up an A, a 3 mm, and an A, and sew through the center A in the next picot (**figure 12, a–b**). Repeat this stitch once (**b–c**), sew through the beadwork as shown to exit the center A in the picot on the bottom edge (**c–d**), and repeat the stitch twice on this edge (**d–e**).

FIGURE 4

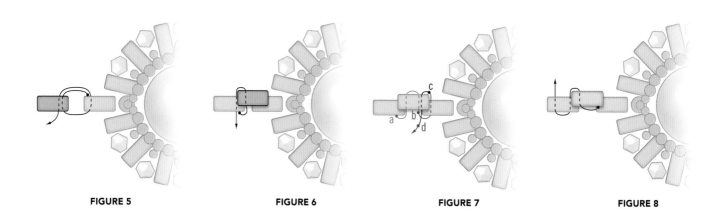

FIGURE 5   **FIGURE 6**   **FIGURE 7**   **FIGURE 8**

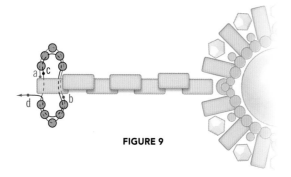

FIGURE 9

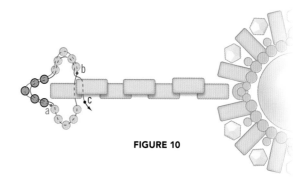

FIGURE 10

Sew through the beadwork as needed to retrace the thread path of the beads just added, and end the thread.

16) Work as in steps 1–15 to make a second end component.

Center components

Work as in steps 1–6 of "End components," leaving an 8-in. (20 cm) tail, to make a total of three center components.

Joining

1) Place two center components horizontally on your work surface, with the working thread of each exiting from the right-hand side. With the working thread of the left-hand component, sew through the open hole of the tab on the adjacent component. Continue through the Half Tila your thread exited at the start of this step, going in the same direction, and retrace the thread path **(figure 13)**.

2) Working as in steps 8–9 of "End components," stitch a Half Tila on top of the two Half Tila tabs to create a double layer. Sew through the beadwork to exit the Half Tila on the top layer.

3) Pick up an A, a 3 mm, and an A, and sew back through the 3 mm **(figure 14, a–b)**. Pick up an A, and sew through the other hole of the same Half Tila **(b–c)**. Repeat these stitches to add embellishment on the opposite side **(c–d)**. Retrace the thread path of both embellishments, and end the thread.

4) Work as in steps 1–3 to connect the remaining center component to the previous center component, and then work in the same manner to attach the end components.

5) Use a 5 mm jump ring to attach half of the clasp to an end picot on an end component. Repeat on the other end. B B

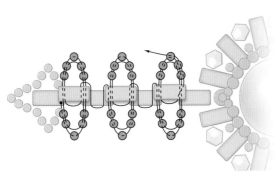

FIGURE 11

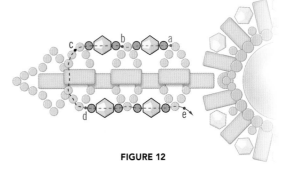

FIGURE 12

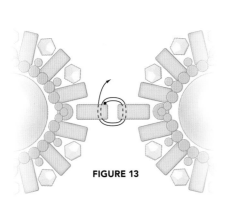

FIGURE 13

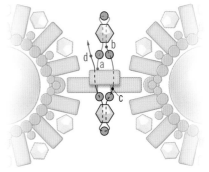

FIGURE 14

GOLDEN PATHS NECKLACE

designed by Mandi Olaniyi

DIFFICULTY ●●●●○

herringbone stitch

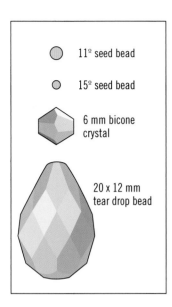

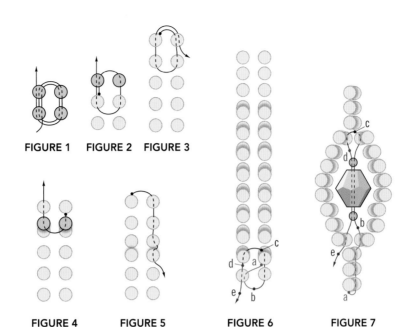

FIGURE 1   FIGURE 2   FIGURE 3

FIGURE 4   FIGURE 5   FIGURE 6   FIGURE 7

Take an adventurous winding journey in herringbone stitch and create clever bezel settings in this gorgeous necklace.

materials
necklace 17 in. (43 cm)
- **1** 20 x 12 mm gemstone teardrop bead (aventurine)
- **11** 6 mm bicone crystals (Swarovski, aquamarine golden shadow)
- **17 g** 11º seed beads (Toho 557PF, permanent finish galvanized gold)
- **1 g** 15º seed beads (Toho 557PF, permanent finish galvanized gold)
- Fireline, 6 lb. test
- beading needles, #11 or #12

basics, p. 13
- herringbone stitch: tubular
- ladder stitch: making a ladder, forming a ring
- ending and adding thread

NECKLACE
Bezeled bicone components
1) On 1 yd. (.9 m) of thread, pick up four 11º seed beads, and sew through the beads again, leaving a 6-in. (15 cm) tail. Position the beads to form two columns of two beads each. Retrace the thread path (not shown in the figure for clarity), and continue through the first two 11ºs (**figure 1**).

2) Work a two-bead-wide herringbone strip: Pick up two 11ºs, sew down through the next bead in the previous row, and continue up through the bead your thread exited at the start of this step and the first bead just added (**figure 2**). Repeat this step seven times to make a strip 10 rows long.

3) Retrace the thread path through the last two rows, and continue through the adjacent bead of the last row (**figure 3**).

4) Pick up two 11ºs, and sew up through the adjacent 11º in the end row (**figure 4**). These two beads will sit on top of and in between rows 9 and 10 and will become row 1 of the matching half of the component.

5) Work as in step 2 to stitch two more herringbone rows off of the end row to form a tab.

6) Working in the opposite direction, sew down through the adjacent 11º in the end row and the following two 11ºs, and continue through the corresponding 11º in row 1 of the new section started in step 4 (**figure 5**).

7) Work as in step 2 to add seven more herringbone rows to form another strip. Align the two strips on top of each other. Note that the second strip will not overlap row 1 of the first strip.

8) Still working in the opposite direction, make a join: Sew diagonally through the opposite end 11º in the first strip (**figure 6, a–b**) and the adjacent 11º in the same row, and continue back through the 11º your thread exited at the start of this step (**b–c**). Sew through the adjacent 11º in the same row of this strip (**c–d**) and the end 11º in the opposite strip (**d–e**). Retrace the thread path to reinforce the connection.

9) Work two rows of herringbone off this end row to form a tab.

10) Working in the opposite direction, sew through the adjacent 11º in this end row, and continue through the next three 11ºs as shown (**figure 7, a–b**).

11) Pick up a 15º seed bead, a 6 mm bicone crystal, and a 15º, skip the next six 11ºs, and sew through the following 11º in this strip (**b–c**) and the corresponding 11º in the opposite strip (**c–d**). Sew back through the 15º, crystal, and 15º, skipping the next six 11ºs in this strip, and sew through the following 11º (**d–e**). End the threads.

12) Work as in steps 1–11 to make a total of 10 components.

FIGURE 8   FIGURE 9   FIGURE 10   FIGURE 11

BEZELED TEARDROP PENDANT

The pendant is made similarly to the "Bezeled bicone components," except it has an additional row of 15°s around each edge, and there is only one joined corner instead of two. The herringbone strip can easily be adjusted to fit your particular size gemstone.

1) Work as in steps 1–2 of "Bezeled bicone component" to make a strip long enough to fit snugly around the circumference of the teardrop gemstone. Make sure the ends meet. Our 20 x 12 mm bead required a strip with 34 rows. Stitch one additional row, and retrace the thread path of the last row.

2) Sew through the adjacent bead in the end row (**figure 8, a–b**). Work in square stitch: Pick up a 15° seed bead, sew through the 11° your thread is exiting, going in the same direction, and continue through the next 11° in the following row (**b–c**). Repeat this stitch for the remainder of this edge, except do not add a 15° to the end row (**c–d**). Sew through the adjacent 11° and the following 11° on the opposite edge (**d–e**), and work as before to add 15°s along this edge (**e–f**). End and add thread as needed.

3) Fold the beadwork, and align the two ends. Form a corner join: With the working thread, sew up through the corresponding bead on the opposite end, and continue down through the adjacent end bead and the next bead on the end you started from (**figure 9, a–b**). Retrace the thread path to secure the join (not shown in figure for clarity), and sew through the 11° your thread exited at the start of this step and the next 11° on the opposite end (**b–c**).

4) Work a two-bead wide strip of herringbone stitch using 11°s for two rows, and then make another row using 15°s to make a tab that will be used for joining the pendant to the ropes.

5) Sew through the beadwork to exit a 15° along one inner edge of the bezel. Sew through all the edge 15°s on this side of the bezel, pull the thread tight, and retrace the thread path. This will be the back of the pendant. Sew through the beadwork to exit a 15° on the front.

6) Place the teardrop gemstone in the center of the beadwork, and sew through the 15°s on this edge. Pull the thread tight, and retrace the thread path to secure the teardrop.

7) Sew through the beadwork to the back of the bezel, and exit the center 11° on the bottom of the pendant. Pick up a crystal and a 15°, and sew back through the crystal and the 11° your thread exited at the start of this step, going in the same direction (**figure 10**). Retrace the thread path, and end the threads.

ROPES

1) On a comfortable length of thread and leaving a 6-in. (15 cm) tail, make a four-bead ladder using 11°s, and join the ends to form a ring.

2) Work in tubular herringbone stitch for 136 rows or for your desired length.

3) With the working thread, work two rows of two-bead-wide herringbone stitch using 11°s off the end row to form a tab. This will be used to attach the pendant. End the tail but not the working thread.

4) Work as in steps 1–3 to make a second rope.

ROPE EMBELLISHMENT

1) With the working thread from one rope and working in the opposite direction, sew through the adjacent 11° in the end row, and continue through the next six 11°s (**figure 11, point a**).

2) Position the rope vertically on your work surface and align a bezeled bicone component on the right side of the rope with one tab of the bezeled bicone adjacent to the 11° your working thread is exiting.

3) Sew up through the corresponding 11° on the bezeled bicone tab (**a–b**), and continue down through the adjacent 11° (**b–c**) and the adjacent 11° in the same row on the rope your thread exited at the start of this step (**c–d**).

4) Sew up through the 11° your thread exited at the start of step 3, and continue through the next 14 11°s (**d–e**). Sew down through the corresponding 11° on the other tab of the bicone component (**e–f**), and work as before to attach this tab of the component to the rope.

5) Sew through the beadwork to exit an 11° on the opposite side of the herringbone rope (in the same row to which this end of the bezel is attached), with the needle facing toward the opposite end. Continue working in a similar manner to attach a bezeled bicone to this side of the rope as (**figure 12**).

6) Repeat steps 2–5 once, and then repeat steps 2–4 once again.

7) Work as in steps 1–6 to embellish the other rope.

FIGURE 12

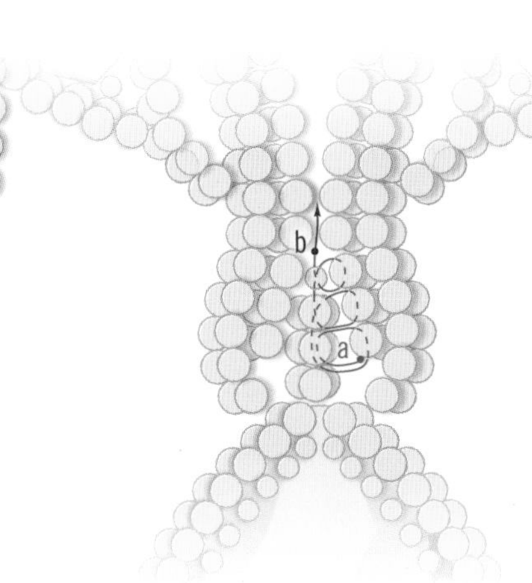

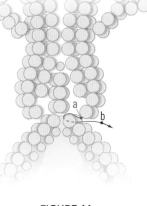

FIGURE 13

FIGURE 14

FIGURE 15

ASSEMBLY

1) Position the two ropes vertically on your work surface with the tabs at the bottom. Center the bezeled teardrop pendant faceup between the tabs.

2) Using the working thread from the rope to the right of the pendant, sew through the tab to exit the end 11º in the last row of the tubular herringbone section **(figure 13, point a)**. Work a square stitch thread path to attach the pendant tab to the corresponding end three rows of the tubular herringbone rope **(figure 13, a–b)**. Repeat these stitches on the back surface.

3) Repeat steps 1–2 on the opposite side of the pendant, attaching it to the other rope.

4) Sew through the beadwork to exit the end tab 11º of the rope to the right of the pendant, with the needle facing toward the pendant **(figure 14, point a)**.

5) Sew through the adjacent 11º on the pendant as shown to secure the front of the rope to the pendant **(a–b)**. Repeat this step on the back of the pendant. End the thread.

6) Work as in steps 4–5 to attach the end of the other rope to the pendant.

SQUARE TOGGLE CLASP

1) Work as in steps 1–2 of "Ropes" to make a strip of tubular herringbone that is eight rounds long. Retrace the thread path of the last round to secure the beads, and exit an 11º in round 7 with the needle facing back toward row 6 **(figure 15, point a)**.

2) Pick up two 11ºs, and sew through the 11º your thread is exiting, going in the same direction to form the base for the next leg of the toggle **(a–b)**. Retrace the thread path. Flip the beadwork over, and repeat this step on the opposite side.

3) Work seven rounds of tubular herringbone stitch off the four 11ºs just added to form the

next leg of the square. Retrace the thread path of the last round to secure the beads.

4) Repeat steps 2–3 twice to form the remaining two legs of the square.

5) To join the square: Exit an 11º in round 7 of the last leg, sew through the adjacent end 11º in round 1 of the first leg, and then continue through the adjacent 11º in the same round and the 11º your thread exited at the start of this step, going in the same direction **(figure 16)**. Retrace the thread path to secure the join. Flip the beadwork over, and repeat this step on the opposite surface. End the tail but not the working thread.

6) To make the toggle bar, make a strip of tubular herringbone with four 11ºs in each round that is 19 rounds long. End the tail but not the working thread.

7) Attach the toggle bar: With the working thread, sew through the beadwork to exit an 11º in the center of the bar. Pick up three 11ºs, sew through an 11º in an end round of the rope, the adjacent 11º in the same round, and continue back through the three 11ºs just added and the adjacent 11º in the same round of the toggle bar **(figure 17)**. Retrace the thread path to secure the join, connecting the rope to the center bead in the other column. End the thread.

8) With the working thread of the toggle ring, sew through the beadwork to exit between the two center 11ºs on an outside edge, and then center the toggle ring to the end of the rope. With the working thread of the toggle ring, sew through the corresponding 11º in the end round of the rope, and continue through the adjacent 11º in the same round and the center two 11ºs on the edge of the toggle ring, going in the same direction **(figure 18)**. Retrace the thread path to reinforce the connection.

9) Flip the beadwork over, and work as in step 8 to attach the opposite surface. End the thread. **B&B**

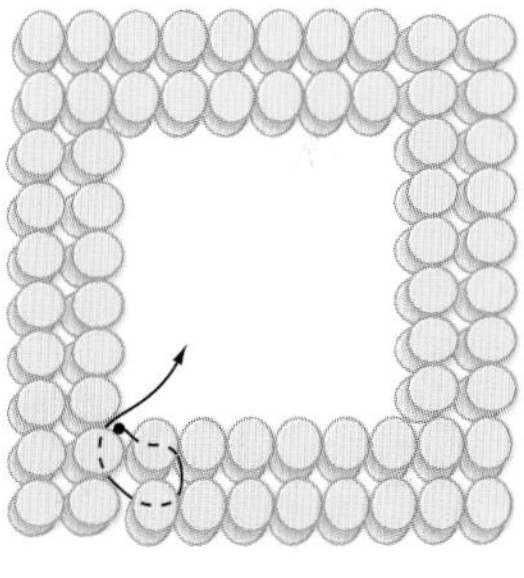

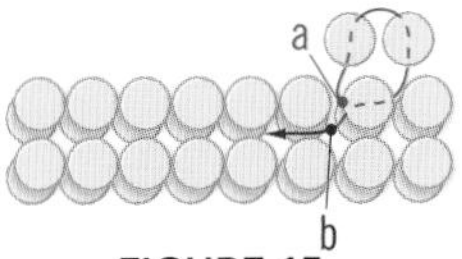

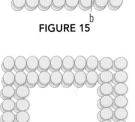

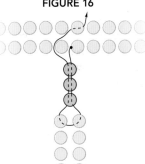

FIGURE 16

FIGURE 17

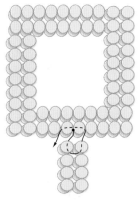

FIGURE 18

ENCASED IN ELEGANCE SET

designed by
Josane Demuylder

DIFFICULTY ●●●○○

prismatic right-angle weave

Showcase captured pearls in this prismatic right-angle weave stitched necklace and earrings.

NECKLACE

1) On a comfortable length of thread, pick up five color A 11º seed beads, sew through the beads again to form a ring, and continue through the next A, leaving a 6-in. (15 cm) tail. This is the base of the first prismatic right-angle weave (PRAW) unit. Work the following PRAW units as follows:

Unit 1:

• **Side 1:** Pick up three As, sew through the A your thread is exiting, and continue through the next A in the ring **(figure 1, a–b)**.

• **Sides 2–4:** Pick up two As, sew through the adjacent A from the previous side **(b–c)**, and continue through the A your thread exited at the start of this stitch and the following A in the ring **(c–d)**. Repeat this stitch twice **(d–e)**.

• **Side 5:** Sew through the adjacent A in side 1, pick up an A, and sew through the adjacent A in side 4 and the A in the ring your thread exited at the start of this step **(e–f)**. Step up by continuing through the adjacent A in side 1 and the A added on this side **(f–g)**.

• Complete the PRAW unit by sewing through the top A in each of the five sides, and continue through the A your thread exited at the start of this stitch **(g–h)**. This completes one PRAW unit.

Units 2–5: Working off the top ring of As in the previous round, repeat "Unit 1" four times.

Unit 6: Work as in "Unit 1," but substitute color B 11ºs for the As.

Unit 7: Continue working in the same manner, but with the following changes:

• **Side 1:** Color C 11º seed bead, 8º seed bead, C **(figure 2, a–b)**.

• **Sides 2–4:** C, 8º **(b–c)**.

• **Side 5:** 8º **(c–d)**. Do not sew through the top 8ºs from each side.

• Pick up a B, and sew through the next top 8º **(d–e)**. Repeat this stitch four times to complete the round **(e–f)**.

Unit 8 (pearl cage): Work in the same manner, making the following changes. After adding each side, sew through the 8º your thread is exiting, and continue through the next B and 8º in the ring.

• **Side 1:** Seven 15º seed beads, 8º, seven 15ºs **(figure 3, a–b)**.

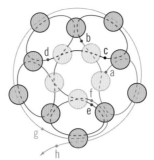

FIGURE 1

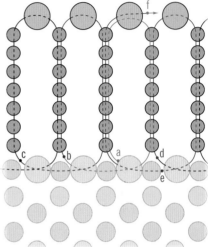

FIGURE 2

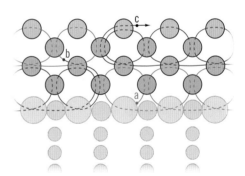

FIGURE 3

FIGURE 4

• **Sides 2–4:** Seven 15ºs, 8º; sew down through the adjacent seven 15ºs, and continue through the adjacent 8º, B, and 8º **(b–c)**. Repeat this stitch twice **(c–d)**.

• Place a color D 6 mm pearl into the center of the beadwork (not shown in the figure for clarity).

• **Side 5:** Sew up through the adjacent seven 15ºs in the first side, pick up an 8º, and sew down through the adjacent seven 15ºs in the last side added and the 8º your thread exited at the start of this stitch to enclose the pearl in the beadwork **(d–e)**. Continue through the next B, 8º, seven 15ºs, and 8º **(e–f)**.

• Add a B between the top 8ºs.

Unit 9: After adding each side, sew through the 8º your thread is exiting and the next B and 8º in the ring **(figure 4, a–b)**.

• **Side 1:** C, B, C.

• **Sides 2–4:** C, B.

• **Side 5:** B.

• Sew through the top B in each of the five sides.

Unit 10: Work as in "Unit 1," using bead colors as follows:

• **Side 1:** B, A, B.

• **Sides 2–4:** B, A.

• **Side 5:** A **(b–c)**.

2) Repeat units 6–10 for the desired length, allowing approximately 1⅜ in. (3.5 cm) for the clasp. End and add thread as needed. Our 18-in. (46 cm) necklace features an alternating pattern of eight color D and seven color E pearl units. When you've complete all the desired pearl units, repeat units 1–5 with all As.

3) Add a length of thread as long as the necklace plus 6 in. (15 cm), exiting just before the first pearl cage. Sew through the center of the beadwork and pearls to center the pearls and hide the holes. End the thread after the last pearl cage.

CLASP

1) Pick up an 8º, a color D 6 mm pearl, an 8º, a 10 mm pearl, an 8º, and an A, and sew back through the 8º, 10 mm, 8º, D, and 8º. Skip the next A in the ring, and sew through the following two As, using a tight tension **(figure 5)** (only the end round of As is shown in the figure for clarity). Retrace the thread path several times, and end the working thread.

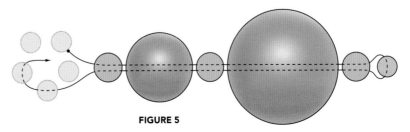

FIGURE 5

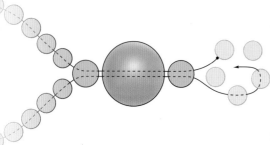

FIGURE 6

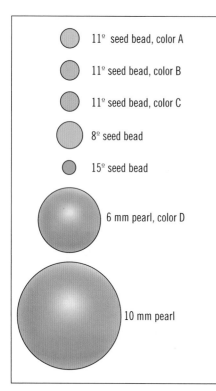

- 11° seed bead, color A
- 11° seed bead, color B
- 11° seed bead, color C
- 8° seed bead
- 15° seed bead
- 6 mm pearl, color D
- 10 mm pearl

2) With the tail, pick up an 8°, a D, an 8°, and 21 As, sew back through the 8°, 6 mm, and 8° to form a loop, skip the next A in the ring, and sew through the following two As in the round, using a tight tension (**figure 6**) (only the end round of As is shown in figure for clarity). Check the fit of the loop over the 10 mm, and add or remove 11°s in the loop if necessary. Retrace the thread path several times, and end the tail.

EARRINGS

1) Work PRAW units as in the necklace as follows:
• On a comfortable length of thread, pick up five 15°s, sew through the beads again to form a ring, and continue through the next 15°, leaving an 8-in. (20 cm) tail. This is the base of the first unit.
Unit 1: After adding each side, sew through the 15° your thread is exiting, and continue through the next 15° in the ring.
• **Side 1:** 11°, 8°, 11°.
• **Sides 2–4:** 11°, 8°.
• **Side 5:** 8°; do not sew through the top 8° from each side.
• Pick up an 11°, and sew through the next top 8°. Repeat this stitch four times to complete the round.
Unit 2: Work a pearl cage as in "Unit 8" of the necklace.
Unit 3: After adding each side, sew through the 8° your thread is exiting, and the next 11° and 8° in the ring.
• **Side 1:** 11°, 15°, 11°.
• **Sides 2–4:** 11°, 15°.
• **Side 5:** 15°; sew through the top 15° in each of the five sides.
Units 4–9: Work six units using 15°s, or vary the length of the earring by adding or omitting units as desired. End the working thread.
2) With the tail, pick up five 15°s, skip the next 15° in the ring, and sew through the following two 15°s to form a loop. Retrace the thread path several times, and end the tail.
3) Open the loop of an ear wire, and attach it to the loop just added.
4) Repeat steps 1–3 to make another earring. B⬡B

materials
bronze necklace 18 in. (46 cm)

- Swarovski pearls
  - **1** 10 mm (bronze)
  - **10** 6 mm, color D (bronze)
  - **7** 6 mm, color E (turquoise)
- **4 g** 8° seed beads (Miyuki 457, metallic dark bronze)
- 11° seed beads
  - **4 g** color A (Miyuki 457, metallic dark bronze)
  - **4 g** color B (Miyuki 2006, matte metallic dark bronze)
  - **2 g** color C (Toho 1611, opaque lagoon luster)
- **4 g** 15° seed beads (Miyuki 2006, matte metallic dark bronze)
- Fireline, 6 lb. test
- beading needles, #11 or #12

bronze earrings 1¼ in. (3.2 cm)

- **2** 6 mm pearls (Swarovski, bronze)
- seed beads (Miyuki 457, metallic dark bronze)
  - **1 g** 8°
  - **30** 11°
  - **1 g** 15°
- Fireline, 6 lb. test
- beading needles, #11 or #12
- **1** pair of earring findings
- **2** pairs of chainnose, bent-nose, and/or flatnose pliers

Find info for the alternate colorway at
FacetJewelry.com/resourceguide

basics, p. 13
- ending and adding thread
- opening and closing loops and jump rings

Beads, buttons & filigree

Use lentil beads, filigree, and craft store buttons to make lively lilies with a secret support system.

by Carolyn Cave

Flat-backed floral components make for great earrings, pendants, bracelets, and more. What can you create with this versatile design?

I was given some single-hole lentil beads and decided to make beaded flowers with them, pairing them with curved petal beads and craft store buttons to mimic the look of a blooming water lily. I added metal filigree stampings for extra panache.

PENDANT

The lentil beads shown in this project are coated on one side so they look green on one surface and silver on the other. The instructions will tell you from which side you should pick up each lentil. Pick up each petal bead with the curved side facing up.

1) On 2 ft. (61 cm) of thread and leaving a 6-in. (15 cm) tail, pick up six 15° seed beads. Sew through the beads again to form a ring, tie a square knot, and sew through the first 15° in the ring **(figure 1, a–b)**.

2) Pick up an 11° seed bead, an O-bead, a lentil (from the green side), a lentil (from the silver side), an 11°, a 15°, an 11°, a lentil (silver side), a lentil (green side), an 11°, a 15°, an 11°, a lentil (green side), a lentil (silver side), an O-bead, and an 11°. Sew through 15° your thread is exiting, going in the same direction to form a loop, and

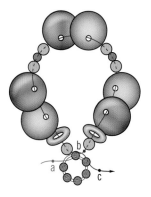

FIGURE 1

continue through the next 15º in the ring (b–c). Pull the thread tight.

3) Pick up an 11º, an O-bead, a lentil (green side), a lentil (silver side), an 11º, a 15º, an 11º, a lentil (silver side), a lentil (green side), an 11º and a 15º. Sew through the 11º, two lentils, O-bead, and 11º in the adjacent loop (**figure 2, a–b**). Continue through the same 15º in the center ring, going in the same direction, and continue through the next 15º (**b–c**). Pull the thread tight.

4) Repeat step 3 three more times (**figure 3, a–b**). Sew through the adjacent 11º, O-bead, two lentils, and 11º in the first loop (**b–c**). Pick up a 15º, an 11º, a lentil (silver side), a lentil (green side), an 11º, and a 15º. Sew through the adjacent 11º, two lentils, O-bead, and 11º in the previous loop, and continue through the 15º your thread exited at the start of this step and the following 15º in the center ring (**figure 4, a–b**). Sew through the first 10 beads in the first loop to exit an 11º (**b–c**).

5) Pick up a petal bead from the right, when the tip is curving upward and the hole is at the lower end of the bead. Sew through the 11º, two lentils, and 11º in the next outer loop (**figure 5, a–b**). Repeat this stitch five times to complete the round, and continue through the first petal added in the round (**b–c**). Pull the thread tight to make the beadwork dome.

6) Flip your work. You will be stitching in the opposite direction now. Pick up two 15ºs, an 11º, and two 15ºs, and sew through the next petal

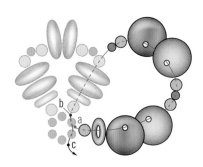

FIGURE 2

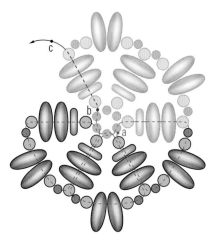

FIGURE 3

DIFFICULTY ●●○○○
filigree

materials
both projects
- beading needles, #12
- Fireline, 8 lb. test
- **2** pairs of chainnose, flat-nose, and/or bentnose pliers

pendant 1¾ in. (4.4 cm)
- **24** 6 mm lentil beads (crystal vitrail)
- **6** 6 x 4 mm curved petal beads (polychrome viridian; glitznkitz.com)
- **6** 3.8 mm O-beads (matte transparent peridot vitrail)
- **1 g** 11º seed beads (Miyuki 4204, Duracoat Champagne)
- **1 g** size 15º seed beads (Miyuki 457, metallic dark bronze)
- **1** 35–45 mm brass metal filigree stamping
- **1** 15 mm flat button, domed top, up to 3 mm thick (dark green or black; available at craft or fabric stores)
- **1** 6 mm jump ring (16-gauge, brass)

earrings 1¼ in. (3.2 cm)
(same colors as pendant)
- **48** 6 mm lentil beads
- **12** 6 x 4 mm curved petal beads
- **12** 3.8 mm O-beads
- **1 g** size 11º seed beads
- **1 g** size 15º seed beads
- **2** 15 mm flat buttons, domed top, up to 3 mm thick
- **1** pair of earring findings

basics, p. 13
- ending thread
- square knot
- opening and closing loops and jump rings

SUPPLY NOTE

The metal filigree I used in my pendant at left is vintage and you're unlikely to find one just like it, so I made a few more lilies using modern filigree designs, and changed the color scheme to ignite your imagination. My favorite sources for filigree findings include:

- round (right): artbeads.com
- five-petal flower (top, right): michaels.com
- BeadFX, Fusion Beads, vintagejewelrysupplies.com, and Vintaj

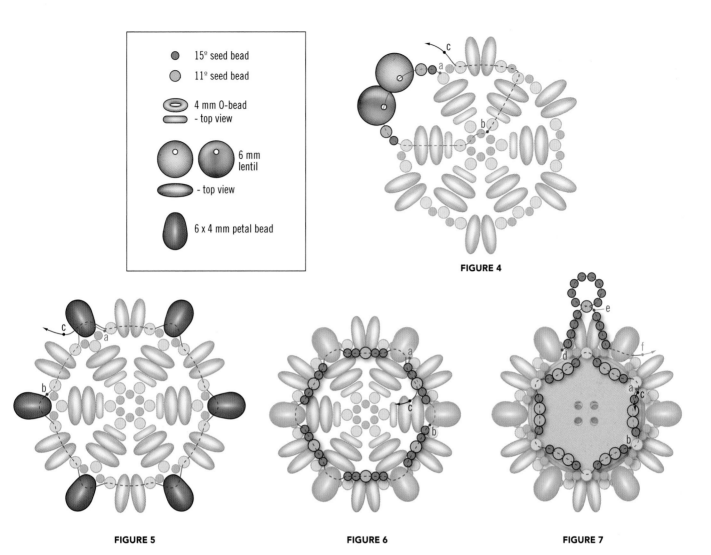

FIGURE 4

FIGURE 5

FIGURE 6

FIGURE 7

bead **(figure 6, a–b)**. Repeat this stitch five times to complete the round, and sew through the first two 15ºs and 11º **(b–c)**. Insert a button facedown into the dome of lentils and under the ring of seed beads just added, and tighten.

7) Pick up a 15º, two 11ºs, and a 15º, and sew through the next 11º in the previous round **(figure 7, a–b)**. Repeat this stitch five times **(b–c)** to complete the round. Sew through several more beads in this round, tying a few half-hitch knots along the way to secure. Exit a petal bead. End the tail but not the working thread.

8) Attach a 6 mm jump ring to the metal stamping to mark the top of the pendant.

9) Center the beadwork on the front of the metal stamping with a petal bead centered at the top. Using the working thread, attach the flower to the metal stamping by sewing down between the spaces in the metal stamping and through each petal bead to evenly secure the flower. When the flower is secure, end the thread.

N O T E Stitch through the metal stamping so that the thread passes through it at a 90-degree angle. This ensures that the thread is not cut on the sharp edge of the metal. You may wish to add some 15ºs to the stitches to hide and protect the thread.

EARRINGS

1) On 28 in. (71 cm) of thread, work as in steps 1–7 of "Pendant" to make a flower.

2) Pick up four 15ºs, an 11º, and eight 15ºs, and sew through the 11º again to form a loop **(d–e)**. Retrace the thread path of the loop (not shown in the figure for clarity), pick up four 15ºs, and sew through the next petal bead **(e–f)**. End the thread.

3) Open the loop of an ear wire, and attach it to the loop of 15ºs.

4) Repeat steps 1–3 to make another earring. **B&B**

Navette
necklace

Capture stunning crystals and chatons with a classic collectionof seed beads to create a timeless accessory.

designed by **Melissa Grakowsky Shippee**

Necklace

12 mm rivoli components

1 On 1 yd. (.9 m) of thread, pick up 32 color A 11º cylinder beads, and sew through the beads again to form a ring, leaving a 6-in. (15 cm) tail. Continue through the next two As.

2 Pick up a color B 11º cylinder bead, skip the next A in the ring, and sew through the following seven As in the round **(figure 1, a–b)**. Repeat this stitch three times to complete the round, positioning the Bs to the inside of the ring, and sew through the first B added **(b–c)**.

3 Pick up six color C 15º seed beads, and sew through the next B in the ring **(figure 2, a–b)**. Repeat this stitch three times to complete the round **(b–c)**, and sew through the first group of Cs added **(c–d)**. Check the fit. If this round is too tight, add seven Cs instead of six for each stitch. There should be a small open space between the ring of As and Cs.

4 Pick up a color D 15º seed bead, and sew through the following group of Cs in the inner ring **(d–e)**. Repeat this stitch three times to complete the round **(e–f)**. Retrace the thread path (not shown in the figure for clarity), and continue through the next B in the previous round. Reverse direction, and sew back through the adjacent A in round 1 **(f–g)**.

5 Center a 12 mm rivoli facedown on the beadwork. You will now work the back of the bezel. Working as in step 3, pick up seven Cs, and sew through the next "up" A in round 1 **(figure 3, a–b)**. Repeat this stitch three times to complete the round **(b–c)**. Check the fit. If this round is too tight, add eight

Cs instead of seven for each stitch. Retrace the thread path (not shown in the figure for clarity), and sew through the first group of Cs added **(c–d)**.

6 Working as in step 4, add a C next to each up-A, sewing through each group of Cs added in the previous round and stepping up through the first C added **(d–e)**.

7 Working as in step 3, add groups of six Cs between the up-beads added in the previous round **(e–f)**. Check the fit, and add or remove a C in each stitch if needed. Retrace the thread path, skipping the C up-beads in the previous round to cinch up the beads.

8 Flip the component over, and sew through the beadwork to exit the middle A in the outer ring **(figure 4, point a)**. Pick up three 11º seed beads, and sew through the middle A again and the following As in the group to form a picot **(a–b)**. Pick up a B, and sew through the outer round to exit the next middle A **(b–c)**. Repeat these two stitches three times to complete the round **(c–d)**. Retrace the thread

path, and end the tail but not the working thread.

9 Work as in steps 1–8 to make a total of nine 12 mm rivoli components.

14 mm rivoli component

Work as in "12 mm rivoli components" with the following changes:

• Work as in steps 1–2, except pick up 40 As to form the ring, and sew through nine instead of seven As after picking up the B in each stitch.

• Work as in steps 3–4, except pick up eight Cs in each group instead of six.

• Work as in step 5, except pick up eight Cs instead of seven, and use a 14 mm rivoli.

• Work as in step 6, sewing through eight Cs instead of seven Cs after adding each C.

• Skip step 7.

• Work as in step 8. After retracing the thread path, exit the tip 11º in a picot. End the tail, but not the working thread.

Chaton components

1 On 1 yd. (.9 m) of thread, pick up a repeating pattern of an 11º, two As, a B, and two As four times, and sew through all the beads again, leaving a 6-in. (15 cm) tail. Continue through the first three beads in the ring.

2 Pick up an A, skip the next B in the ring, and sew through the next five beads **(figure 5, a–b)**. Repeat this

FIGURE 1

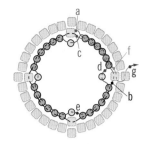

FIGURE 2

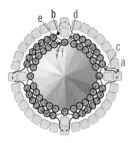

FIGURE 3

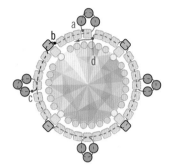

FIGURE 4

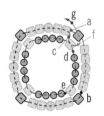

FIGURE 5

- ▢ 11º cylinder bead, color A
- ▢ 11º cylinder bead, color B
- ● 15º seed bead, color C
- ○ 15º seed bead, color D

12 mm rivoli

-back surface

● 11º seed bead

8 mm chaton

-back surface

32 x 17 mm navette crystal

14 mm rivoli

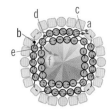

FIGURE 6

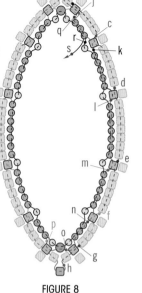

FIGURE 7

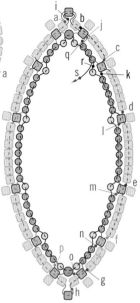

FIGURE 8

FIGURE 9

stitch three times to complete the round **(b–c)**, and continue through the following B **(c–d)**.

3 Pick up four Cs, and sew through the following B **(d–e)**. Repeat this stitch three times to complete the round **(e–f)**. Check the fit. If this round is too tight, add five Cs instead of four in each stitch. Reverse direction, and sew back through the adjacent A **(f–g)**.

4 Position a chaton facedown in the center of the beadwork. Pick up five Cs, and sew through the following up-A **(figure 6, a–b)**. Repeat this stitch three times to complete the round **(b–c)**. Retrace the thread path, skipping the As (not shown in the figure for clarity), and continue through the first five Cs added **(c–d)**.

5 Add a C next to each up-A in the ring, stepping up through the first C added **(d–e)**.

6 Add groups of four Cs between the Cs added in the previous round **(e–f)**. Check the fit. If this round is too tight, add five Cs instead of four in each stitch. Retrace the thread path, skipping the Cs added in the previous round, and sew through the beadwork to exit between an A and a B on the front of the component, with the needle pointing toward the B **(figure 7, point a)**.

7 Add a B next to each previous B, and step up through the first B added **(a–b)**. End the tail, but not

the working thread.

8 Work as in steps 1–7 to make a total of 10 chaton components.

Navette component

1 On a comfortable length of thread, pick up 62 As, and sew through the beads again to form a ring, leaving a 6-in. (15 cm) tail. Continue through the first two As.

2 Pick up an A, and sew through the next A in the ring **(figure 8, a–b)**. Pick up a B, skip an A, and sew through the next three As **(b–c)**. Repeat this last stitch five times, but sew through five As **(c–d)**, seven As **(d–e)**, five As **(e–f)**, three As **(f–g)**, and one A **(g–h)** in that order.

3 Repeat step 2 to complete the round **(h–i)**. Sew through the first A added in this round, and continue through the following A and B **(i–j)**.

4 Pick up three Cs, and sew through the next B **(j–k)**. Repeat this stitch four times with five Cs **(k–l)**, seven Cs **(l–m)**, five Cs **(m–n)**, and three Cs **(n–o)**. Pick up an 11º, and sew through the following B **(o–p)**.

5 Repeat step 4 **(p–q)**, and continue through the first three Cs added **(q–r)**.

6 Work a round with Ds, adding a D next to each adjacent B **(r–s)**.

7 Sew through the beadwork to exit an up-A in the outer ring as shown **(figure 9, a–b)**. Pick up eight Cs, and sew through the next up-A **(b–c)**. Repeat this stitch once with six Cs **(c–d)**, once with three Cs **(d–e)**, once with two Cs **(e–f)**, once with three Cs **(f–g)**, and once with six Cs **(g–h)**. Repeat this sequence of stitches to complete the round **(h–i)**, and sew through the first eight Cs added **(i–j)**.

8 Work a round with Ds, adding a D next to each adjacent A, and step up through the first D added **(j–k)**.

9 Position the navette crystal facedown in the beadwork, and hold it in place while completing the remaining rounds. Work as in step 7, except start the pattern with picking up six (instead of eight) Cs, pick up only one instead of two Cs at the end points, and step up through the first six Cs added **(k–l)**.

10 Work as in step 8 **(l–m)**.

11 Pick up three Cs, and

Difficulty rating

◆ ◆ ◆ ◆ ◯

Materials
adjustable necklace 14–19 in. (36 x 48 cm)

• **1** 32 x 17 mm navette (4227) crystal (Swarovski, ultra blue AB)
• rivolis (Swarovski)
  - **1** 14 mm (ultra blue AB)
  - **9** 12 mm (fuchsia)
• **10** 8 mm (SS39) chatons (Swarovski 1088, ruby glacier blue)
• 11º cylinder beads
  - **5 g** color A (Miyuki Delica 2049, luminous hot pink)
  - **1 g** color B (Toho Aiko 2117, aqua opal silver-lined permanent)
• **5 g** 11º seed beads (Toho 221, bronze)
• **15º** seed beads
  - **6 g** color C (Toho 221, bronze)
  - **1 g** color D (Miyuki 574, lilac silver-lined alabaster)
• Fireline, 6 lb. test
• beading needles, #11 or #12

Basics, p. 13
• ending and adding thread

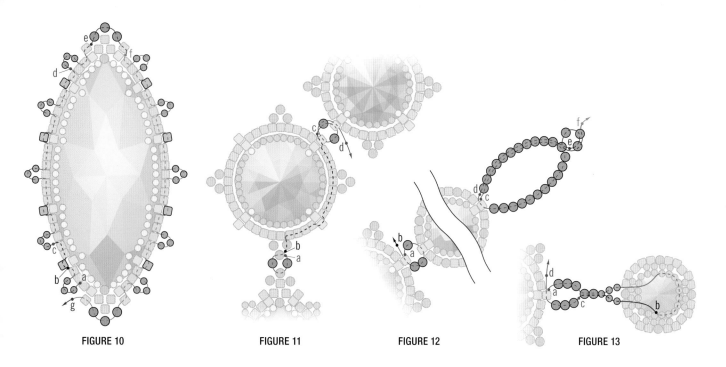

FIGURE 10   FIGURE 11   FIGURE 12   FIGURE 13

sew through the next two Ds
(m–n). Work this side of the
bezel with the same number
of Cs as in the previous round
of Cs **(n–o).** Repeat all of
these stitches to complete
the round **(o–p)**.
12 Sew through the ring of
As on the front of the bezel,
and exit at **figure 10, point a.**
13 Pick up three Cs, skip
the next A in the round, and
sew through the following A
to form a picot **(a–b)**. Pick
up a B, skip the next B, and
sew through the next two
As **(b–c)**. Repeat these two
stitches three times, adjusting
the number of As you sew
through so each picot is
made over the center A
in its section **(c–d)**. Pick up
three Cs, skip the next A,
and sew through the following A in the same section
and the next up-A **(d–e)**.
Pick up three 11ºs, skip the
three As at the tip, and sew
through the corresponding
up-A on the other edge **(e–f)**.
Position the 11ºs on the tip to
sit behind the As. Work in the
same manner to add picots
and Bs to this edge and bottom tip of the component
(f–g). Retrace the thread
path, and end the threads.

Assembly
1 Position the 14 mm rivoli
component above the
navette on your bead mat.
With the working thread from
the 14 mm rivoli, work a join:
Pick up an 11º, sew through
the tip 11º on the top picot
of the navette, pick up an
11º, and sew through the
11º your thread exited at the
start of this step **(figure 11,
a–b)**. Retrace the thread
path several times (not
shown in the figure for
clarity), and sew through
the beadwork as shown
to exit the upper outer B
on the right-hand side of
the 14 mm rivoli **(b–c)**.
2 To make the first half of
the neck strap, position a
12 mm rivoli component to
the right of the 14 mm rivoli.
Using the working thread
from the 14 mm rivoli, join
to the adjacent up-B on
the 12 mm using 11ºs. **(c–d)**.
End the thread. With the working thread from the 12 mm,
sew through the beadwork
to exit the B opposite the join
(figure 12, point a).
3 Position a chaton component to the right of the 12 mm,
and work a curving join: Pick
up an 11º, and sew through

the corresponding B on the
chaton component. Pick up
two 11ºs, and sew through
the B your thread exited
on the 12 mm component
(a–b). Retrace the thread
path several times.
4 Continue attaching 12 mm
components and chatons
in an alternating pattern with
a curving join three more
times. On the end chaton,
sew through the beadwork
to exit the B opposite the
join **(point c)**. Do not end
this thread, but end any
other remaining threads
on the neck strap.
5 Pick up 23 11ºs, and sew
through the B your thread
is exiting to form a loop
(c–d). Retrace the thread
path twice (not shown in
the figure for clarity), and
continue through the first
12 11ºs added **(d–e)**.
6 Pick up three 11ºs, and sew
through the 11º your thread
is exiting to form a picot.
Retrace the thread path
twice (not shown in the
figure for clarity), and sew
through the first two 11ºs
added **(e–f)**.
7 Work as in steps 5–6
to make four more loops
and picots.

8 Work as in steps 2–7 on
the left side of the navette
to complete the second
half of the neck strap.

Clasp
The clasp consists of a
double button made of two
chaton components and
a 12 mm rivoli component.
1 With the working thread of
the 12 mm rivoli component,
sew through the beadwork
to exit an outer B **(figure 13,
point a)**. Pick up five 11ºs
and three Cs, and sew
through 10 inner-round Cs
on the back of a chaton
component as shown **(a–b)**.
Pick up two Cs, and sew
through the first C added
and the next two 11ºs **(b–c)**.
Pick up three 11ºs, and sew
through the B your thread
exited at the start of this step
(c–d). Retrace the thread
path several times.
2 Work as in step 1 to attach
the remaining chaton com-
ponent to the B on the adjacent side of the 12 mm rivoli
component. To secure the
necklace, pass a chaton
button component through
a loop on each side of the
chain. ●

RAY OF LIGHT EARRINGS

designed by
Margherita Fusco

DIFFICULTY ●●○○○

bead weaving

materials
earrings 2 in. (5 cm)

- **60** 2.5 x 5 mm SuperDuo beads (matte gold)
- **60** 4 mm bicone crystals (Swarovski, rose water opal AB2X)
- 11º seed beads
  - **4 g** color A (Toho PF557, permanent finish galvanized starlight)
  - **1 g** color B (Miyuki 4219, Duracoat galvanized magenta)
- **2 g** 11º Delica cylinder beads (Miyuki DB410, galvanized yellow gold)
- **1 g** 15º seed beads (Toho PF557, permanent finish galvanized starlight)
- **1** pair of earring findings
- Fireline, 6 lb. test
- beading needles, #12
- **2** pairs of chainnose, bent-nose, and/or flatnose pliers

basics, p. 13
- ending thread
- square knot
- opening and closing loops

⬡	4 mm bicone crystal
⬮	2.5 x 5 mm SuperDuo bead
○	11º seed bead, color A
○	11º seed bead, color B
▢	11º cylinder bead

Sometimes a special evening just needs big, sparkly earrings. Create these stunners by circling around and around with bicone crystals, seed beads, Delicas, and SuperDuo beads.

EARRINGS

1) On 5 ft. (1.5 m) of thread, pick up a repeating pattern of a 4 mm bicone crystal and an 11º cylinder bead 15 times. Leaving a 6-in. (15 cm) tail, tie a square knot to form a ring, and sew through the first 4 mm again **(figure 1, a–b)**.

2) Pick up a cylinder, and sew through the next 4 mm **(b–c)**. Repeat this stitch 14 times, and step up through the first cylinder in this round **(c–d)**.

3) Pick up four color A 11º seed beads, and sew through the next cylinder **(d–e)**. Repeat this stitch 14 times to create a round of arches **(e–f)**.

4) Repeat step 3 to make another round of arches that sit next to the previous round. When the round is complete, sew through the first three As added in this round **(figure 2)**.

5) Pick up a color B 11º seed bead, a cylinder, and a B, and sew through the second and third As of the next arch on the this edge **(figure 3, a–b)**. Repeat this stitch 14 times, and step up through the first B and cylinder added in this step **(c–d)**.

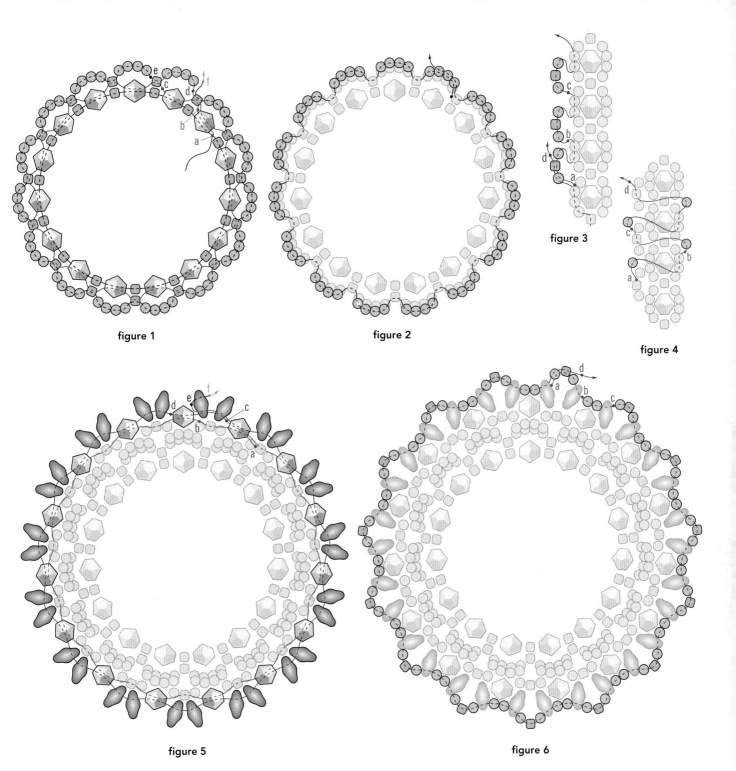

figure 1

figure 2

figure 3

figure 4

figure 5

figure 6

6) To join the two arches together, pick up a B, and sew through the second and third As of the next arch on the other edge **(figure 4, a–b)**. Pick up a B, and sew through the next cylinder added in the previous round **(b–c)**. Repeat these two stitches **(c–d)** 14 times. Don't step up.

7) Pick up a 4 mm, and sew through the next cylinder **(figure 5, a–b)**. Repeat this stitch 14 times, and step up through the first 4 mm added in this round **(b–c)**.

8) Pick up two SuperDuos, and sew through the next 4 mm in the previous round **(c–d)**. Repeat this stitch 14 times, and sew through the inner holes of the first two SuperDuos added in this step **(d–e)**. Continue through the open hole of the SuperDuo your thread is exiting **(e–f)**.

9) Pick up a B, a cylinder, and a B, and sew through the open hole of the next SuperDuo, pulling tight to form a picot **(figure 6, a–b)**. Pick up two Bs, and sew through the open hole

of the next SuperDuo **(b–c)**. Repeat these stitches 14 times, and sew through the first B and cylinder added in this round **(c–d)**.

10) Pick up seven 15⁰s, and sew through the cylinder your thread is exiting to create a loop. Retrace the thread path several times, and end the working thread and tail.

11) Open the loop of an earring finding, and attach it to the loop of 15⁰s.

12) Make a second earring. B⬚B

HONEYCOMB DELIGHT BRACELET

designed by Isabella Lam

DIFFICULTY ●●●○○

---

cubic right-angle weave

HIDDEN SUPERDUOS

Because the SuperDuos will be on the bottom of the base and do not show very much when the bracelet is complete, the color can vary slightly from the color listed without changing the overall look.

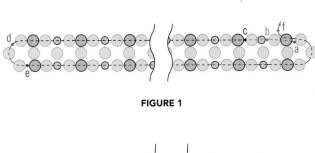

FIGURE 1

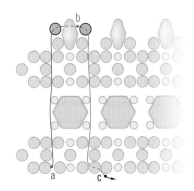

FIGURE 3

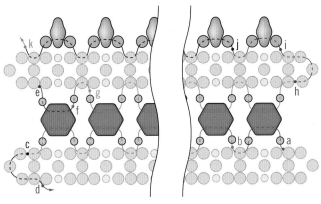

FIGURE 2

⬡	6 mm Honeycomb bead
⬭	2.5 x 5 mm SuperDuo bead
⬡	3 mm bicone crystal
⬡	2 mm druk bead
○	15º seed bead

Everybody will be buzzing when they see this Honeycomb-bead bracelet with an embellished cubic right-angle weave base.

BASE

1) On a comfortable length of thread, and leaving a 6-in. (15 cm) tail, use 2 mm druk beads to work a cubic right-angle weave (CRAW) strip to the desired length, ending with an even number of units that is divisible by four. Allow ½ in. (1.3 cm) for the clasp, and end and add thread as needed. A 7½-in. (19.1 cm) bracelet has 44 units. Sew through the beadwork to exit an end edge 2 mm with your needle pointing toward the other end. End the tail but not the working thread. Make another strip of the same length.

2) Pick up a 2 mm, and sew through the next edge 2 mm (**figure 1, a–b**). For clarity, only one side of the CRAW strip is shown in the figures. Pick up a 15º seed bead, and sew through the following edge 2 mm (**b–c**). Repeat these steps for the remainder of the strip, ending with a 2 mm (**c–d**). Do not use tight tension or the beadwork will curve. Sew through the next two 2 mms in the end unit to exit the opposite edge 2 mm (**d–e**). Repeat these stitches for this edge of the strip, and continue through the first 2 mm added in this step (**e–f**). Repeat this step on the other strip. End and add thread throughout the beadwork as needed.

3) With the working thread from either strip, pick up a 15º, a Honeycomb bead, and a 15º, skip the next three edge beads, and sew through the following 2 mm added in the last round (**figure 2, a–b**).

NOTE If your Honeycombs have different colors on each side, pick up so the side you do not want to show on the front of the bracelet faces up. The side facing downward right now will be the side that faces the top of the bracelet when it is complete.

Repeat this stitch for the remainder of this edge of the strip (**b–c**). You should end with an odd number of Honeycombs. Sew through the next four end beads (**c–d**), and set this thread aside.

4) Position the other strip next to the first one as shown, with the embellished face upward, and the working thread exiting the 2 mm at **figure 2, point e**. With this working thread, pick up a 15º, and sew through the open hole of the next Honeycomb (**e–f**). Pick up a 15º, skip the next three edge beads, and sew through the following 2 mm (**f–g**). Repeat this stitch for the remainder of this strip (**g–h**). Sew through the next four end beads as shown (**h–i**).

5) Pick up a 2 mm, a SuperDuo bead, and a 2 mm, skip the next three edge beads, and sew through the following 2 mm (**i–j**). Repeat this stitch for the remainder of the edge (**j–k**), and set this thread aside.

6) With the working thread from the first strip, pick up a 2 mm, and sew through the open hole of the adjacent SuperDuo in the opposite

materials
red-and-gold bracelet
7½ in. (19.1 cm)

- **21** 6 mm Honeycomb beads (red lumi)
- **21** 2.5 x 5 mm SuperDuo beads (halo razzmatazz)
- **44** 3 mm bicone crystals (Swarovski, scarabaeus green)
- **1000** (approximately) 2 mm True2 round druk beads (Czech, 24k gold plated)
- **2 g** 15º seed beads (Miyuki 961, bright sterling plated)
- **1** 17 x 13 mm box clasp (Elegant Elements serpentine design, gold; naturecoastsupplies.etsy.com)
- Fireline, 6 lb. test
- beading needles, #11 or #12

basics, p. 13
- cubic right-angle weave
- ending and adding thread

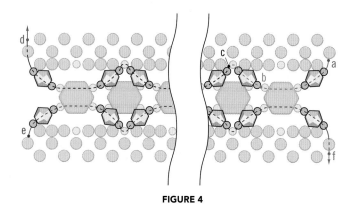

FIGURE 4

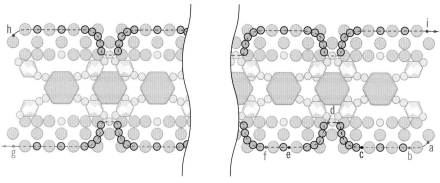

FIGURE 5

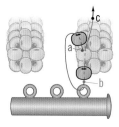

FIGURE 6

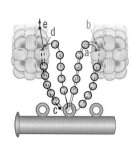

FIGURE 7

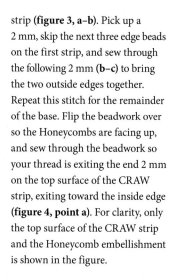

strip (**figure 3, a–b**). Pick up a 2 mm, skip the next three edge beads on the first strip, and sew through the following 2 mm (**b–c**) to bring the two outside edges together. Repeat this stitch for the remainder of the base. Flip the beadwork over so the Honeycombs are facing up, and sew through the beadwork so your thread is exiting the end 2 mm on the top surface of the CRAW strip, exiting toward the inside edge (**figure 4, point a**). For clarity, only the top surface of the CRAW strip and the Honeycomb embellishment is shown in the figure.

EMBELLISHMENT

1) Pick up a 15º, a 3 mm bicone crystal, and a 15º, and sew through the next 15º, Honeycomb, and 15º (**a–b**). Pick up a 15º, bicone, and 15º, and sew through the following top-edge 15º adjacent to the next Honeycomb (**b–c**). Repeat the last two stitches for the remainder of the base, except for the last stitch,

sew through the end 2 mm on the top surface (**c–d**).
2) With the working thread from the other strip, sew through the beadwork to exit the top end 2 mm on this strip (**point e**), and work as in step 1 to embellish this side of the beadwork (**e–f**).
3) With the same working thread, sew through the next end edge 2 mm (**figure 5, a–b**).
4) Pick up a 15º, and sew through the next 2 mm. Repeat this stitch once more (**b–c**).
5) Pick up five 15ºs, and sew through the next 15º on the inside edge (**c–d**). Pick up five 15ºs, skip two edge 2 mms, and sew through the following 2 mm (**d–e**). Pick up a 15º, and sew through the next 2 mm (**e–f**). Repeat these stitches for the remainder of the base, ending with two single stitches using 15ºs as in step 4 (**f–g**). End this thread.
6) With the working thread from the other strip, work as in steps 3–5

to embellish this side of the base (**h–i**). End this thread.

CLASP

1) Add 12-in. (30 cm) of thread to the end of the beadwork with your thread exiting the end inside-edge 2 mm as shown (**figure 6, point a**). Only the end of the strips are shown in the figure for clarity. Pick up a 2 mm, and sew down through the end loop of the clasp (**a–b**). Pick up a 2 mm, and sew up through the 2 mm your thread exited at the start of this step (**b–c**). Retrace the thread path to reinforce the connection.
2) Pick up five 15ºs, and sew down through the center loop of the clasp. Pick up five 15ºs, and sew up through the 2 mm your thread exited at the start of this step (**figure 7, a–b**) (the 2 mms added in step 1 are not shown in the figure for clarity). Retrace the thread path (not shown in the figure for clarity), and continue

through the first five 15ºs picked up and the center loop (**b–c**).
3) Pick up five 15ºs, and sew up through the end inside-edge 2 mm on the other strip (**c–d**). Pick up five 15ºs, and sew down through the center loop of the clasp, the first five 15ºs added, and the same inside-edge 2 mm (**d–e**).
4) Work as in step 1 to attach the remaining clasp loop, and end the thread.
5) Repeat steps 1–4 to attach the other end of the clasp. **B⊗B**

materials

three-strand necklace
19 in. (48 cm)

- 8º Demi beads
  - **16 g** color A (Toho 1F, crystal transparent matte)
  - **15 g** color B (Toho PF21, crystal silver-lined, permanent finish)
- **1** three-strand box clasp (Claspgarten, 14155/03)
- Fireline, 6 lb. test
- beading needle, #10
- disposable lighter or thread burner
- microcrystalline wax

three-ring earrings
1½ in. (3.8 cm)

- 8º Demi beads
  - **1 g** color A (Toho 1F, crystal transparent matte)
  - **1 g** color B (Toho PF21, crystal silver-lined, permanent finish)
- **2** 4 mm soldered jump rings
- **1** pair of ear wires
- **2** pairs of chainnose, bentnose, and/or flatnose pliers

triple dangle earrings
1¾ in. (4.4 cm)

- 8º Demi beads
  - **16 g** color A (Toho 1F, crystal transparent matte)
  - **15 g** color B (Toho PF21, crystal silver-lined, permanent finish)
- 11º hex-cut cylinder beads (Miyuka Delica DBC0035, galvanized silver)
- **2** 4 mm soldered jump rings
- **1** pair of ear wires
- **2** pairs of chainnose, bentnose, and/or flatnose pliers

basics, p. 13

- peyote stitch: circular
- ending and adding thread
- opening and closing jump rings

This frothy concoction combines matte- and silver-lined Demi beads for a delicate and versatile project.

NECKLACE

1) Center a needle on 1 yd. (.9 m) of conditioned thread. Align the ends, and tie an overhand knot. Trim the tails 1 mm from the knot, and melt slightly with a lighter or thread burner to form a finished end.

2) Pick up 12 color A Demi beads. Push the beads to within 1 in. (2.5 cm) of the knot. Separate the strands between the beads and the knot. Pass the needle between the strands and then back through the last bead added. Pull tight to form a ring **(figure 1)**.

3) Working in circular peyote stitch, pick up a color B Demi bead, and sew through the following A. Repeat this stitch 11 times to complete the round, and step up through the first B added **(figure 2, a–b)**.

4) Pick up an A, and sew through the center clasp loop **(b–c)**. Sew back through the A and the B just exited, going in the same direction **(c–d)**. End your thread.

5) Repeat steps 1–4 33 times, but in step 4, attach the new ring to the B opposite the previous connection **(figure 3)**. After completing 34 rings, attach the last ring to the center loop on the other clasp half as in step 4.

6) Repeat steps 1–5 twice, but make one strand with a total of 33 components and one strand with a total of 35 components, attaching each strand to an open clasp loop. **B B**

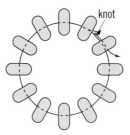

FIGURE 1

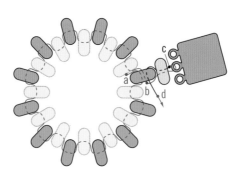

FIGURE 2

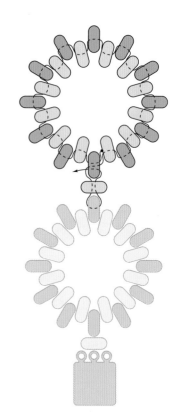

FIGURE 3

OPTION Convert this project from a three-strand necklace into one long strand without a clasp. This super-long necklace could be looped two or three times around your neck to suit your style.

THREE-RING EARRINGS

1) Attach a soldered jump ring to an ear wire.

2) Work as in steps 1–4 of "Necklace" to make three connected rings, attaching an end ring to the soldered ring instead of a clasp **(figure 4)**.

3) Repeat to make a second earring.

TRIPLE DANGLE EARRINGS

1) Attach a soldered jump ring to an ear wire.

2) Work as in steps 1–3 of "Necklace."

3) Pick up an A, 21 11º hex-cut cylinder beads, and the soldered ring on the ear wire. Sew back through all the cylinders, and end the thread.

4) Work as in steps 1–3 of "Necklace," pick up an A and 15 cylinders, and sew through the last cylinder in the first strand and the soldered ring. Sew back through all the cylinders again, and end the thread.

5) Work as in step 4, but pick up 10 cylinders **(figure 5)**.

6) Repeat to make a second earring.

	8º Demi bead, color A
	8º Demi bead, color B
	11º hex-cut cylinder bead

FIGURE 4

FIGURE 5

STAR BRIGHT EARRINGS

You'll sparkle brightly when
wearing these gorgeous earrings
with rivolis, SuperDuos, Rullas,
and bicone crystals.

designed by **Margherita Fusco**

Earrings

1 On 5 ft. (1.5 m) of thread, pick up
a repeating pattern of a Rulla bead
and a 15º seed bead six times. Leaving
a 6-in. (15 cm) tail, tie a square knot
to form the beads into a ring, and
sew through the first Rulla again
(figure 1, a–b).

2 Sew through the open hole of the
same Rulla **(b–c)**. Pick up two SuperDuo
beads, and sew through the open hole
of the next Rulla **(c–d)**. Repeat this stitch
five times to complete the round **(d–e)**.
Sew through the first SuperDuo, and
continue through the open hole of
the same SuperDuo **(e–f)**.

3 Pick up a Rulla, and sew through
the open hole of the next SuperDuo
(f–g). Pick up a SuperDuo, and sew
through the open hole of the following
SuperDuo **(g–h)**. Repeat these stitches
five times to complete the round **(h–i)**.
Sew through the first Rulla added in
this round, and continue through

the open hole of the same Rulla **(i–j)**.

4 Position a rivoli faceup in the center
of the beadwork. The rivoli will overlap
the inner round of Rullas. Pick up a 15º,
a 4 mm bicone crystal, and a 15º, and
sew through the open hole of the next
Rulla **(figure 2, a–b)**. Pull the thread
tight. Make sure the 4 mm is positioned
on the top edge of the rivoli. Repeat this
stitch five times to complete the round
(b–c). Retrace the thread path (not
shown in the figure for clarity), and
continue through the first 15º, 4 mm,
and 15º added **(c–d)**.

5 Pick up five 15ºs, and sew through
the same 15º, 4 mm, and 15º your
thread exited at the start of this step,
going in the same direction to form
a picot **(figure 3, a–b)**. Sew through
the next Rulla and the following set

of three beads **(b–c)**. Repeat this stitch
five times to complete the round, except
on the last stitch, don't sew through
the Rulla and the following three
beads **(c–d)**.

6 Sew through the next three 15ºs in
the picot just added, exiting the center
15º **(d–e)**. Pick up three 15ºs, and sew
through the center 15º in the following
picot **(e–f)**. Repeat this last stitch five
times to complete the round **(f–g)**.
Check the fit. If needed, add four 15ºs
instead of three in each stitch. Retrace
the thread path (not shown in the figure
for clarity), and sew through the beadwork as shown to exit the open hole
of a SuperDuo in the outer ring **(g–h)**.

7 Using tight tension, pick up a
SuperDuo and three 15ºs, sew through
the open hole of the same SuperDuo,
and continue through the outer
hole of the next Rulla **(h–i)**. Pick up a
SuperDuo and three 15ºs, sew through
the open hole of the same SuperDuo,
and continue through the open hole
of the following SuperDuo **(i–j)**. Repeat
these stitches five times to complete
the round **(j–k)**, and continue through
the first SuperDuo and three 15ºs added
at the start of this step **(k–l)**.

8 Using tight tension, pick up three
15ºs, and sew through the inner hole
of the next Rulla **(figure 4, a–b)**. Pick
up three 15ºs, and sew through the

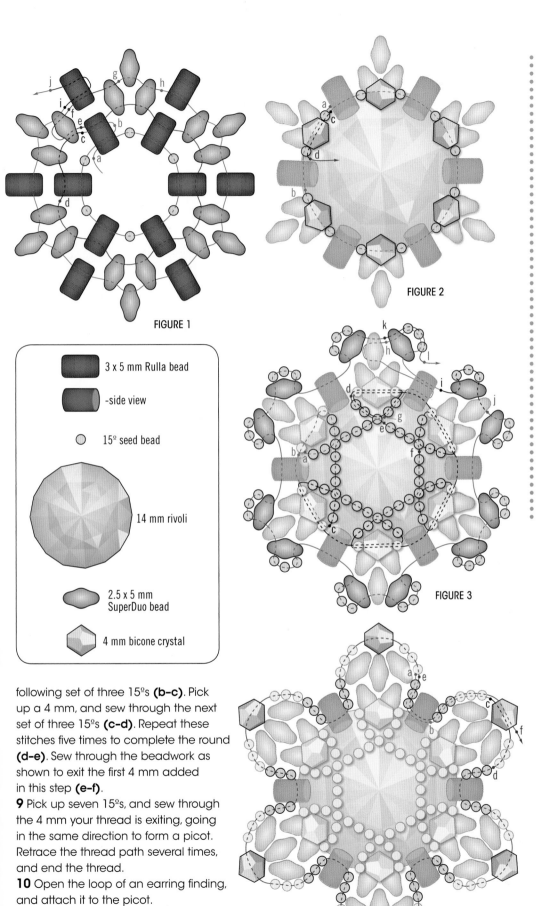

FIGURE 1

FIGURE 2

FIGURE 3

FIGURE 4

3 x 5 mm Rulla bead

-side view

15º seed bead

14 mm rivoli

2.5 x 5 mm SuperDuo bead

4 mm bicone crystal

Difficulty rating

Materials
brown earrings
1⅝ in. (4.1 cm)
- **2** 14 mm Swarovski rivolis (light Colorado topaz)
- **24** 4 mm Swarovski bicone crystals (light smoked topaz AB)
- **24** 3 x 5 mm Rulla beads (metallic dark bronze)
- **6 g** 2.5 x 5 mm SuperDuo beads (crystal bronze copper)
- **2 g** 15º seed beads (Toho PF557, permanent finish galvanized starlight)
- **1** pair of earring findings
- Fireline, 6 lb. test
- beading needles, #12
- **2** pairs of chainnose, bentnose, and/or flatnose pliers

Basics, p.13
- ending thread
- square knot
- opening and closing loops

following set of three 15ºs **(b–c)**. Pick up a 4 mm, and sew through the next set of three 15ºs **(c–d)**. Repeat these stitches five times to complete the round **(d–e)**. Sew through the beadwork as shown to exit the first 4 mm added in this step **(e–f)**.

9 Pick up seven 15ºs, and sew through the 4 mm your thread is exiting, going in the same direction to form a picot. Retrace the thread path several times, and end the thread.

10 Open the loop of an earring finding, and attach it to the picot.

11 Make a second earring. ⊙

Shimmering lights ornament

Adorn your holiday tree with an ornament trimmed with flowers that twinkle with crystals, peanut beads, and seed beads.

designed by **Cary Borelli**

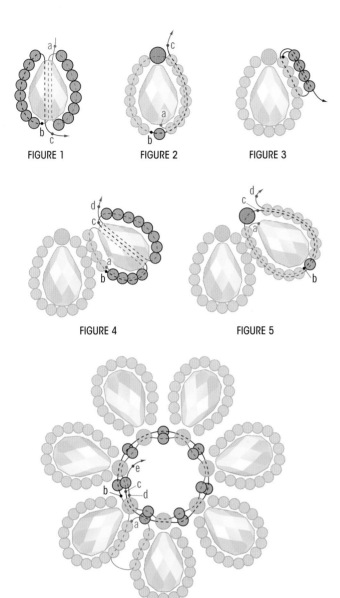

FIGURE 1   FIGURE 2   FIGURE 3

FIGURE 4   FIGURE 5

FIGURE 6

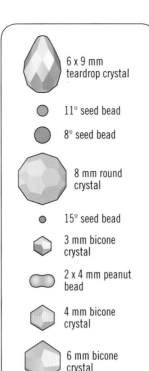

6 x 9 mm teardrop crystal

11º seed bead

8º seed bead

8 mm round crystal

15º seed bead

3 mm bicone crystal

2 x 4 mm peanut bead

4 mm bicone crystal

6 mm bicone crystal

Materials
blue/gold ornament
- **1** 2½ in. (6.4 cm) diameter glass ball ornament (gold)
- **14** 6 x 9 mm center-drilled teardrop crystals (Swarovski 5500, aqua AB)
- **2** 8 mm faceted round crystals (Swarovski 5000, emerald AB)
- bicone crystals (Swarovski 5328, jet AB2X)
  - **18** 6 mm
  - **44** 4 mm
  - **64** 3 mm
- **13 g** 2 x 4 mm peanut beads (metallic gold)
- **1 g** 8º seed beads (Toho 457A, metallic copper)
- **5 g** 11º seed beads (Toho 221, bronze)
- **4 g** 15º seed beads (Toho 221, bronze)
- Fireline, 6 lb. test
- beading needles, #11 or #12
- thread bobbin or piece of cardboard

Basics, p.13
- ending and adding thread
- square knot

Ornament
Flower motif
1 On 2 yd. (1.8 m) of thread, pick up a 6 x 9 mm teardrop crystal through the narrow end and eight 11º seed beads. Sew through the teardrop again in the same direction, leaving a 6-in. (15 cm) tail **(figure 1, a–b)**. This forms a loop of 11ºs around one side of the teardrop. Pick up eight 11ºs, and sew through the teardrop again to form a loop on the other side of the teardrop **(b–c)**.

2 Sew through the first eight 11ºs, pick up an 8º seed bead, and sew through the next eight 11ºs on the other side of the teardrop **(figure 2, a–b)**. Pick up an 11º, and sew through the next eight 11ºs **(b–c)**. Retrace the thread path of all the beads in the ring. This forms the first flower petal.

3 Pick up four 11ºs, sew through the last four 11ºs your thread exited, going in the same direction, and continue through the four new 11ºs **(figure 3)**.

4 Pick up four 11ºs and a teardrop through the wide end, and sew through the four 11ºs your thread just exited **(figure 4, a–b)**. Continue through the four 11ºs and teardrop just added **(b–c)**. Pick up eight 11ºs, and sew through the teardrop, going in the same direction, to form a loop on the other side of the teardrop **(c–d)**.

5 Sew through the eight 11ºs on the first side of this teardrop **(figure 5, a–b)**, pick up an 11º, and continue through the following eight 11ºs **(b–c)**. Pick up an 8º, and sew through all the 11ºs in the ring around this teardrop **(c–d)**.

6 Repeat steps 3–5 five more times to make a total of seven flower petals.

7 Join the petals: Sew through the corresponding four 11ºs on the first and last petals, and exit the 8º in the last petal **(figure 6, a–b)**.

8 Pick up an 11º, and sew through the next 8º. Repeat this stitch six times to complete the round **(b–c)**.

9 Work as in step 8 to add a second layer of 11ºs that

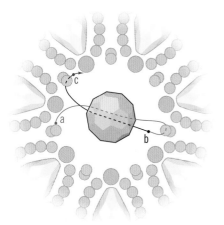

FIGURE 7

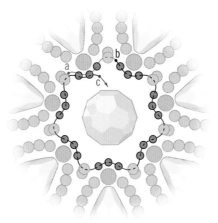

FIGURE 8

FIGURE 9

will sit on top of the previous 11ºs in the ring **(c-d)**, and continue through the first 11º added in this round **(d-e)**.
10 Pick up an 8 mm round crystal, skip the next three 11ºs on the top layer of the ring, and sew through the following 11º on the top layer **(figure 7, a-b)**. Continue back through the 8 mm and the next 11º in the top layer of the ring, going in the same direction **(b-c)**. Pull the thread tight.
11 Pick up three 15º seed beads, and sew through the next 11º in the top layer of the ring to form a picot **(figure 8, a-b)**. Repeat this stitch six times to complete the round, and step up through the first two 11ºs added in the first picot **(b-c)**.
12 Pick up three 15ºs, and sew through the center 15º in the next picot **(figure 9, a-b)**. Repeat this stitch six times to complete a second round of picots **(b-c)**. Do not step up.
13 Pick up a 15º, a 3 mm bicone crystal, and a 15º, and sew through the center 15º in the next picot from the first round **(figure 10, a-b)**. Repeat this stitch six times to complete the round **(b-c)**. This is now the front of the flower. Sew through eight beads as shown to exit a side 11º in the next flower petal **(c-d)**.
14 Pick up a 3 mm, sew

down through the corresponding five 11ºs on the adjacent petal **(d-e)**, and continue through the next 8º and up through the following five 11ºs on the same petal **(e-f)**. Repeat this stitch six times to complete the round **(f-g)**. Sew through the first 3 mm added **(g-h)**.
15 Pick up nine peanut beads, and sew through the next 3 mm between the petals to form a loop **(h-i)**. Repeat this stitch six times to complete the round **(i-j)**. If needed, position each loop to sit behind the petals. End the working thread and tail.
16 Work as in steps 1–15 to make a second flower motif.

Top ring

1 On 3 yd. (2.7 m) of thread, pick up an alternating pattern of an 11º and a 3 mm eighteen times, and center them on the thread. Tie the beads into a ring with a square knot. Wrap one of the threads around a thread bobbin or piece of cardboard. With the working thread, sew through the next 11º in the ring. Slide the ring on top of the ornament to check the fit. If the ring is too tight, loosen it slightly until it fits. Remove the ring from the ornament.
2 Pick up two 15ºs, a peanut, and two 15ºs. Sew through the 11º your thread just exited,

FIGURE 10

going in the same direction to form a loop, and continue through the next 3 mm and 11º **(figure 11, a-b)**. Repeat this stitch 17 times to complete the round **(b-c)**, and continue through the first two 15ºs and peanut added in the first loop **(c-d)**.
3 Pick up a 4 mm bicone crystal, and stitching in the opposite direction, sew through the next peanut **(d-e)**. Repeat this stitch 17 times to complete the round, and step up through the first 4 mm added **(e-f)**.
4 Pick up three peanuts, a 4 mm, and three peanuts, and sew through the 4 mm

your thread just exited, going in the same direction to form a loop **(figure 12, a-b)** Retrace the thread path to reinforce the connection (not shown in the figure for clarity), and continue through the next three peanuts and 4 mm in the loop **(b-c)**.
5 Repeat step 4 once **(c-d)**.
6 Connect the flower motif: Position a flower motif face up and centered below the last stitch. Pick up three peanuts, sew through the three center peanuts on the petal, pick up three peanuts, and sew through the 4 mm your thread is exiting, going in

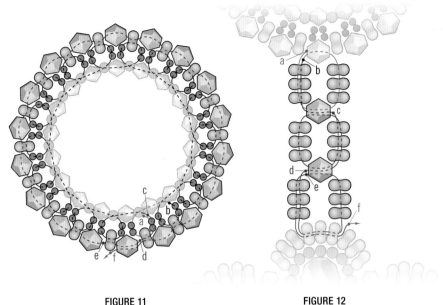

FIGURE 11

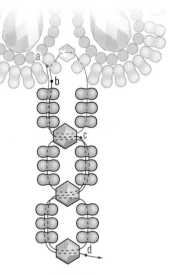

FIGURE 12

FIGURE 13

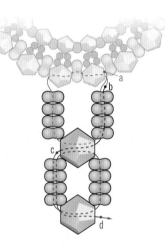

FIGURE 14

the same direction **(d–e)**. Sew through the beads again to reinforce the connection (not shown in the figure for clarity), and continue through the next six peanuts in the connection as shown **(e–f)**.

7 Sew through the peanuts and 3 mms along the perimeter of the flower motif to exit the 3 mm on the opposite edge of the flower motif, and then continue through the next peanut **(figure 13, point a)**. Pick up three peanuts, a 4 mm, and three peanuts, and sew through the peanut, 3 mm, and peanut your thread is exiting, going in the same direction **(a–b)** to form a loop. Continue through the next three peanuts and 4 mm in the loop **(b–c)**. Repeat step 4 twice **(c–d)**. Set this working thread aside.

8 Unwind the thread from the bobbin or piece of cardboard, and attach a needle on this working thread. Sew through the outer ring of 4 mms and peanuts in the top ring to exit a 4 mm directly opposite the first connector strip.

9 Work as in steps 4–7 to attach the other flower motif to the opposite side.

Bottom ring

The bottom ring will be stitched in the opposite order of the top ring, going from the outside and working toward the center of the ring.

1 With a working thread remaining from either connector strip, pick up a peanut and a 4 mm in a repeating pattern eight times, and then pick up another peanut. Sew through the corresponding end 4 mm on the opposite connector strip, going in the same direction. Repeat to form the outer section of the bottom ring. Retrace the thread path, and continue through the next peanut in the ring.

2 Pick up two 15ºs, an 11º, and two 15ºs, sew through the peanut your thread is exiting, going in the same direction to form a loop, and continue through the next 4 mm crystal and peanut. This loop should sit on the inside of the ring. Repeat this stitch 17 times to complete the round, and sew through the next 4 mm, two 15ºs and 11º in the next loop.

3 Pick up a 3 mm, and sew through the center 11º in the next loop. Repeat this stitch 17 times to complete the round. Retrace this

thread path, and end this working thread.

Side connectors

1 Add 2 yd. (1.8 m) of thread to the top ring, exiting the fifth 4 mm crystal away from the upper flower connection points **(figure 14, point a)**. Pick up four peanuts, a 6 mm bicone crystal, and four peanuts, and sew through the last three beads your thread is exiting (4 mm, peanut, and 4 mm) to form a loop **(figure 14, a–b)**. Continue through the next four peanuts and 6 mm in the loop **(b–c)**. Position the beadwork on the ornament with the top and bottom ring centered in the proper position on the bulb. The flowers should be on opposite sides.

2 Using your fingers to keep the beadwork stable on the ornament, pick up four peanuts, a 6 mm, and four peanuts, and sew through the 6 mm your thread is exiting, going in the same direction. Retrace the thread path (not shown in the figure for clarity), and continue through the next four peanuts and 6 mm in the loop **(c–d)**. Depending on the bulb's diameter, repeat this stitch six to seven times,

making sure the connector fits snugly when attached to the bottom ring.

3 To attach this side connector to the bottom ring: Pick up four peanuts, sew through the corresponding 4 mm, peanut, and 4 mm at the center of this side of the bottom ring. Pick up four peanuts, and sew through the 6 mm your thread exited at the start of this step, going in the same direction. Retrace the thread path, and end the thread.

4 Work as in steps 1–3 to add a second side connector to the opposite side of the ornament. ●

DOUBLE V BRACELET

designed by Joanie Jenniges

DIFFICULTY ●●○○○

bead weaving

New Ava beads form a path of diamond shapes in this quick but elegant bracelet.

Bracelet

How to pick up the Ava beads: Sew through the hole on the point of the bead (PH), the hole on a tip entering from the outside edge (TO), or the hole on a tip entering from the inside edge (TI), per the instructions.

materials

silver bracelet 7 in. (18 cm)
- **14** 10 x 4 mm Ava beads (crystal Labrador full)
- bicone crystals (Swarovski)
  - **21** 4 mm (crystal light chrome 2X)
  - **12** 3 mm (crystal comet argent light)
- **2 g** 11º seed beads (Toho P470, permanent galvanized silver)
- **1 g** 15º seed beads (Toho 711, nickel plated silver)
- **1** toggle clasp
- **2** 5 mm jump rings
- Fireline, 6 lb. test
- beading needles, #11 or #12

earrings 1 in. (2.5 cm)
- **4** 10 x 4 mm Ava beads (crystal Labrador full)
- bicone crystals
  - **2** 4 mm (Swarovski, Montana AB)
  - **4** 3 mm (Swarovski, black diamond AB)
- **26** 11º seed beads (Toho 705, matte metallic blue iris)
- **52** 15º seed beads (Miyuki 360, lined light amethyst AB)
- **1** pair of earring findings
- Fireline, 6 lb. test
- beading needles, #11 or #12

basics, p. 13
- ending and adding thread
- square knot
- opening and closing jump rings

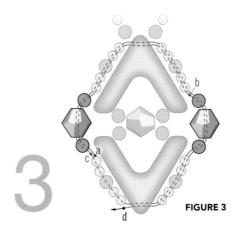

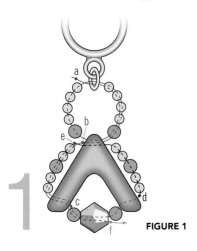

FIGURE 1

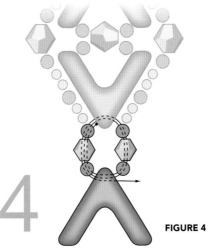

FIGURE 3

1) Attach a 5 mm jump ring to the loop of a toggle ring.

2) On 2 yd. (1.8 m) of thread, pick up the jump ring with the attached clasp, four 15º seed beads, an 11º seed bead, an Ava bead (PH), an 11º, and four 15ºs, and tie the working thread and tail together with a square knot, leaving a 6-in. (15 cm) tail. Continue through the jump ring, first four 15ºs, 11º, and Ava (PH) **(figure 1, a–b)**.

3) Pick up two 15ºs, an 11º, and two 15ºs, and sew through the Ava (TO) **(b–c)**. Pick up an 11º, a 4 mm bicone crystal, and an 11º, and sew through the open hole of the Ava (TI) **(c–d)**. Pick up two 15ºs, an 11º, and two 15ºs, and sew through the Ava (PH) **(d–e)**. Continue through the next eight beads to exit the 4 mm **(e–f)**.

5) Pick up an 11º, a 4 mm, and an 11º, and sew the next five beads, the Ava (PH), and the following five beads **(figure 3, a–b)**. Repeat this stitch once more **(b–c)**, and continue through the beadwork to exit the point of the last Ava added **(c–d)**.

Make matching earrings

For each earring, work as in steps 1–5 of "Bracelet" using 2 ft. (61 cm) of thread and sewing through the loop of an ear wire instead of a jump ring with an attached clasp. Then pick up an 11º, a 3 mm, a 15º, an 11º, a 15º, a 3 mm, and an 11º, and sew through the Ava (PH). End the threads.

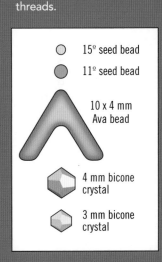

◯	15º seed bead
◯	11º seed bead
∧	10 x 4 mm Ava bead
⬡	4 mm bicone crystal
⬡	3 mm bicone crystal

TIP Always check to make sure that all holes of multi-hole beads are unplugged before using them. Sometimes, you can clear a plugged hole with a beading needle or a head pin.

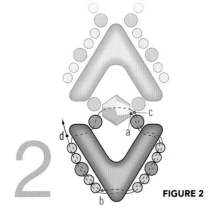

FIGURE 2

FIGURE 4

4) Pick up an 11º, an Ava (TI), two 15ºs, an 11º, and two 15ºs, and sew through the Ava (PH) **(figure 2, a–b)**. Pick up two 15ºs, an 11º, and two 15ºs, and sew through the open hole of the Ava (TO). Pick up an 11º, and sew through the 4 mm your thread exited at the start of this step **(b–c)**. Continue through the beadwork to exit the second set of five beads added in this step as shown **(c–d)**.

6) Pick up an 11º, a 3 mm bicone crystal, an 11º, an Ava (PH), an 11º, a 3 mm, and an 11º, and sew through the Ava (PH) your thread exited at the start of this step. Retrace the thread path, and continue through the first 11º, 3 mm, 11º, and Ava (PH) added **(figure 4)**.

7) Work as in steps 3–6 five times, then work as in steps 3–5 once more. End and add thread as needed.

8) Attach a jump ring to the toggle bar, and stitch the toggle bar to this end of the beadwork using the same bead counts as in step 2. Test the toggle to make sure it works properly, and add additional 15ºs if necessary. Retrace the clasp connection several times, and end the working thread.

9) With the tail, retrace the clasp connection several times, and end the thread. **B&B**

ISLAND RHYTHMS CUFF

designed by
Cecil Rodriguez

DIFFICULTY ●●○○○

bead weaving

Short hole

FIGURE 1

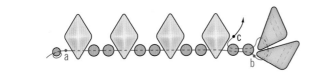

FIGURE 2

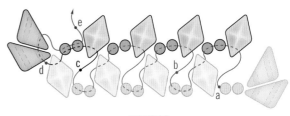

FIGURE 3

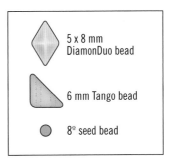

5 x 8 mm
DiamonDuo bead

6 mm Tango bead

8º seed bead

materials
butter pecan cuff
7 x 2 in. (18 x 5 cm)

- **160 (23 g)** 5 x 8 mm
  DiamonDuo beads (butter
  pecan)
- **82 (14 g)** 6 mm Tango beads
  (lumi green)
- **6 g** 8º Czech seed beads
  (Preciosa 10140, smoky
  topaz)
- **2** 16 mm buttons with shank
- Fireline, 6 lb. test
- beading needle, #12

basics, p. 13
- stop bead
- ending and adding thread

Tango beads dance along the edges of
this cuff as seed beads follow DiamonDuos
across the woven base.

Each Tango bead has two parallel
holes — a long hole and a short hole
that run from a shorter base edge to
a longer diagonal edge (**figure 1**). In
this project, you will always sew
through the short hole, picking up
the beads from the base edge.

The DiamonDuos have a beveled
side (top) and a flat side (bottom).
Pick up each DiamonDuo through
the bottom hole from either the
right side (BR) or left side (BL), per
the instructions.

For all two-hole beads, check to
ensure that all holes are open.

LINE 'EM UP
To avoid picking up the
Tangos the wrong way,
before starting the base,
line up two rows of 40
Tangos each, with the short
holes pointing inward so
the rows mirror each other.
To ensure you have the
DiamonDuos all facing the
same way, arrange each one
so the beveled surface faces
up and there is a top hole
and a bottom hole.

Base
1) Attach a stop bead to a comfortable length of thread, leaving
a 17-in. (43 cm) tail.

2) Pick up a repeating pattern
of a DiamonDuo (BL) and two 8º
seed beads four times (**figure 2,
a–b**). Pick up two Tango beads, and
sew back through the last two 8ºs
just added (**b–c**). Pull the beads
to tighten.

EVEN TENSION
When tightening your beads,
do not pull too taut or the
base may curve.

3) Pick up a DiamonDuo (BR) and
two 8ºs, and sew through the open
hole of the next DiamonDuo and
the following two 8ºs (**figure 3,
a–b**). Repeat this stitch two times
(**b–c**). Pick up a DiamonDuo (BR)
and two 8ºs and sew through the
open hole of the next DiamonDuo
(**c–d**). Pick up two Tangos, and sew

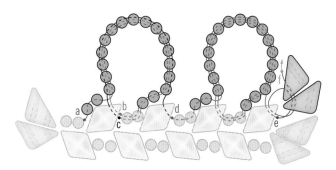

FIGURE 4

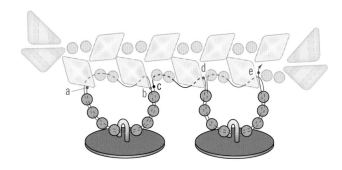

FIGURE 5

back through the last two 8ºs just added **(d–e)**. Tighten the beads to straighten the row.

4) Repeat step 3 38 times (a total of 40 rows) for a 7-in. (18 cm) bracelet, but when working rows from the left, pick up the Diamon-Duo from the left side. To maintain even tension and straight lines, push down on the beads as you build the rows. End and add thread as needed. To alter the length, add or omit rows as desired, allowing approximately ½ in. (1.3 cm) for the clasp.

Clasp

1) With the working thread, pick up 19 8ºs, and sew back through the next two 8ºs in the last row **(figure 4, a–b)**. Sew through the adjacent Diamon-Duo, skip the first two 8ºs just picked up, and then continue through the next 19 8ºs **(b–c)**. Continue through the DiamonDuo, 15 8ºs, and the open hole of the next DiamonDuo to reinforce the loop **(c–d)**. Sew through two 8ºs, and then repeat this step to make the next clasp loop **(d–e)**. Pick up two Tangos, and sew through the adjacent DiamonDuo and the two new Tangos **(e–f)**. End the working thread.

2) Remove the stop bead from the tail thread, and attach a needle. Pick up four 8ºs, a button shank, and four 8ºs **(figure 5, a–b)**. Sew through the adjacent DiamonDuo, two 8ºs, DiamonDuo, and the beads just added **(b–c)**. Reinforce the loop a few times (not shown in the figure for clarity). Sew through the next two 8ºs and DiamonDuo **(c–d)**, and then attach another button as shown **(d–e)**. Reinforce the loop a few times, and end the working thread. **B&B**

Make a narrower cuff by building rows with two groups of one DiamonDuo and two 8º seed beads, plus only one button clasp. End by adding one 8º seed bead instead of two Tangos. You'll need only half the beads, except for the Tangos. The result produces a more casual composition.

materials

green pendant 2¼ in. (5.7 cm)

- **1** 27 mm crystal stone (Swarovski 1201, crystal AB)
- **15** 6 mm two-hole lentil beads (CzechMates, matte metallic flax)
- **15** 4 mm fire-polished beads (milky aqua)
- 2.5 x 5 mm SuperDuos
  - **75** color A (green metallic matte)
  - **15** color B (matte apollo gold)
- **2 g** 8º seed beads (Toho PF562F, permanent finish galvanized saffron)
- **3 g** 11º seed bead (Miyuki 4204, duracoat galvanized champagne)
- **1 g** 15º seed beads (Miyuki 0457L, metallic opaque bronze)
- **1** 6 mm jump ring or split ring
- Fireline, 6 lb. test
- beading needles, #11 or #12
- **2** pairs of chainnose, flatnose, and/or bentnose pliers

basics, p. 13

- square knot
- ending thread
- opening and closing loops

Circles of SuperDuos, seeds, and fire-polished beads encase the substantial crystal stone for a lavish accent piece.

Front Bezel

1) On 7 ft. (2.1 m) of thread, pick up a repeating pattern of two color A SuperDuos and one 11º seed bead 15 times. Tie a square knot to form a ring, and sew through the open hole of the first A **(figure 1, a–b)**.

2) Pick up an 8º seed bead, and sew through the open hole of the next two As **(b–c)**. Repeat this stitch 14 times to complete the round, and sew through the first 8º added **(c–d)**.

3) Pick up an A and three 11ºs, sew through the open hole of the same A, and continue through the next 8º **(d–e)**. Repeat this stitch 14 times to complete the round, and sew through the first SuperDuo and two 11ºs added **(e–f)**.

4) Place the crystal facedown in the center of your work. Pick up two 8ºs, and sew through the center

11º in the next picot **(figure 2, a–b)**. Repeat this stitch 14 times to complete the round, and sew through the first two 8ºs added **(b–c)**. Push down on the crystal as you pull the thread tight so the beadwork cups.

Back Bezel

1) Pick up an 11º, and sew through the next two 8ºs **(figure 3, a–b)**. Repeat this stitch 14 times to complete the round, and step up through the first 11º added **(b–c)**.

2) Pick up two 11ºs, and sew through the next 11º **(c–d)**. Repeat this stitch 14 times to complete the round, and step up through the first two 11ºs added **(d–e)**.

3) Pick up one 11º, and sew through the next two 11ºs **(figure 4, a–b)** Repeat this stitch 14 times

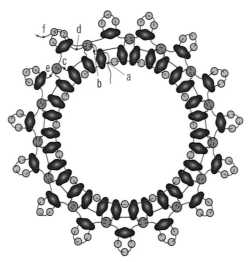

FIGURE 1

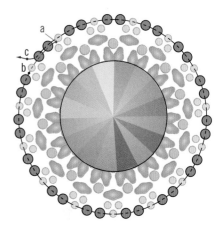

FIGURE 2

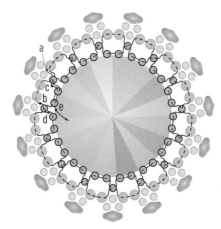

FIGURE 3

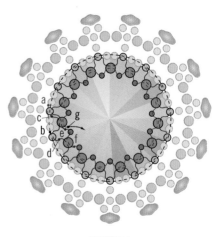

FIGURE 4

to complete the round, and sew through the first 11º added **(b–c)**.

4) Pick up an 8º and sew through the next 11º in the previous round **(c–d)**. Repeat this stitch 14 times to complete the round, and sew through first 8º added **(d–e)**.

5) Pick up a 15º seed bead, and sew through the next 8º **(e–f)**. Repeat this stitch 14 times to complete the round **(f–g)**, and retrace the thread path of the 15ºs and 8ºs again using tight tension.

Embellishments

1) Sew through the beadwork to exit an 8º in the outer edge **(figure 5, point a)**, and flip over the beadwork so the rivoli faces upward.

2) Pick up an 11º, two As, and an 11º, and sew through the next 8º **(a–b)**. Repeat this stitch 14 times to complete the round, and sew through the first 11º and the open hole of the adjacent A **(b–c)**.

3) Pick up a lentil bead, an 11º, a color B SuperDuo, and three 15ºs, and sew through the open hole of the same B **(c–d)**. Pick up an 11º, and sew through the open hole of the adjacent lentil and the open hole of the next A **(d–e)**. Pick up an 8º, and sew through the open hole of the following A **(e–f)**. Repeat these stitches 14 times to complete the round, and sew through the adjacent hole of the first lentil, 11º, B, three 15ºs, other hole of the same B, and next 11º **(f–g)**.

4) Pick up a 4 mm fire-polished bead, and sew through the next 11º, B, three 15ºs, other hole of the same B, and next 11º **(figure 6, a–b)**. Repeat this stitch 14 times to complete the round, but after the last stitch sew through only the next 11º, B, and two 15ºs **(b–c)**. Pick up five 15ºs and a jump ring or split ring, and sew through the 15º your thread is exiting, going in the same direction to form a loop **(c–d)**. Retrace the thread path of the loop, and end the working thread and tail. **B&B**

FIGURE 5

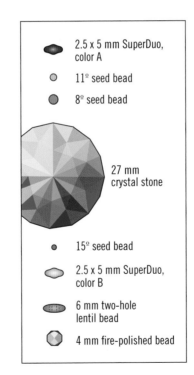

- 2.5 x 5 mm SuperDuo, color A
- 11º seed bead
- 8º seed bead
- 27 mm crystal stone
- 15º seed bead
- 2.5 x 5 mm SuperDuo, color B
- 6 mm two-hole lentil bead
- 4 mm fire-polished bead

TIP The key to this bezel is using tight thread tension throughout the project. This will keep your rows in place and provide a cohesive look throughout the work.

FIGURE 6

Earring options

To make mini-pendant earrings, work as in steps 1–4 of "Front Bezel," but repeat patterns only seven times and use a 12 mm rivoli. Embellish with 15ºs, add a dangle, and attach an earring finding. Repeat to make a pair.

For rivoli-free earrings, work as in steps 1–3 of "Front Bezel," but repeat patterns six times. Embellish as desired.

FALL FLAMES
rope

Work a subtle color gradation into a chenille stitch rope for a necklace that reflects nature's beautiful seasonal colors.

by **Marsha Wiest-Hines**

Prepare the cord necklace

Fold the necklace in half, aligning the ends, to find the exact center, and mark that point with a marker or pen. Open the necklace and lay it out straight. On each side of the center, mark the cord at the ½ in. (1.3 cm), 2 in. (5 cm), 3½ in. (8.9 cm), 5 in. (13 cm), and 6½ in. (16.5 cm) points. Clasp the necklace, and lay it flat on your workspace, making sure you can see these "balance marks."

Gradated chenille stitch sheath

1 On a comfortable length of conditioned thread, pick up eight color A 11º seed beads. Wrap the beads around the cord at one end, and leaving a 6-in. (15 cm) tail, sew through all eight beads again to form them into a ring. Sew through one more bead **(figure 1)**, pulling snug from both ends, to secure the ring of beads next to the cord end. Grasp the cord end and thread tail securely to keep the beadwork from slipping around the cord.
2 Work rounds of chenille stitch as follows:
Round 2: Pick up one color F 11º seed bead, and sew

through the next two As. Repeat this stitch three times to complete the round, and step up through the first F **(figure 2)**.
Round 3: Pick up two As and, sew through the next F. Repeat this stitch three times to complete the round, and step up through the first A added in this round **(figure 3)**.
Round 4: Pick up one F, and sew through the next two As. Repeat this stitch three times to complete the round, and step up through the first F **(figure 4)**.

These four rounds comprise one "unit" of chenille stitch. Counting in units will be necessary for the remainder of this project.
3 Repeat rounds 3 and 4 twice to work another unit of chenille stitch for two complete units. At this point, if your beads are slipping around the necklace, coat your tail with microcrystalline wax, and sew through the original eight As with a tight tension once or twice until the beads are securely anchored to the cord by tension.
4 Continue working in chenille stitch with As and Fs until you reach your first balance mark.
5 Next comes the first color transition, which will be

completed over the next eight units (32 rounds), finishing at the next balance mark. You will gradually reduce the number of As in a round, while increasing the number of color B beads. You will keep the new color beads as far apart from each other as possible in each unit. Beginning at the first round in the transition,

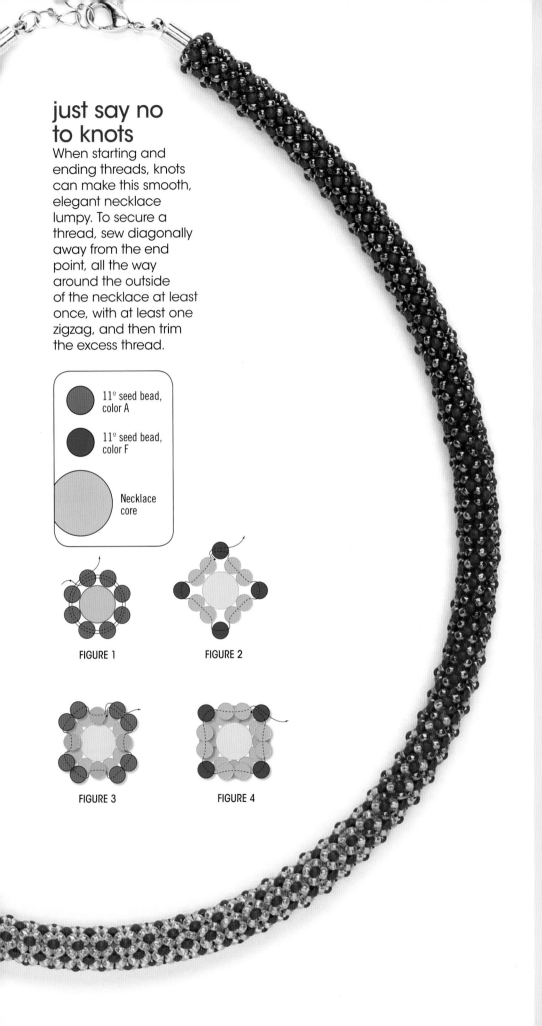

just say no to knots

When starting and ending threads, knots can make this smooth, elegant necklace lumpy. To secure a thread, sew diagonally away from the end point, all the way around the outside of the necklace at least once, with at least one zigzag, and then trim the excess thread.

11º seed bead, color A

11º seed bead, color F

Necklace core

FIGURE 1

FIGURE 2

FIGURE 3

FIGURE 4

Difficulty rating

Materials
rope 18 in. (46 cm) with 1½-in. (3.8 cm) extender chain

- 11º seed beads
  - **4 g** color A (Miyuki 356, purple-lined amethyst AB)
  - **3 g** color B (Toho 165C, dark ruby transparent rainbow)
  - **3 g** color C (Toho 165, ruby hyacinth transparent rainbow)
  - **3 g** color D (Toho 2030, hyacinth silver-lined rainbow)
  - **3 g** color E (Toho 175, citrine transparent rainbow)
  - **8 g** color F (Toho 2609F, semi-glazed marsala)
- 1 3 mm x 18-in. (46 cm) pre-finished satin covered cord necklace, with clasp and chain (burgundy; www.satincord.com/d_necklaces_ssc3mm.html)
- nylon beading thread, size D (beige or brown; should blend with the cord)
- contrasting thread used for "balance marks"
- microcrystalline wax
- needles, #11 and 12 Straw or Sharp (the length of a beading needle is awkward for this project)
- marker or pen

Basics, p. 13
- conditioning thread
- ending and adding thread
- square knot

note
You can use other types of cord for the core — try leather, cotton bolo cord, or just about any other 3 mm thick cord. Finish the ends with glue-in end caps or a magnetic clasp.

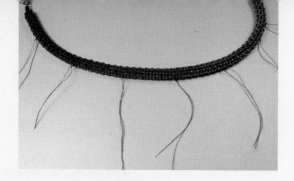

keep your place

Using transparent rainbow beads makes the necklace mysterious and subtle, but it is easy to get lost in your count. To help keep track of your progress, tie a bright thread with a square knot into one of the final F beads in each transition, so you never need to count more than eight units to know where you are. Leave these threads a couple inches long, and hold them out of the way with your fingers.

work four stitches per round as follows, stepping up at the end of each round:
Round 1: AA, AA, AA, AA
Round 2: F, F, F, F
Round 3: AA, AA, AA, AA
Round 4: F, F, F, F; this completes unit 1 of this section.
Round 5: AB, AA, AA, AA
Round 6: F, F, F, F
Round 7: AA, AA, AB, AA
Round 8: F, F, F, F; this completes unit 2.
Round 9: AB, AA, AB, AA
Round 10: F, F, F, F
Round 11: AA, AB, AA, AB
Round 12: F, F, F, F; this completes unit 3.
Round 13: AB, AA, AB, AB
Round 14: F, F, F, F
Round 15: AB, AB, AA, AB
Round 16: F, F, F, F; this completes unit 4.
Round 17: AB, AB, AB, AB
Round 18: F, F, F, F
Round 19: AB, AB, AB, AB
Round 20: F, F, F, F; this completes unit 5.
Round 21: BB, AB, AB, AB
Round 22: F, F, F, F
Round 23: AB, AB, BB, AB
Round 24: F, F, F, F; this completes unit 6.
Round 25: BB, AB, BB, AB
Round 26: F, F, F, F
Round 27: AB, BB, AB, BB
Round 28: F, F, F, F; this completes unit 7.
Round 29: BB, AB, BB, BB
Round 30: F, F, F, F
Round 31: BB, BB, BB, AB
Round 32: F, F, F, F; this completes unit 8.

6 You will notice that the work is somewhat elastic, and can be stretched longer or condensed shorter as you work. The balance marks indicate a relaxed position for the end of each gradation transition. The rope needs to be relaxed to curve easily around your neck, so use the balance marks to orient the work to the correct amount of stretch.

7 You will use the same chart for each transition on the first half of the necklace by putting away the beads you just eliminated in the transition, moving the color you transitioned to into the "A" position, and placing your next color of beads in the "B" position. The Fs remain constant throughout the piece. Work three more color transitions, transitioning from color B to color C, color C to color D, and color D to color E, using your balance marks to double check that your work is going according to plan.

When your have finished the transition to color E, you should be at the mark ½ in. (1.2 cm) short of the center line. Stretch or condense your work as needed.

8 Work three units with color E, and tie a bright thread to an F in the last round. This is the center of your necklace and should align with your center balance mark.

9 Work three more units of color E. This is the end of the center E color block.

10 You are now ready to begin your next color transition, from color E to color D. On the first side of the necklace, you worked a unit of the new color to begin. On this side, to keep our necklace symmetrical, you will want that new color unit to be at the end of the transition. On this side, the chart looks like this:
Round 1: ED, EE, EE, EE
Round 2: F, F, F, F
Round 3: EE, EE, ED, EE
Round 4: F, F, F, F; this completes unit 1.
Round 5: ED, EE, ED, EE
Round 6: F, F, F, F
Round 7: EE, ED, EE, ED
Round 8: F, F, F, F; this completes unit 2.
Round 9: ED, EE, ED, ED
Round 10: F, F, F, F
Round 11: ED, ED, EE, ED
Round 12: F, F, F, F; this completes unit 3.
Round 13: ED, ED, ED, ED
Round 14: F, F, F, F
Round 15: ED, ED, ED, ED
Round 16: F, F, F, F; this completes unit 4.
Round 17: DD, ED, ED, ED
Round 18: F, F, F, F
Round 19: ED, ED, DD, ED
Round 20: F, F, F, F; this completes unit 5.
Round 21: DD, ED, DD, ED
Round 22: F, F, F, F
Round 23: ED, DD, ED, DD
Round 24: F, F, F, F; this completes unit 6.

Round 25: DD, ED, DD, DD
Round 26: F, F, F, F
Round 27: DD, DD, DD, ED
Round 28: F, F, F, F; this completes unit 7.
Round 29: DD, DD, DD, DD
Round 30: F, F, F, F
Round 31: DD, DD, DD, DD
Round 32: F, F, F, F; this completes unit 8.

11 Use the same chart for each transition on the second half of the necklace by putting away the beads you just eliminated in the transition, moving the color you transitioned to into the "E" position, and placing your next color of beads in the "D" position. Stitch this gradation transition four times in total, moving from E to D (finished), D to C, C to B, and B to A. Each transition will have eight units, ending with a unit of the newly established color. End and add thread as needed.

12 To complete the rope, stitch in rounds using As to equal the number of rounds of As at the other end. If your work is twisted, align it now. Wax your remaining thread with Microcrystalline wax, switch to a size 12 needle, and secure this end by passing your needle through the last row of eight As at least three or four times, with very snug tension, until the beads are anchored securely at the end of the cord. ●

Join strips of crescent beads together to make a bracelet with a delicate, feathery look.

How to pick up the crescent beads: With the tips of the crescent facing down, pick up the bead through the left hole (LH) or the right hole (RH).

First strip

1) Attach a stop bead to a comfortable length of thread, leaving a 6-in. (15 cm) tail.

2) Pick up a crescent (RH), a crescent (LH), an 11º seed bead, a crescent (LH), and an 11º, and sew back through the same hole of the last crescent, the next 11º, and the following two crescents **(figure 1)**.

3) Pick up three 11ºs, skip the crescent your thread is exiting, and sew through the open hole of the next crescent **(figure 2, a–b)**. Pick up an 11º, and sew through the open hole of the following crescent **(b–c)**.

4) Pick up a repeating pattern of a crescent (LH) and an 11º twice **(c–d)**, and sew back through the same hole of the last crescent, the next 11º, and the following two crescents **(d–e)**.

5) Repeat steps 3–4 for the desired length, allowing ½ in. (1.3 cm) for the clasp, and ending with step 3. Do not use a tight tension or the beadwork will twist. End and add thread as needed.

6) Pick up two 11ºs and sew through the adjacent 11º and crescent **(figure 3, a–b)**. Pick up two 11ºs, skip the next 11º and crescent, and sew through the following 11º and crescent **(b–c)**. Repeat these stitches for the remainder of the strip, except on the last stitch pick up three 11ºs, skip the next 11º and crescent, and sew through the open hole of the following crescent **(figure 4, a–b)**. Pick up an 11º, and sew back through the same hole of the crescent and the last two 11ºs added **(b–c)**.

7) Pick up an 11º, a 3 mm English-cut round bead, and an 11º, skip the next 11º, crescent, and 11º, and sew through the following 11º **(c–d)**. Repeat this stitch for the remainder of the strip. The beads should lie flat along the edge of the strip. End and add thread as needed; end the working thread but not the tail.

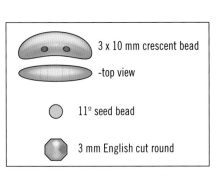

3 x 10 mm crescent bead -top view

11º seed bead

3 mm English cut round

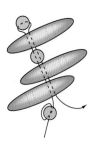

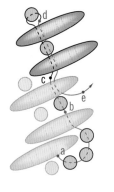

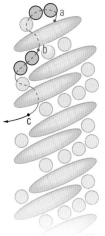

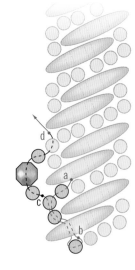

FIGURE 1   **FIGURE 2**   **FIGURE 3**   **FIGURE 4**

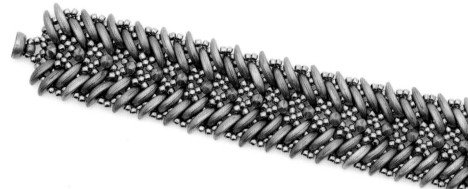

Second strip

Work steps 1–6 of "First strip" with the following changes to make it a mirror image:
• Work as in step 1, but leave a 12-in. (30 cm) tail.
• In step 2, pick up a crescent (LH), a crescent (RH), an 11º seed bead, a crescent (RH), and an 11º, and complete the step as directed.
• In step 4, pick up each crescent through the RH.
• Do not end the working thread or tail after step 6.

Join

1) Position the first strip vertically with the 3 mms on the left edge and the stop bead closest to you. Position the second strip to the left of the first strip, with the stop bead closest to you. The crescents should be angled as shown in **figure 5** and the tips of the crescents facing downward.
2) With the working thread from the left-hand strip, pick up an 11º, and sew through the adjacent 3 mm on the right-hand strip **(figure 5, a–b)**. Pick up an 11º, and sew through the center 11º in

the next set of three 11ºs on the left-hand strip **(b–c)**. Repeat these stitches for the remainder of the strips using an even tension so the beadwork lies flat.
3) Pick up an 11º, a 3 mm, and an 11º, and sew through the center 11º in the three-bead set on the end of the left-hand strip **(figure 6, a–b)**. Pick up two 11ºs, half of the clasp, and two 11ºs, and sew through the corresponding 11º in the end three-bead set of the right-hand strip **(b–c)**. Pick up an 11º, and sew through the 3 mm just added. Pick up an 11º, and sew through the center 11º in the next three-bead set on the right-hand strip **(c–d)**. Sew through the beadwork, and retrace the thread path of the clasp connection. End this thread.
4) Remove the stop bead from the right-hand strip, and end this tail. Remove the

stop bead from the left strip, and attach a needle to the tail. Pick up two 11ºs, and sew through the next end 11º **(figure 7, a–b)**. Pick up two 11ºs, half of the clasp, and two 11ºs, and sew through the corresponding 11º on the right-hand strip **(b–c)**. Pick up two 11ºs, and sew through the following 11º **(c–d)**. Sew through the beadwork, retrace the thread path of the clasp connection, and end the tail. **B⦂B**

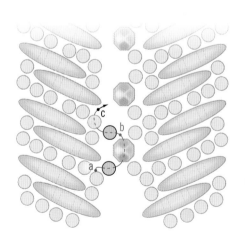

FIGURE 5

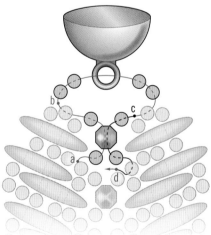

FIGURE 6

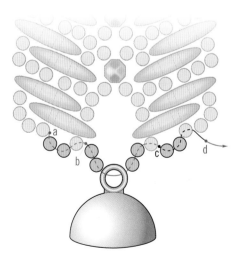

FIGURE 7

TWIST AND TURN EARRINGS

designed by Puca

DIFFICULTY ●●○○○

bead weaving

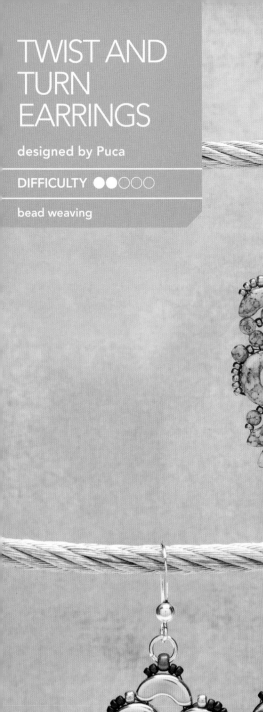

5 x 10 mm
Arcos par Puca bead

15º seed bead

2.5 x 3 mm Minos
par Puca bead

5 x 7 mm Pip bead

3 x 5 mm pinch bead

8º seed bead

11º seed bead

materials
purple earrings 1⅞ x ⅞ in.
(4.8 x 2.2 cm)

- **20** 5 x 10 mm Arcos par
  Puca beads (opaque mix
  rose gold ceramic)
- **2** 5 x 7 mm Pip beads
  (pastel burgundy)
- **2** 3 x 5 mm pinch beads
  (metallic suede pink)
- **16** 2.5 x 3 mm Minos par
  Puca beads (opaque mix
  rose gold ceramic)
- **2** 8º seed beads (Miyuki
  4220, Duracoat eggplant)
- **4** 11º seed beads (Miyuki
  4204, Duracoat galvanized
  champagne)
- **1 g** 15º seed beads (Miyuki
  4218, Duracoat galvanized
  dusty orchid)
- **1** pair of earring findings
- **2** 4 mm jump rings
- Fireline, 6 lb. test
- beading needles, #11 or #12
- **2** pairs of chainnose, flatnose, and/or bentnose pliers

Basics, p. 13
- ending and adding thread
- attaching a stop bead
- opening and closing loops
  and jump rings

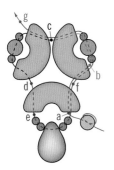

STASH BUSTER!

Use what you have on hand in place of the pinch beads and Pip beads.

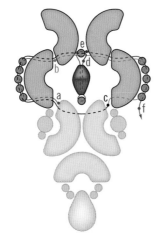

FIGURE 1

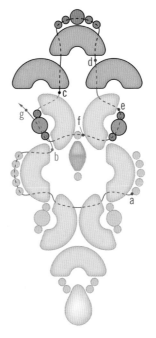

FIGURE 2

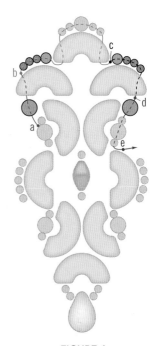

FIGURE 3

FIGURE 4

New shaped beads give these earrings a unique look that's stylish and elegant, and can be worked up in a short time.

EARRINGS

How to pick up the Arcos beads: Sew through the side holes entering from the inside edge (IE) or the outside edge (OE). The center holes will not be used for this pattern.

1) On 1 yd. (.9 m) of thread, attach a stop bead, leaving a 6-in. (15 cm) tail. Pick up an Arcos (IE), an Arcos (OE) **(figure 1, a–b)**, a 15º seed bead, a Minos bead, and a 15º, and sew through the open side hole (IE) of the last Arcos added **(b–c)**.

2) Pick up an Arcos (OE), a 15º, a Minos, and a 15º, and sew through the open side hole (IE) of the same Arcos **(c–d)**. Continue through the open hole (OE) of the adjacent Arcos **(d–e)**.

3) Pick up two 15ºs, a Pip bead, and two 15ºs, and sew through the other hole (IE) of the same Arcos **(e–f)**. Continue through the beadwork as shown to exit the tip of the third Arcos **(f–g)**. Remove the stop bead.

4) Pick up an Arcos (IE) and five 15ºs, and sew through the open hole (OE) of the same Arcos

(figure 2, a–b). Pick up an Arcos (IE), a 15º, an Arcos (OE), an Arcos (IE), and five 15ºs, and sew through the open hole (OE) of the last Arcos just added **(b–c)**. Continue through the next three Arcos, five 15ºs, the other hole (OE) of the same Arcos, the following Arcos (IE) and the next 15º as shown **(c–d)**.

5) Pick up a pinch bead and a 15º, and sew back through the pinch bead and the 15º your thread exited at the start of the step, going in the same direction **(d–e)**. Continue through the next two Arcos and the following five 15ºs **(e–f)**.

6) Sew through the beadwork as shown **(figure 3, a–b)**. Pick up a 15º, a Minos, and a 15º, and sew through the open hole (IE) of the adjacent Arcos **(b–c)**.

7) Pick up two Arcos (IE), two 15ºs, an 8º, and two 15ºs, and sew through the open hole (OE) of the last Arcos added **(c–d)**. Pick up an Arcos (OE), and sew through the open hole (OE) of the adjacent Arcos **(d–e)**.

8) Pick up a 15º, a Minos, and a 15º, and sew through the other hole (IE) of the same Arcos **(e–f)**. Continue through the next 15º, Arcos, 15º, and Minos **(f–g)**.

9) Pick up a Minos, and sew through the open hole (IE) of the adjacent Arcos **(figure 4, a–b)**. Pick up three 15ºs and an 11º seed bead, and sew through the following Arcos (IE), the next five beads, and the other hole (OE) of this Arcos **(b–c)**.

10) Pick up an 11º and three 15ºs, and sew through the open hole (OE) of the adjacent Arcos **(c–d)**. Pick up a Minos, and sew through the following 15º, Minos, and 15º **(d–e)**.

11) Pick up a 15º and a Minos, and sew through the beadwork as shown to exit the five 15ºs on the opposite side **(figure 5, a–b)**. Pick up a Minos and a 15º, and sew through the next 15º and Minos **(b–c)**. End the threads.

12) Open a jump ring, and attach it to the 8º at the top of the beadwork and an earring finding.

13) Repeat steps 1–12 to make another earring. B&B

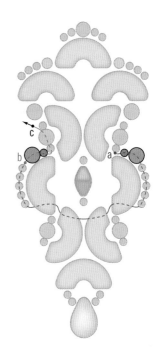

FIGURE 5

PEYOTE STITCH

VICTORIAN FLOWER BRACELET

Make a festive bracelet of sturdy but delicate hexagonal components and pearl-embellished flowers.

designed by **Lorraine Coetzee**

Base components

1 On 4 ft. (1.2 m) of thread, pick up a repeating pattern of a color A 11º cylinder bead and five color B 11º cylinder beads six times. Retrace the thread path to form a ring, leaving a 16-in. (41 cm) tail, and sew through the first six beads to exit the fifth B in the ring.
2 Work in rounds as follows, keeping a tight tension:
Round 2: Pick up two As, skip the next A, and sew through the following B **(figure 1, a–b)**.

Work two peyote stitches using Bs **(b–c)**. Repeat these stitches five times to complete the round, and step up through the first A added in this round **(c–d)**.
Round 3: Pick up one A, and sew through the next A. Work three peyote stitches using Bs **(d–e)**. Repeat these stitches five times to complete the round, and step up through the first A added in this round **(e–f)**.
Round 4: Work four peyote stitches using Bs **(f–g)**.

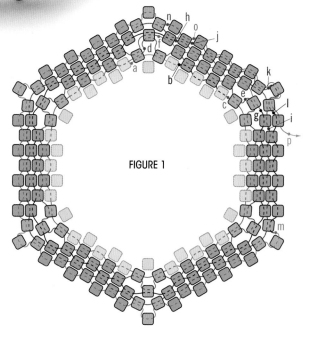

FIGURE 1

98

Repeat these stitches five times to complete the round, and step up through the first B added **(g–h)**.

Round 5: Work three peyote stitches using Bs. Pick up two As, and sew through the next B **(h–i)**. Repeat these stitches five times to complete the round, and step up through the first B added **(i–j)**.

Round 6: Work three peyote stitches using Bs **(j–k)**. Pick up one A, and sew through the next A **(k–l)**. Work four peyote stitches using Bs **(l–m)**. Continue around, adding an A at each corner and four Bs on each side **(m–n)**. Work one more stitch using a B to complete the round **(n–o)**. Sew through the next nine beads as shown to exit the first B on the following side **(o–p)**, and set this thread aside. Attach a needle to the tail.

Round 7: The beads added in the next three rounds will begin to curve upward. With your tail exiting an A **(figure 2, point a)**, work three peyote stitches using Bs **(a–b)**. Repeat these three stitches five times to complete the round, and step up through the first B added **(b–c)**.

Round 8: Work two peyote stitches using Bs. Pick up two As, and sew through the next B **(c–d)**. Repeat these stitches five times to complete the round, and step up through the first B added **(d–e)**.

Round 9: Work two peyote stitches using Bs. Pick up one A, and sew through the next A **(e–f)**. Continue around, adding three Bs on each side and one A at each corner for the next five sides **(f–g)**. Work one peyote stitch using a B to complete the round **(g–h)**. End this thread.

3 Using the working thread **(point l)**, work in flat odd-count peyote using Bs to add seven rows to form a tab that is seven beads wide. End with three up-beads **(i–j)**.

4 Repeat steps 1–3 to make four more components.

5 To connect the base components, position two components face up next to each other with the tabs to the right. With the thread on the first component, zip the tab on the first component to the center row edge opposite the tab on the second component. Retrace the join, and end this thread. Repeat this step with the remaining components.

Toggle ring

1 Repeat steps 1–2 of "Base components" with the following changes:

• In step 1, pick up the repeating pattern only five times so the shape has five sides instead of six, and leave a 2-ft. (61 cm) tail.

• In step 2, work the repeats for completing the rounds for a five-sided ring, not six.

• At the end of round 9, step up through the first B added in the round, and do not end the thread.

2 Continue working in rounds as in the "Base components." Rounds 1–7 in figure 3 are not shown in the illustration for clarity:

Difficulty rating

   ◇

Materials

bracelet 7¼ in. (18.4 cm)

• **4** 10 mm Swarovski rivolis (light vitrail)
• **52** 4 mm Swarovski pearls (creamrose)
• **2 g** 11º seed beads (Miyuki 4220, Duracoat galvanized eggplant)
• 11º Delica cylinder beads
  - **3 g** color A (Miyuki DB1851F, Duracoat galvanized matte light pewter)
  - **10 g** color B (Miyuki DB1850, Duracoat galvanized eggplant)
• **3 g** 15º seed bead (Miyuki 2008, matte metallic patina iris)
• **1 g** 13º Charlotte beads (silver)
• Fireline, 6 lb. test
• beading needles, #11 or #12

Basics, p.13

• peyote stitch: tubular, flat odd-count, zipping up
• ending and adding thread
• attacing a stop bead

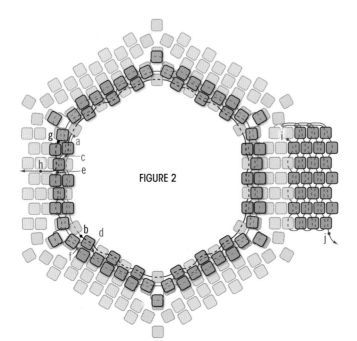

FIGURE 2

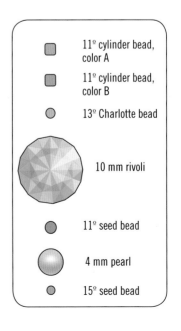

	11º cylinder bead, color A
	11º cylinder bead, color B
	13º Charlotte bead
	10 mm rivoli
	11º seed bead
	4 mm pearl
	15º seed bead

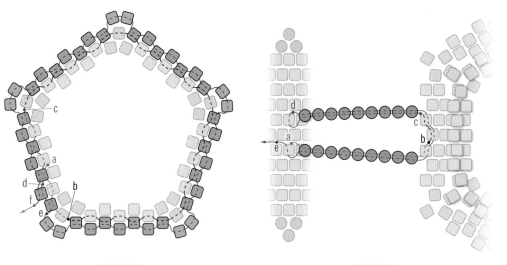

FIGURE 3

FIGURE 4

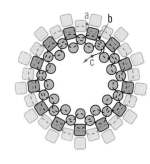

FIGURE 5

Round 10: Work two peyote stitches using Bs **(figure 3, a–b)**. Work four peyote stitches using Bs, and then repeat three times to add four Bs per side **(b–c)**. Work two peyote stitches using Bs, and step up through the first B added to complete the round **(c–d)**.
Round 11: Work one peyote stitch using a B **(d–e)**. Continue around, picking up two As at each corner and working three stitches with Bs on each side, stepping up through the first B **(e–f)**.
3 Zip up round 11 and round 6 (the opposite edge) by sewing through the next B in round 6. Continue through the following A in round 11, the tip A in round 6, and the next A in round 11. Continue to zip up the remaining edges and corners, and end the threads.
4 With the thread from the tab on the end base component, attach the tab to the toggle ring by zipping it to the center row on one edge of the toggle ring. Retrace the join, and end this thread.

Toggle bar
1 On 2 ft. (61 cm) of thread, attach a stop bead, leaving a 6-in. (15 cm) tail. Pick up 11 Bs. These beads will shift to become the first two rows of the toggle bar as the next row is added.
2 Using Bs, work in flat odd-count peyote until you have eight rows. Zip up rows 1 and 8 to form a tube.
3 Sew through the center of the tube to the other end, pick up three 11ºs, sew back through the tube to the first end, pick up three 11ºs, and sew through the tube again. Retrace the thread path twice, and then sew through the beads to exit a B five beads from the end edge **(figure 4, point a)**. End the tail, but not the working thread.
4 Pick up nine 11ºs, and sew through the second B on the bottom edge of the end base component, opposite the tab **(a–b)**. Sew through the beadwork to exit the next B in the same row **(b–c)**. Pick up nine 11ºs, and sew through the next B in the same row

on the bar **(c–d)**. Retrace the thread path back through the beads to exit the B on the bar your thread exited at the start of this step, going in the same direction **(d–e)**. End the thread.

Flower
1 On 4 ft. (1.2 m) of thread, pick up 26 Bs. Sew through the beads again to form a ring, and continue through the first bead again, leaving an 8-in. (20 cm) tail.
2 Work in rounds of tubular peyote stitch for the front of the bezel as follows, stepping up after each round:
Round 3: Work a round using Bs **(figure 5, a–b)**.
Rounds 4–5: Work both rounds using 13º Charlottes **(b–c)**.
3 Flip the beadwork over, and place the rivoli face-down in the bezel. The bezel will not fit on the rivoli very well until the second round of 13º Charlottes are added to the back and tightened.
4 Using the tail, work two rounds of 13º Charlottes for

the back of the bezel, using a tight tension. End the tail. With the working thread, sew through the beadwork to exit the second (center) round of cylinders. Flip the bezel to the front.
5 Pick up an 11º seed bead, a 4 mm pearl, and three 15º seed beads, and sew back through the pearl. Pick up an 11º, and sew through the next cylinder in the same round **(figure 6, a–b)**. Repeat these stitches 12 times using a tight tension to complete the round **(b–c)**, and sew through the next cylinder in round 1 **(c–d)**.
6 Pick up three 15ºs, and sew through the next cylinder in the same round **(figure 7, a–b)**. Repeat this stitch 12 times using a tight tension to complete the round **(b–c)**. Sew through the beadwork to exit the last round of cylinder beads near the center on the back of the bezel.
7 Repeat steps 1–6 to make a total of four flowers.

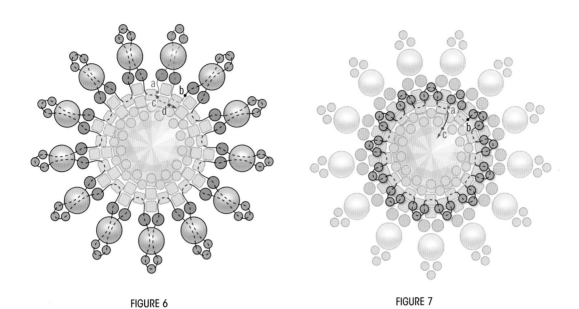

FIGURE 6   FIGURE 7

Attaching the flowers to the base

Position a flower over the tab between two base components, with the working thread from the flower near the adjacent top outer edge B of the base component. Sew through the first top outer edge B in the base component, and continue through the next B in the same round of the flower. Continue to attach the flower by sewing through the next B in the top outer edge of the base component and the following B in the same round of the flower. Sew through the last top outer edge B in the base component, and sew back through the join using a tight tension **(figure 8 and photo)**. The beadwork is shown loose so you can see the thread path. Sew through the flower to exit the opposite side, and attach it to the edge of the next base component. End this thread. Repeat to attach the remaining flowers. **◐**

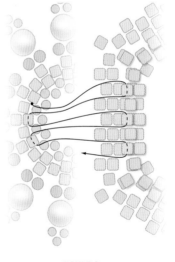

FIGURE 8

ADJUST THE LENGTH
If you need to adjust the length, try one of these tips:
• Use more or fewer base components and flowers
• Adjust the tab connecting the toggle ring
• Shorten or lengthen the toggle bar attachment

Ivy *trails* NECKLACE

Stitch a lovely necklace that follows a lush winding path of leaves, pearls, and crystals.

designed by **Isabella Lam**

Necklace

1 On a comfortable length of thread, attach a stop bead, leaving an 8-in. (20 cm) tail. Pick up an 8º seed bead.

2 Pick up an 8 mm pearl and nine 11º seed beads, and sew through the pearl again, going in the same direction **(figure 1, a–b)** to form a loop around one side of the pearl.

3 Pick up an 11º, a 4 mm bicone crystal, and an 11º **(b–c)**.

4 Work as in steps 2–3 for the desired length, ending after step 2 **(c–d)**. Our 19-in. (48 cm) necklace has a total of 30 pearls.

5 Pick up an 8º and three 11ºs, and sew back through the 8º and the end pearl **(figure 2, a–b)** to form a picot on this end.

6 Sew through the first seven 11ºs in the loop around the pearl **(b–c)**. Pick up a 15º, an 11º, an O-bead, a leaf bead, an O-bead, a Super-Duo, and an 11º, skip the first two 11ºs in the loop, and sew through the remaining seven 11ºs, going in the same direction **(c–d)**. Sew through the adjacent pearl, 11º, 4 mm crystal, 11º, and the next pearl **(d–e)**.

7 Work as in step 6 to embellish the next 28 pearls, except pick up an 11º, a SuperDuo, an O-bead, a leaf bead, an O-bead, a SuperDuo, and an 11º for each embellishment **(e–f)**.

8 Embellish the last pearl as a mirror image of the first pearl by picking up an 11º, a SuperDuo, an O-bead, a leaf bead, an O-bead, an 11º, and a 15º **(f–g)** and continue through the next 8º **(g–h)**.

9 Remove the stop bead. Using the working thread, pick up three 11ºs, sew back through the 8º your thread is exiting, and continue through the first five 11ºs in the adjacent loop around the end pearl **(figure 3, a–b)**.

10 Pick up three 15º seed beads, a 3 mm bicone crystal, and two 15ºs, and sew through the open hole of the next SuperDuo **(b–c)**.

11 Pick up a 15º, an 8º, and a 15º, and sew through the open hole of the next SuperDuo **(c–d)**.

12 Pick up two 15ºs, a 3 mm crystal, and three 15ºs, and sew through the center 11º in the loop around the next pearl **(d–e)**.

13 Work as in steps 10–12 for the remainder of the necklace **(e–f)**.

Clasp

1 Sew through the next four 11ºs in the loop, the following 8º, and the next two 11ºs in the end picot **(f–g)**. Pick up three 11ºs, the loop of the toggle ring, and three 11ºs, and sew through the 11º your thread is exiting, going in the same direction **(g–h)**. Retrace the thread path several times, and end the working thread.

2 With the tail, sew through the adjacent two 11ºs in the adjacent picot, exiting the center 11º. Work as in step 1 to add the toggle bar. ●

Difficulty rating

Materials

necklace 19 in. (48 cm)

- **30** 8 mm pearls (Swarovski, iridescent green)
- **30** 12 x 7 mm leaf beads (Czech, iris brown)
- **5 g** 2.5 x 5 mm SuperDuo beads (opaque green luster)
- bicone crystals (Swarovski)
  - **29** 4 mm (chrysolite AB2X)
  - **58** 3 mm (chrysolite AB2X)
- **2 g** 3.8 mm O-beads (crystal golden rainbow)
- **2 g** 8º seed beads (Miyuki 457, metallic dark bronze)
- **3 g** 11º seed beads (Toho 221, bronze)
- **3 g** 15º seed beads (Toho 221, bronze)
- **1** toggle clasp
- Fireline, 6 lb. test
- beading needles, #11 or #12

Basics, p.13

- ending and adding thread
- attaching a stop bead

Bead legend:

- 8º seed bead
- 8 mm pearl
- 11º seed bead
- 4 mm bicone crystal
- 15º seed bead
- 3.8 mm O-bead
- 12 x 7 mm leaf bead
- 2.5 x 5 mm SuperDuo bead
- 3 mm bicone crystal

FIGURE 1

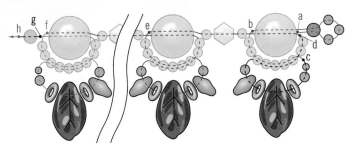

FIGURE 2

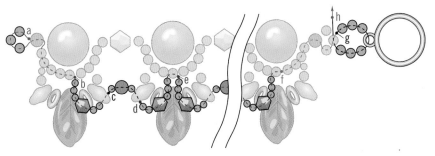

FIGURE 3

NAUTILUS EARRINGS

designed by
Graziella Malara

DIFFICULTY ●●●○○

peyote stitch

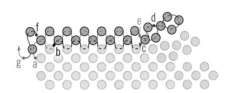

FIGURE 1

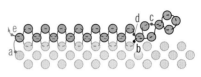
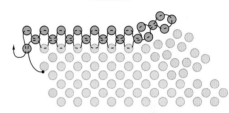

FIGURE 2

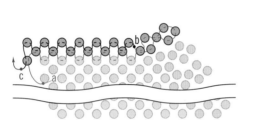

FIGURE 3

FIGURE 4

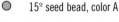
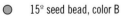

FIGURE 5

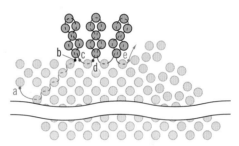

FIGURE 6

- ⬤ 15º seed bead, color A
- ⬤ 15º seed bead, color B
- ⬡ 4 mm bicone crystal

Aquatic-inspired spirals of seed beads coil to create exotic earrings ready for beachwear.

Nautilus earring

1) On a comfortable length of thread, leave an 18-in. (46 cm) tail, and pick up one color A 15º seed bead, 15 color B 15º seed beads, and five As (**figure 1, a–b**). These 21 beads will shift to form rows 1 and 2 as the next row is added. End and add thread as needed.

2) Work in flat odd-count peyote stitch as follows:

Row 3: Work 10 peyote stitches using two As and eight Bs (**b–c**).

Row 4: Work seven peyote stitches using one B per stitch (**figure 2, a–b**).

Tendril 2: Pick up six As, skip the last three As, and sew back through the next A (**b–c**). Work one peyote stitch using an A (**c–d**).

NOTE The first "tendril" is the color A portion of the first row. The tendrils will be used to hold the edging crystals in place.

Row 5: Work seven peyote stitches using one B per stitch (**d–e**).

Row 6: Pick up two As, and sew through the last B added in the previous row (**figure 3, a–b**). Work five peyote stitches using one B per stitch (**b–c**).

Tendril 3: Pick up six As, skip the last three As, and sew back through the next A (**c–d**). Work

one peyote stitch using an A (**d–e**).

Row 7: Work six peyote stitches using one B per stitch, sewing through an A after the last stitch (**e–f**). Pick up one B, and sew through the next A (**f–g**).

3) Repeat row 6, tendril 3, and row 7 (**figure 4**) 13 times for a total of 16 tendrils.

4) Repeat row 6 and tendril 3 once more (**figure 5, a–b**). To finish the edge, work seven stitches with one A per stitch (**b–c**).

5) Sew through the beadwork to exit the fourth bead added in the last row (**figure 6, a–b**). Work a tendril as before (**b–c**), and sew through the next edge A (**c–d**). Repeat twice to add two more tendrils (**d–e**). Set the working thread aside.

6) With the tail, work nine peyote stitches with one A per stitch off of

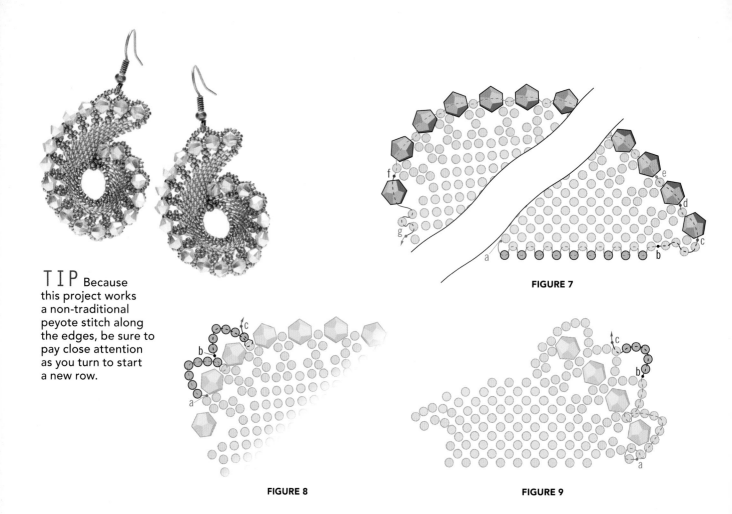

TIP Because this project works a non-traditional peyote stitch along the edges, be sure to pay close attention as you turn to start a new row.

FIGURE 7

FIGURE 8

FIGURE 9

row 1 (**figure 7, a–b**), and then sew through the first tendril to exit the tip bead (**b–c**).

Pick up a 4 mm bicone crystal, and sew through the tip bead of the next tendril (**c–d**). Repeat (**d–e**) until you have a total of 19 crystals (**e–f**). Pick up one more crystal, skip the next edge A, and sew through the following three As (**f–g**).

7) Sew through the beadwork to exit the tip bead of the nearest tendril (**figure 8, point a**). Pick up seven As, sew through the tip bead of the next tendril, and sew back through the seventh bead just added (**a–b**).

8) Pick up six As, sew through the tip bead of the next tendril, and sew back through

the last bead added (**b–c**). Repeat this step to add a loop of As around the outer edge of each of the remaining crystals.

9) To add a hanging loop, sew through the beadwork to exit the center A in the loop above the second-to-last crystal (**figure 9, a–b**). Pick up five As, and sew through the center A on the next loop (**b–c**). Sew through several more beads, and end the thread.

10) With the remaining thread, sew through the beadwork to exit an A on one end of the flat bottom edge, opposite the crystals. Zigzag through the bottom edge beads to cinch the edge beads together. The beadwork should curve.

When you reach the other end, form the beadwork into a spiral, with the end with the hanging loop on the outside and the end with the unembellished crystal near the center. Overlap the three beads on each end, and tack into this position, sewing through beads as needed. Gently fan the outer-edge beads outward. End the thread.

11) Open the loop of an ear wire, and attach it to the hanging loop.

12) Repeat steps 1–11 to make another earring. When forming the spiral, curve the beadwork in the opposite direction so the earrings are mirror images of each other. **B&B**

PINWHEEL
PENDANT

designed by
Debora Hodoyer

DIFFICULTY ●●●○○

bead weaving

materials
purple/grey pendant
2 in. (5 cm)

- **1** 14 mm rivoli (Swarovski, light rose)
- **6** 5 x 10 mm Arcos par Puca bead (opaque blue ceramic look)
- **6** 6 mm two-hole cabochon beads (jet hematite)
- fire-polished beads (saturated lavender)
  - **6** 6 mm
  - **6** 4 mm
  - **6** 3 mm
- **18** 2 x 4 mm MiniDuo beads (chalk lilac luster)
- **1 g** 3.8 mm O-bead (chalk white lila vega luster)
- **12** 2.5 x 3 mm Minos par Puca beads (opaque blue ceramic look)
- **6** 8º seed beads (Toho 611, matte opaque gray)
- **1 g** 11º seed beads (Toho 611, matte opaque gray)
- **1 g** 15º seed beads (Toho 52, opaque lavender)
- **2** 6 mm jump rings
- Fireline, 6 lb. test
- beading needles, #11 or #12
- **2** pairs of chainnose, flatnose, and/or bentnose pliers

basics, p. 13
- ending and adding thread
- opening and closing jump rings

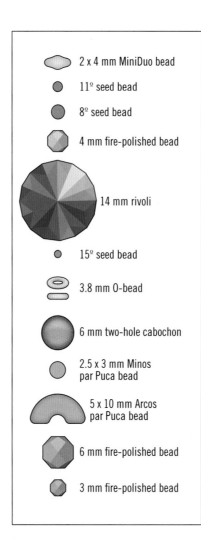

2 x 4 mm MiniDuo bead

11º seed bead

8º seed bead

4 mm fire-polished bead

14 mm rivoli

15º seed bead

3.8 mm O-bead

6 mm two-hole cabochon

2.5 x 3 mm Minos par Puca bead

5 x 10 mm Arcos par Puca bead

6 mm fire-polished bead

3 mm fire-polished bead

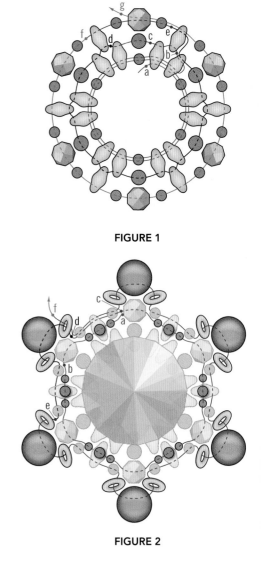

FIGURE 1

FIGURE 2

A variety of beads give this fun and pretty pinwheel-inspired pendant a one-of-a-kind look.

Pendant

How to pick up the two-hole cabochons: With the dome facing up and the holes running vertically, pick up the cabochon through the left hole. How to pick up the Arcos beads: Sew through the center and end holes, entering from the inside edge (IE) or the outside edge (OE).

1) On 7 ft. (2.1 m) of thread, pick up a repeating pattern of two MiniDuos and an 11º seed bead six times, and sew through the beads again, leaving a 6-in. (15 cm) tail. Continue through the first two MiniDuos and the open hole of the second MiniDuo **(figure 1, a–b)**. End the tail thread.
2) Pick up a MiniDuo, and sew through the open hole of the next MiniDuo **(b–c)**. Pick up an 8º seed bead, and sew through the open hole of the next MiniDuo **(c–d)**. Repeat these stitches

five times to complete the round, and sew through the open hole of the first MiniDuo added in this round **(d–e)**, using a tight tension so the beadwork begins to cup slightly.
3) Pick up an 11º, a 4 mm fire-polished bead, and an 11º, and sew through the open hole of the next MiniDuo **(e–f)**. Repeat this stitch five times to complete the round, and sew through the first 11º and 4 mm fire-polished bead added **(f–g)**. Place the 14 mm rivoli faceup into the beadwork.
4) Pick up a 15º seed bead, an 11º, and a 15º, and sew through the next 4 mm fire-polished bead **(figure 2, a–b)**. Repeat this stitch five times using a tight tension to complete the round **(b–c)**, retrace the thread path to tighten (not shown in the figure for clarity), and sew through the adjacent 11º, MiniDuo, and 11º **(c–d)**.
5) Pick up an O-bead, a two-hole cabochon,

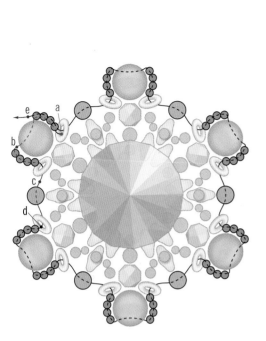

FIGURE 3

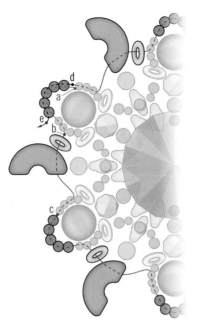

FIGURE 4

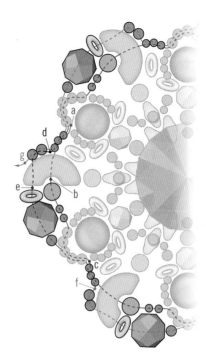

FIGURE 5

and an O-bead, and sew through the next 11º, MiniDuo, and 11º **(d–e)**. Repeat this stitch five times to complete the round, retrace the thread path (not shown in the figure for clarity), and continue through the first O-bead added **(e–f)**.

6) Pick up four 15ºs, and sew through the open hole of the next cabochon **(figure 3, a–b)**. Pick up four 15ºs, and sew through the following O-bead **(b–c)**. Pick up a Minos bead, and sew through the next O-bead **(c–d)**. Repeat these stitches five times to complete the round, and sew through the first four 15ºs added **(d–e)**.

7) Pick up five 11ºs, and sew through the next two 15ºs **(figure 4, a–b)**. Pick up an O-bead and the end hole of an Arcos (OE), skip the next

Minos and 15º, and sew through the following three 15ºs **(b–c)**. Repeat these stitches five times to complete the round **(c–d)**. Retrace the thread path (not shown in the figure for clarity), and sew through the first five 11ºs added **(d–e)**.

8) Pick up three 15ºs, and sew through the center hole of the Arcos (OE) **(figure 5, a–b)**. Pick up a Minos and two 15ºs, and sew through the next five 11ºs **(b–c)**. Repeat these stitches five times to complete the round, retrace the thread path (not shown in the figure for clarity), and sew through the first three 15ºs added **(c–d)**.

9) Pick up two 11ºs, and sew through the open hole of the next Arcos (OE) **(d–e)**. Pick up an O-bead, a 6 mm fire-polished bead, and an 11º, skip the next Minos, two 15ºs, and two 11ºs, and sew through the following three 11ºs and three 15ºs **(e–f)**. Repeat these stitches five times, and sew through the first two 11ºs added **(f–g)**.

10) Pick up four 11ºs, and sew through the next O-bead, 6 mm fire-polished bead, and 11º **(figure 6, a–b)**. Pick up an 11º, a 3 mm fire-polished bead, and an 11º, skip the next three 11ºs and three 15º, and sew through the following two 11ºs **(b–c)**. Repeat these stitches five times to complete the round, and sew through the first three 11ºs added in this round **(c–d)**.

11) Pick up eight 15ºs, and sew through the same 11º, going in the same direction to form a loop. Retrace the thread path. Sew through all the beads on the outside edge to tighten the beadwork, and end the thread. Open two jump rings, and attach them to the loop. **B⋅B**

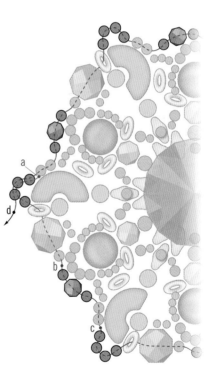

FIGURE 6

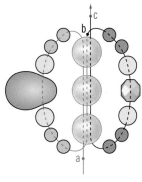

FIGURE 1

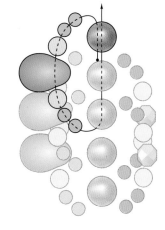

FIGURE 2

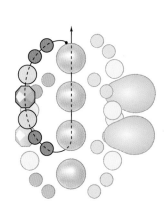

FIGURE 3

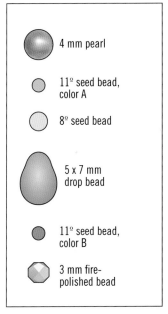

FIGURE 4

STASH BUSTER!

As shown in the purple bracelet, swap accent beads of similar shape and size to utilize whatever beads you have on hand.

○ 4 mm pearl

○ 11º seed bead, color A

○ 8º seed bead

○ 5 x 7 mm drop bead

● 11º seed bead, color B

◇ 3 mm fire-polished bead

materials
green bracelet 8½ in. (21.6 cm)

- **46** 5 x 7 mm drop beads (mint gold)
- **48** 4 mm pearls (Swarovski, brown)
- **50** 3 mm fire-polished beads (transparent aqua gold)
- **5 g** 8º seed beads (Toho 4204, Duracoat galvanized champagne)
- 11º seed beads
  - **5 g** color A (Toho 2103, lime opal silver-lined)
  - **5 g** color B (Toho 221, bronze)
- **1** ¾-in. (1.9 cm) glass button (Czech)
- Fireline, 6 lb. test
- beading needles, #11 or #12

basics, p. 13
- ending and adding thread

Create a dramatic double spiral with a secret treasure hidden within the twists of the bracelet.

BASE

1) On a comfortable length of thread, and leaving a 12-in. (30 cm) tail, pick up three 4 mm pearls to start the formation of the spiral core.

2) Pick up two color A 11º seed beads, an 8º seed bead, a drop bead, an 8º, and two As, and sew through the first three pearls added, going in the same direction, to form a "drop bead loop" on the left side of the pearls **(figure 1, a–b)**.

3) Pick up two color B 11º seed beads, an 8º, a 3 mm fire-polished bead, an 8º, and two Bs, and sew through the first three pearls added in step 1, going in the same direction, to form a "fire-polished loop" on the right side of the pearls **(b–c)**.

4) Pick up a pearl and the same sequence of beads as in step 2, and sew through the last two pearls in the core and the pearl just added, going in the same direction. Pull the thread tight, and push this loop to the left side of the pearls so it rests on top of the previous drop bead loop **(figure 2)**.

5) Flip the beadwork so that the fire-polished loop is on the left. Pick up the same sequence of beads as in step 3, and sew through the last three pearls in the core, going in the same direction to form another loop. Push this loop to the left so it rests on top of the previous fire-polished loop **(figure 3)**.

6) Flip the beadwork so the drop bead loops are on the left again. Work as in step 4 to form another drop bead loop, and push it to the left so it rests on top of the previous drop bead loop **(figure 4)**.

7) Work as in steps 5–6 for the desired length, less 1¼ in. (3.2 cm) for the clasp, ending on step 5. The beadwork will naturally start to spiral. End and add thread as needed.

EMBELLISHMENT

1) Working toward the opposite end of the base, sew through the adjacent A of the end drop bead loop **(figure 5, a–b)**. Pick up an A, and sew through the closest end A in the following drop bead loop **(b–c)**. Repeat this stitch for the remainder of the base **(c–d)**. End and add thread as needed. After the last stitch, continue through the remaining six beads in the end drop bead loop **(d–e)**.

2) Working toward the opposite end of the base, sew through the first B of the adjacent fire-polished loop **(e–f)**. Work as in step 1 to add a B between each fire-polished loop **(f–g)**.

3) To add embellishment to the opposite side of each loop, sew through the core of pearls to exit the opposite end of the base, and repeat steps 2–3 on the other side of each loop.

CLASP

1) Using the tail thread, pick up a 3 mm fire-polished bead, a B, the shank of the button, and a B, and sew back through the fire-polished bead. Sew through the beadwork to retrace this thread path several times, and end the tail.

2) With the working thread exiting the core pearl at the opposite end, pick up a fire-polished bead and a repeating pattern of an 8° and a B 15 times, or enough times for the loop to fit comfortably around the button, and sew back through the fire-polished bead. Following the established thread path in the base, sew through an end loop and back through the end three core pearls. Retrace the thread path through the button loop several times, and end the thread. **B·B**

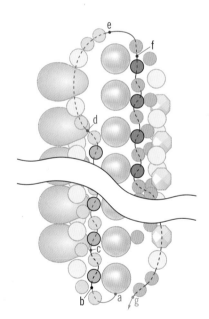

FIGURE 5

LACY
FLOWER
EARRINGS

designed by
Magdalena Dec

DIFFICULTY ●●●○○

peyote stitch

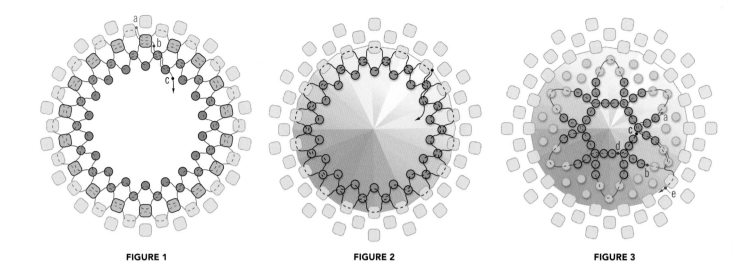

FIGURE 1

FIGURE 2

FIGURE 3

materials
green/blue earrings
2¼ in. (5.7 cm)

- **2** 14 mm rivoli (Swarovski, light Colorado topaz)
- **5 g** 11º seed beads (Toho PF567, permanent finish galvanized polaris)
- **1 g** cylinder beads (Miyuki DB168, opaque gray AB)
- 15º seed beads
  - **5 g** color A (Toho PF570, permanent finish galvanized mint green)
  - **1 g** color B (Toho PF567, permanent finish metallic polaris)
- **1** pair of earring findings
- Fireline, 6 lb. test
- beading needles, #11 or #12

basics
- square knot
- peyote stitch: tubular, flat odd-count
- stop bead
- ending and adding thread

These large and airy earrings are in full bloom and will be the highlight of your favorite summer outfit.

Bezel

1) On 5 ft. (1.5 m) of thread, pick up 36 11º cylinder beads. Leaving a 6-in. (15 cm) tail, tie the beads into a ring with a square knot, and sew through the first few beads again. These beads will form the first two rounds as the next round is added.

2) Work a round of peyote stitch using cylinders, and step up through the first cylinder added **(figure 1, a–b)**.

3) Work one round using color A 15º seed beads and another round using color B 15º seed beads, stepping up at the end of each round **(b–c)**. Pull snug so the beadwork begins to cup.

4) Sew through the beadwork to exit a cylinder in the first round. Place the rivoli facedown into the beadwork. Stepping up at the end of each round, work two rounds using As **(figure 2)**.

5) Pick up five As, skip the next A in the previous round, and sew through the following three As as shown to form a picot **(figure 3, a–b)**. Repeat this stitch five times to complete the round, and step up through the first three As added **(b–c)**.

6) Pick up two As, and sew through the center A in the next picot **(c–d)**. Repeat this stitch five times to complete the round, retrace the thread path to tighten (not shown in the figure for clarity), and sew through the following four As and the adjacent cylinder as shown **(d–e)**. End the tail but not the working thread, and set the bezel aside.

Petals

1) Attach a stop bead to 18 in. (46 cm) of thread, leaving a 6-in. (15 cm) tail. Pick up 37 As. These beads will form the first two rows as the next row is added.

2) Work in odd-count peyote stitch as follows using a tight tension:
Row 3: Work 18 stitches with one A per stitch **(figure 4, a–b)**. Pick up an A, and sew through the next three As as shown to exit the second-to-last A in row 3 **(b–c)**.
Row 4: Work two stitches using As, 12 stitches using 11º seed beads, and two stitches using As **(c–d)**. The beadwork will begin to curve. Sew through the beadwork as shown to exit the last A added **(figure 5, a–b)**.

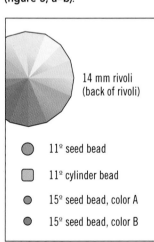

14 mm rivoli (back of rivoli)

- ● 11º seed bead
- ▢ 11º cylinder bead
- ● 15º seed bead, color A
- ● 15º seed bead, color B

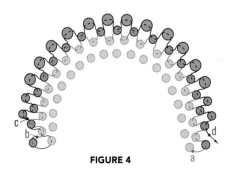

FIGURE 4

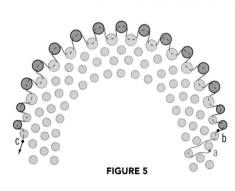

FIGURE 5

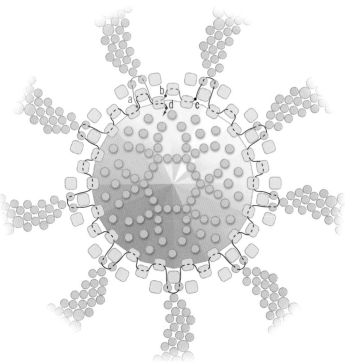

FIGURE 6

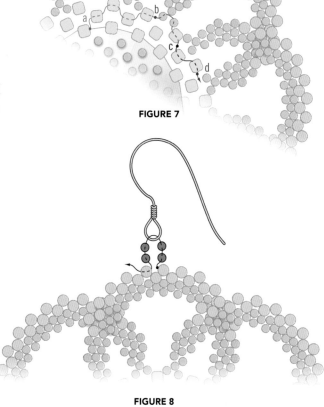

FIGURE 7

FIGURE 8

Row 5: Work two stitches using Bs, 11 using 11ºs, and two using Bs **(b–c)**. Remove the stop bead, and end the threads.

3) Repeat steps 1–2 to make a total of nine petals.

4) With the working thread from the bezel and the back facing up, sew up through the end A on the left arm of a petal, down through the adjacent end A, and through the next cylinder in the same round of the bezel **(figure 6, a–b)**. Sew through the beadwork to exit the following cylinder in the same round **(b–c)**. Repeat these stitches eight times to attach the left arms of the remaining petals **(c–d)**. Sew through the beadwork as shown to exit the cylinder in the outer round of the bezel between the second and third petals **(figure 7, a–b)**.

5) Attach the right arm of the first petal added as before, positioning this arm of the petal behind the left arm of the next petal **(b–c)**. Sew through the beadwork to exit the following cylinder in the same round **(c–d)**. Work as before to connect the remaining right arms of the petals, making sure each petal is positioned behind the next.

6) Sew through the beadwork to exit a bead where two petals overlap. Sew through an adjacent bead in the other petal, and back through a bead in the first petal to join the two layers together. Repeat this stitch two or three times between the two petals. Sew through the outer edge to reach the intersection of the next set of petals, and join them as before. Repeat to join the remaining petals.

7) After joining the last two petals, sew through the nearest petal to exit an outer edge 11º near the center of the petal. Pick up two Bs, the loop of an earring finding, and two Bs, and sew through the following 11º in the outer row **(figure 8)**. Retrace the thread path several times, and end the thread.

8) Make a second earring but when attaching the petals, work in a counter-clockwise direction, and attach the right arms first instead of the left arms. When attaching the other arm of each petal, position the left arm behind the next petal going in a counter-clockwise direction, and attach as before. This makes a mirror image of the first earring. **B⊗B**

Mandala magic

Mix and match a series of five components to create modern mandala jewelry.

by Francesca Walton

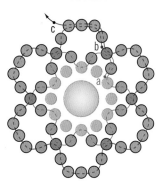

LARGE CIRCLE

1) On 1 yd. (.9 m) of thread, pick up 12 color A 15º seed beads. Leaving a 6-in. (15 cm) tail, tie the beads into a ring with a square knot, and then sew through the first two beads in the ring **(figure 1, a–b)**.

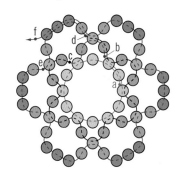

2) Work in rounds as follows:

Round 1: Pick up one color B 15º seed bead, one color C 15º seed bead, and one B. Skip the next A in the ring, and sew through the following A **(b–c)**. Repeat this stitch five times, and step up through the first B and C in this round **(c–d)**.

Round 2: Pick up one B, three color D 15º seed beads, and one B, and sew through the center C in the next stitch in the previous round **(d–e)**. Repeat this stitch five times to complete the round, and step up through the first B and three Ds in this round **(e–f)**.

Round 3: Pick up one D, one B, and one D, and sew through the center three Ds in the next stitch in the previous round **(figure 2, a–b)**. Repeat this stitch five times, and step up through the first D added in this round **(b–c)**.

Round 4: Pick up three Ds, and sew through the next two Ds **(c–d)**. Pick up three color E 15º seed beads, skip the next D, and sew through the following two Ds **(d–e)**. Repeat these two stitches five times, and step up through the first two Ds added in this round **(e–f)**.

Round 5: Pick up one D and two Es, and sew through the center E in the next stitch in the previous round **(f–g)**. Pick up two Es and one D, and sew through the center D in the following stitch **(g–h)**. Repeat these two stitches five times, and step up through the first three beads added in this step **(h–i)**.

Round 6: Pick up one E, one C, and one E, and

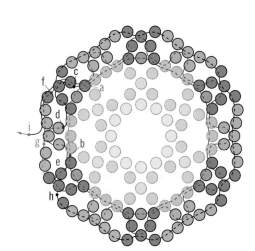

FIGURE 1

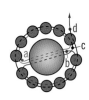

FIGURE 4

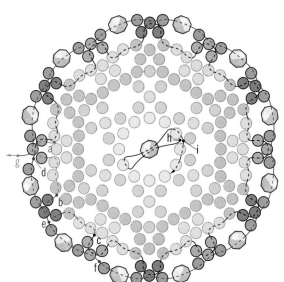

FIGURE 2

FIGURE 3

FIGURE 5

sew through the center C in the next stitch (e–f). Repeat these two stitches five times (f–g), tie a few half-hitch knots, and set this thread aside to use later.

3) Attach a needle to the tail. Pick up one M 2 mm, and sew through the opposite A in the center ring. Sew back through the M 2 mm and the A your thread exited at the start of this step (h–i). End the tail, and set this component aside.

CAT-HEAD CONNECTOR

1) On 1 yd. (.9 m) of thread, pick up one 4 mm round bead and six color F 15º seed beads. Leaving a 6-in. (15 cm) tail, sew through the 4 mm again (figure 4, a–b). Pick up six more Fs, and sew through the 4 mm once more to create a ring of Fs around the 4 mm (b–c). Sew through all the Fs again to cinch up the ring (c–d).

2) Work as in rounds 1–5 of "Large circle" with the following beads:

Round 1: One color G 15º seed bead, one D, one G per stitch (figure 5, a–b).

Round 2: One G, three Bs, and one G per stitch (b–c).

Round 3: One B, one G, and one B per stitch (figure 6, a–b).

Round 4:

Stitch 1: Three Bs (b–c).

Stitch 2: One color H 15º seed bead, one color K 11º cylinder bead, and one H (c–d).

Stitch 3: One B, one K, and one B (d–e).

Atlantis earrings

To make the earrings shown, make two each of the Large and Small circles, two Cat-head connectors, and two Small stars. Connect them as explained on p. 119, and then add a crystal drop at the bottom of each small star. Connect the top of each Large circle to an earring finding, and then use leftover beads to embellish the findings, if desired.

---

sew through the next three beads added in the previous round (figure 3, a–b). Pick up three Ds, and sew through the following three beads added in the previous round (b–c). Repeat these two stitches five times, and step up through the first E and C added in this round (c–d).

Round 7: Pick up one B, one color M 2 mm fire-polished bead, and one B, and sew through the center D in the next stitch in the previous round (d–e). Pick up one B, an M 2 mm, and one B, and

---

Express yourself

Change out the colors to reflect your style — use the patterns as canvases to create mandalas in your favorite palettes. Go to FacetJewelry.com/resourceguide to print blank templates that you can color.

DIFFICULTY ●●○○○

materials
mandala components
½–1-in. (5–10 cm) diameter each

- **1 g** 15º seed beads in each of **9** colors
  - color A (Toho 7BDF, matte transparent zircon)
  - color B (Toho 221, bronze)
  - color C (Toho 23BDAF, silver-lined aqua matte)
  - color D (Toho 28F, silver-lined blue matte)
  - color E (Toho PF569F, matte perma-nent finish turquoise)
  - color F (Toho 48, opaque blue cobalt)
  - color G (Toho 72F, transparent matte emerald)
  - color H (Toho 55D, green opaque turquoise)
  - color J (Toho 55, opaque turquoise)
- **1 g** 110 cylinder beads in each of **2** colors
  - color K (Toho Aiko 1523, blue zircon satin)
  - color L (Toho Aiko 835, light aqua)
- **1 g** 110 seed bead (Toho 2607F, semi-glazed midnight blue)
- 2 mm fire-polished beads
  - **32** color M (gold)
  - **2–12** color N (aqua halo)
- **4** 4 mm druk (aqua halo)
- **2** 10 mm crystal drops
- **2** flower earring findings (firemountaingems.com, H20-A9041FN)
- Fireline, 6 lb. test
- beading needles, #13

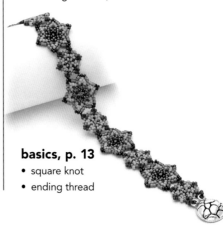

basics, p. 13
- square knot
- ending thread

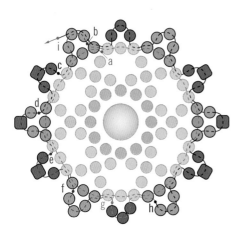

FIGURE 6

Stitch 4: One H, one K, and one H (**e–f**).

Stitch 5: Three Bs (**f–g**).

Stitch 6: Three Hs (**g–h**).

Repeat these six stitches once, and step up through the first two Bs added in this round (**h–i**).

Round 5: Work a stitch with two Cs and one K (**figure 7, a–b**) and a stitch with one K and two Cs (**b–c**). Repeat these two stitches five times (**c–d**).

3) For the final round, sew through the outer edge beads to exit at **point e**. Pick up three Cs,

skip the adjacent B, and sew through the next seven edge beads (**e–f**). Pick up three Cs, skip the next B, and sew through the next 15 beads (**f–g**). Repeat these two stitches (**g–h**). Tie a half–hitch knot, and sew through the next two Cs (**h–i**). Set this component aside.

SMALL CIRCLE

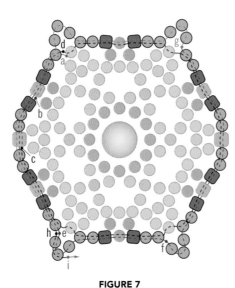

1) On 1 yd. (.9 m) of thread, pick up a repeating pattern of one color J 15° seed bead and one C six times. Leaving a 6-in. (15 cm) tail, tie the beads into a ring with a square knot, and sew through the first two beads to exit a C (**figure 8, a–b**).

2) Work as in rounds 1–5 of "Large circle" with the following beads:

Round 1: Three Cs per stitch (**b–c**).

Round 2: One C, three Fs, and one C per stitch (**c–d**).

Round 3: Three Cs per stitch (**d–e**).

Round 4:

Stitch 1: Three Cs (**e–f**).

Stitch 2: Three Fs (**f–g**).

Repeat these two stitches five times, and step up through the first two Cs added in this round (**g–h**).

Round 5: One B, one 11° seed bead, and one B per stitch (**h–i**). Tie a half-hitch know, and end this thread.

3) Attach a needle to the tail, and add an M 2 mm in the center, as in step 3 of "Large circle." Set this component aside.

SMALL STAR

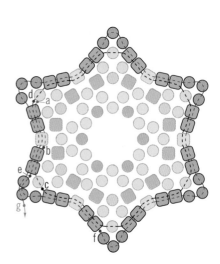

1) On 1 yd. (.9 m) of thread, pick up a repeating pattern of one E and one F six times. Leaving a 6-in. (15 cm) tail, tie the beads into a ring with a square knot, and sew through the first two beads to exit an F.

2) Work in rounds as follows:

Round 1: Three Es per stitch (**figure 9, a–b**).

Round 2: Pick up one K, one B, and one K, and sew through the next center E in the previous round (**b–c**). Repeat this stitch five times, and step up through the first K in this round (**c–d**).

Round 3: Pick up three Bs, and sew through the next K (**d–e**). Pick up one K, and sew through the following K (**e–f**). Repeat these two stitches five times, tie a half–hitch knot, and sew through the first two Bs in this round (**f–g**).

3) Attach a needle to the tail, and add an N 2 mm in the center, as in step 3 of "Large circle." End the tail.

15° seed beads	
⬤	Color A
⬤	Color B
⬤	Color C
⬤	Color D
⬤	Color E
⬤	Color F
⬤	Color G
⬤	Color H
⬤	Color J
⬢	2 mm fire-polished bead, color M
⬤	4 mm round bead
⬤	11° seed bead
▪	11° cylinder bead, color K
▫	11° cylinder bead, color L

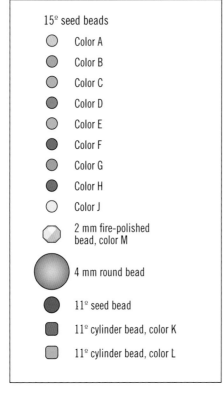

FIGURE 7

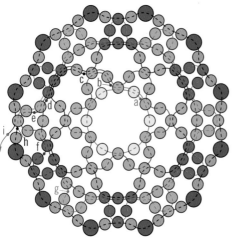

FIGURE 8

FIGURE 9

FIGURE 10

LARGE STAR

The Large star doesn't appear in the Atlantis earrings, but it rounds out the set very nicely. It pairs particularly well with the Small star, as is evident in the bracelet pattern available at FacetJewelry.com/resourceguide.

1) On 1 yd. (.9 m) of thread, pick up an alternating pattern of one E and one F six times. Leaving a 6-in. (15 cm) tail, tie the beads into a ring with a square knot, and sew through the first two beads to exit an E.

2) Work as in rounds 1–3 of "Small star" with the following beads:

Round 1: Three Es per stitch.

Round 2: One color K, one B, and one K per stitch.

Round 3: Pick up three Cs, and sew through the next K. Pick up one color L 11º cylinder bead, and sew through the next K. Repeat these

two stitches five times, and step up through the first two Cs added in this round.

3) Continue working in rounds:

Round 4: Pick up two Ls, skip a C and a K, and sew through the next L (figure 10, a–b). Pick up two Ls, and sew through the next point C (b–c). Repeat these two stitches five times (c–d). Sew through the next five beads to exit the L adjacent to the next point C (d–e).

Round 5: Pick up three Bs, skip the next C, and sew through the following five beads (e–f). Repeat this stitch five times, tie a few half–hitch knots, and then sew through the beadwork to exit a center B added in this round (f–g).

4) Attach a needle to the tail, and add a color M 2 mm in the center, as in step 3 of "Large circle." End the tail.

PUTTING IT ALL TOGETHER

To make the earrings as shown on p. 116, follow these suggestions for attaching your components or devise your own methods.

Earwire to Large circle

With the thread remaining on the Large circle, sew through the next three beads in the outer round to exit a B, with your needle pointing toward the next C. Pick up a 4 mm, sew through the loop of an earwire, and sew back through the 4 mm. Skip the adjacent C in the outer round, and sew through the next B. Retrace the thread path a couple of times, and end the thread.

Large circle to Cat-head connector

With the thread remaining from the Cat-head connector, sew through a B, 2 mm, and B in the outer round of the Large circle, opposite the earwire (figure 11, a–b). Pick up a C, and sew through the next B, 2 mm, and B (b–c). Sew back through the adjacent four beads in the Cat-head connector (c–d), the C just added on the Large circle, and the next K and four Cs on the Cat-head connector (d–e). Sew through the outer edge beads of the Cat-head connector to exit a center C opposite the Large circle.

Cat-head connector to Small circle

With the thread exiting the Cat-head connector, pick up a C, and sew through a B, 11º and B on the outer edge of the Small circle (figure 12, a–b). Pick up C, and sew through the next B, 11º, and B (b–c). Pick up a C, and sew through four beads on the Cat head connector as shown (c–d). Sew through the C just added, skip the adjacent bead on the Cat-head connector, and continue through the next five beads on the Cat-head connector (d–e). End the thread.

Small circle to Small star

With the thread exiting a center B on the Small star, sew through a bottom B, 11º, and B on the Small circle (figure 13, a–b). Sew through the next center K on the Small star, and continue through the next B, 11º, and B on the Small circle (b–c). Retrace the thread path through the connection, and end the thread. **B B**

One, two, and many

I think of this design in terms of the counting systems of some primitive tribes — one, two, and many. The components can be combined and connected in any number of ways. For example, make a simple earring with just one unit (usually the large circle), make a slightly longer earring with two units (e.g., a small circle and a small star), or combine many units for long, dramatic earrings, bracelets, and even necklaces.

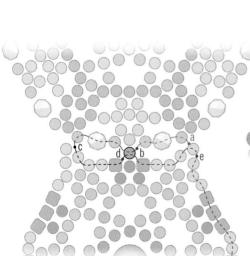

FIGURE 11

FIGURE 12

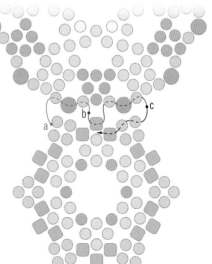

FIGURE 13

FUNKY HEARTS BRACELET

**designed by
Lorraine Coetzee**

DIFFICULTY ●●○○○

peyote stitch

materials
bracelet 7½ in. (19.1 cm)

- 11º Miyuki Delica cylinder
  beads
  - **2 g** color A (DB0200,
    opaque chalk white)
  - **3 g** color B (DB0042, gold-
    lined crystal)
  - **4 g** color C (DB0859,
    matte emerald AB)
  - **3 g** color D (DB0074, lined
    light fuchsia AB)
  - **3 g** color E (DB0795, matte
    opaque vermillion)
  - **2 g** color F (DB0654, dark
    cranberry opaque)
- Fireline, 6 lb. test, or nylon
  beading thread, size D
- beading needles, #12

basics, p. 13

- peyote stitch: flat, even-
  count, flat odd-count,
  zipping up or joining
- ending and adding thread
- attaching a stop bead

For a Word chart of
this pattern, visit

**FacetJewelry.com/
resourceguide**

PATTERN

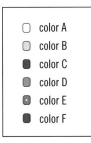

- ⬜ color A
- ⬜ color B
- ⬛ color C
- ⬜ color D
- ⬜ color E
- ⬛ color F

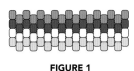

FIGURE 1

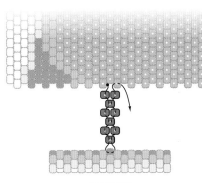

FIGURE 2

FIGURE 3

Show your wild side this Valentine's Day (or any day, for that matter) with this heart-motif bracelet that is bursting with vibrant colors.

PEYOTE BAND

1) On a comfortable length of thread, attach a stop bead, leaving a 6-in. (15 cm) tail. Starting at the upper-right corner of the pattern, pick up 11º cylinder beads for rows 1 and 2: one B, eight As, one B, 10 Cs, one B, and seven As.

2) Following the **pattern** or the Word chart (get it at FacetJewelry.com/resourceguide), work in flat even-count peyote stitch using the appropriate color cylinders. End and add thread as needed while you stitch, and end the working thread and tail when you complete the band.

EDGING

1) Add a comfortable length of thread to one end of the band, and exit the nearest corner cylinder, with your needle pointing away from the beadwork.

2) Pick up three cylinders in colors that match the adjacent cylinders in the band, and sew down through the next edge cylinder and up through the following edge cylinder. Repeat this stitch for the length of the band, picking up colors to extend the design into the edging.

3) Sew through the beadwork to exit the nearest corner cylinder along the other edge, and repeat step 2. End and add thread as needed.

CLASP

1) Refer to **figure 1**: On 18 in. (46 cm) of thread, attach a stop bead, leaving a 6-in. (15 cm) tail. Pick up 17 color D cylinders. Using Cs, work two rows of flat odd-count peyote stitch. Repeat to work two rows with As and two rows with Bs. Zip up the edges to form the toggle bar, and end the working thread and tail.

2) Add 12 in. (30 cm) of thread to one end of the band, and exit one of the middle up-beads in the end row. Pick up six cylinders to match the cylinder you thread is exiting, and sew through a middle cylinder on the toggle bar. Sew back through the sixth cylinder, and then work three peyote stitches, sewing into the adjacent middle up-bead in the end row of the band **(figure 2)**.

3) Add 12 in. (30 cm) of thread to the other end of the band, and exit one up-bead away from the middle up-bead. Pick up approximately 23 Cs, skip the middle up-bead, and sew through the following up-bead to form a loop **(figure 3, a–b)**. Work back around the loop in peyote stitch, using one C per stitch, and sew through the bead your thread exited at the start of this step **(b–c)**. Retrace the thread path through the loop a couple of times, and end the thread. **B&B**

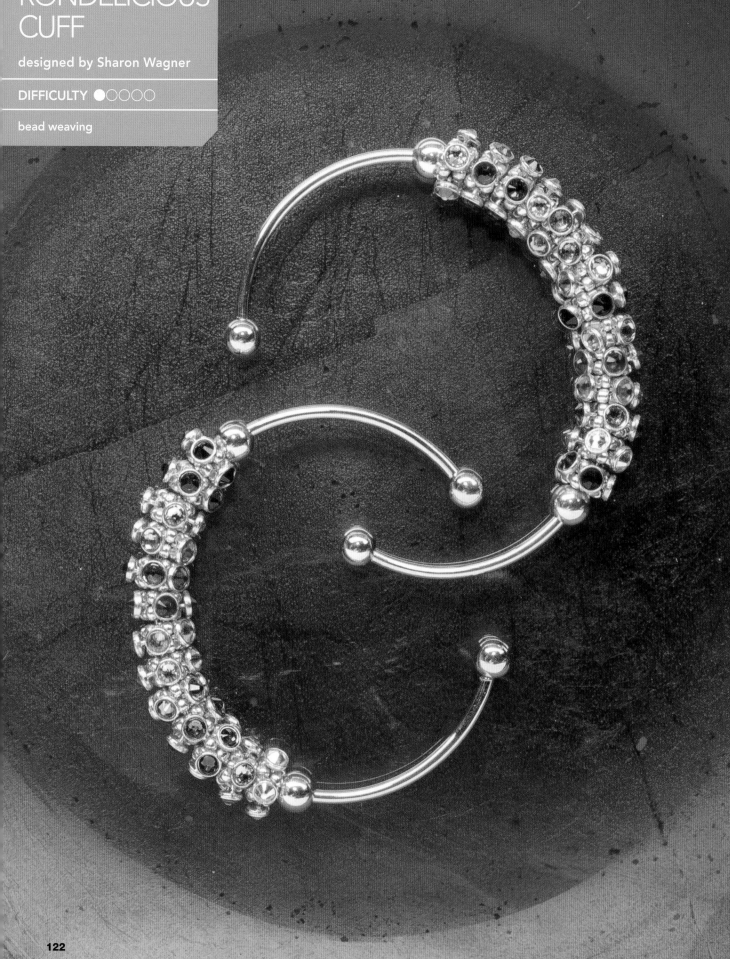

RONDELICIOUS
CUFF

designed by Sharon Wagner

DIFFICULTY ●○○○○

bead weaving

Make fun and sparkly little components to wear on a cuff, hoop earrings, or necklace.

RONDELLE COMPONENT

The rondelles can be made with 11º and 15º seed beads or 8º and 11º seed beads, but the rondelles with 8ºs and 11ºs are a little easier to do and produce a slightly larger rondelle. You may want to try a practice rondelle with 8ºs and 11ºs before trying the 11ºs and 15ºs.

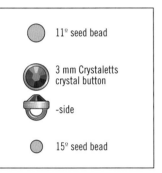

⬤	11º seed bead
⬤	3 mm Crystaletts crystal button
⬤	-side
⬤	15º seed bead

materials
gold cuff 2½ in. (6.4 cm) diameter

- **1** 2½-in. (6.4 mm) Add-a-bead charm cuff with twist-off ball ends and stop beads (gold; beadabead.com)
- **70** 3 mm Crystaletts crystal buttons (assorted crystal colors with gold base)
- **2 g** 11º seed beads (Toho PF557, permanent finish galvanized starlight)
- **1 g** 15º seed beads (Toho PF557, permanent finish galvanized starlight)
- Fireline, 6 lb. test
- beading needles, #11 or #12

basics, p. 13
- ending and adding thread

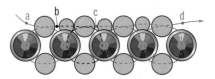

FIGURE 1

1) On 2 ft. (61 cm) of thread, pick up an 11º seed bead, a 3 mm Crystaletts button, an 11º, and a button. Leaving a 6-in. (15 cm) tail, sew through the first 11º again to form a ring (**figure 1, a–b**). Retrace the thread path (not shown in the figure for clarity). The beadwork may be a little loose, but do not tie a knot.

2) Pick up a 15º seed bead, an 11º, a button, and an 11º, and sew through the previous button and the first 11º added in this step (**b–c**). Using a tight tension, retrace the thread path (not shown in the figure for clarity). Repeat twice (**c–d**).

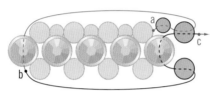

FIGURE 2

3) Pick up a 15º and an 11º, and sew through the end button on the opposite end of the beadwork (**figure 2, a–b**) to form a ring. Pick up an 11º, and sew through the last button and the first 11º added in this step (**b–c**). Retrace the thread path using a tight tension.

4) Pick up a 15º, and sew through the next 11º on this edge of the ring (**figure 3, a–b**). Continue through the remaining 15ºs and 11ºs on this edge of the ring, and then sew through the 15º just added and the next 11º (**b–c**).

FIGURE 3

5) Sew through the adjacent button and 11º on the other edge of the ring. Add 15ºs between the 11ºs on this edge, retrace the thread path using a tight tension, and end the threads.

6) Repeat steps 1–5 to make the desired number of components. Our cuff bracelet samples contain 13–14 components each.

ASSEMBLY

Unscrew the ball end of the cuff, and remove one stop bead. Slide on the desired number of components, and replace the stop bead and ball end of the cuff. Adjust the stop beads to center the components on the cuff. **B&B**

ONE PATTERN, MANY LOOKS BRACELET

designed by Karen Bruns

DIFFICULTY ●●○○○

bead weaving

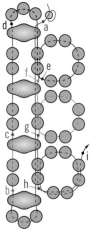

FIGURE 1

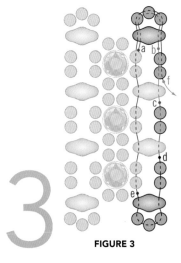

FIGURE 3

BRACELET

1) On a comfortable length of thread, attach a stop bead, leaving a 12-in. (30 cm) tail. Pick up a repeating pattern of a SuperDuo and two 11º seed beads three times, and then pick up a SuperDuo and three 11ºs. Sew through the open hole of the same SuperDuo (**figure 1, a–b**).

2) Pick up two 11ºs, and sew through the open hole of the next SuperDuo (**b–c**). Repeat this stitch twice (**c–d**). Pick up three 11ºs, and sew through the other hole of the same SuperDuo and the next two 11ºs (**d–e**).

3) Pick up six 11ºs, and sew through the two 11ºs your thread just exited, going in the same direction (**e–f**) to form a loop. Continue through the next SuperDuo and two 11ºs (**f–g**). Repeat these stitches twice, but do not sew through the SuperDuo after the last stitch (**g–h**). Instead, sew through the first four 11ºs added in the last loop (**h–i**).

7) Pick up a SuperDuo and three 11ºs, and sew through the open hole of the same SuperDuo (**figure 3, a–b**). Pick up two 11ºs, and sew through the open hole of the next SuperDuo (**b–c**). Repeat this last stitch once more (**c–d**).

8) Pick up two 11ºs, a SuperDuo, and three 11ºs, and sew through the open hole of the same SuperDuo (**d–e**). Continue through the beadwork as shown (**e–f**).

9) Repeat steps 3–8 for the desired bracelet length, allowing ½ in. (1.3 cm) for the clasp. Our 8-in. (20 cm) bracelet has 22 rows of SuperDuos. End and add thread as needed.

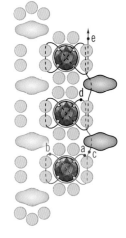

FIGURE 2

4) Pick up a 4 mm rose montée, cross the opening of the loop diagonally, and sew through the two corresponding 11ºs, going in the same direction (**figure 2, a–b**). Make sure the 4 mm is facing up. Sew through the open channel of the 4 mm, and continue through the two 11ºs your thread exited at the start of this step, going in the same direction (**b–c**).

5) Pick up a SuperDuo, and sew through the two corresponding 11ºs in the next loop (**c–d**).

6) Repeat steps 4–5 once, then repeat step 4 once more (**d–e**).

CLASP

1) With the working thread, work as in step 3 of "Bracelet" to add a loop to each set of two 11ºs on this end, retracing each loop three times before adding the remaining loops. End the working thread.

2) On the tail end, remove the stop bead, and sew through the next three 11ºs, SuperDuo, and two 11ºs. Work as before to add three loops, and end the tail.

3) Use a jump ring to attach each loop of the clasp to an end loop on the bracelet. **B&B**

● CHANGE IT UP

Substitute a variety of two-hole beads for a different look. You can alter the width by increasing or decreasing the number of two-hole bead sets picked up in the first row. The number of rose montées in each row will match the number of loops needed for the clasp.

Experiment with a variety of two-hole beads and rose montées for a bracelet that is as versatile as it is pretty.

2.5 x 5 mm
SuperDuo bead

11º seed bead

4 mm rose montée

materials
turquoise/red bracelet
8 x ⅞ in. (20 x 2.2 cm)

- **7 g** 2.5 x 5 mm SuperDuos (opaque turquoise bronze Picasso)
- **63** 4 mm (SS16) rose montées (Swarovski, light Siam)
- **7 g** 11º seed beads (Toho 1706, gilded marble black)
- **1** 3-strand tube clasp
- **6** 6 mm jump rings
- Fireline, 6 lb. test
- beading needles, #11 or #12
- **2** pairs of chainnose, bentnose, and/or flatnose pliers

basics, p. 13
- ending and adding thread
- attaching a stop bead
- opening and closing loops and jump rings

Crescent fringe collar

Learn to make this fringed two-tone collar with seed beads and two-hole crescent beads.

by Adrienne Gaskell

Advance your braiding skills with this new column, featuring a kumihimo project and answers to frequently asked questions!

SETUP

1) Cut four cords to 8 ft. (2.5 m) each, and set up your marudai or disk for an eight-strand kongoh gumi.

NOTE Trim and coat the ends of two of the cords with Fray Check so you can string the crescent and magatama beads directly onto the cord, rather than using a Big Eye needle.

2) String each cord with the beads listed in the **Bead & cord layout**. For a 17-in. (43 cm) necklace, including a 1-in. (2.5 cm) clasp, each cord should have a total of 104 beads.

To adjust the necklace length, simply add or omit equal amounts of beads at the end of each cord. Approximately 6.5 beads on each strand equals 1 in. (2.5 cm) of braid. Be sure to end cords 3e and 3w with an 8º seed bead. This may make it necessary to add an extra bead. When adjusting the finished size, all cords should still have the same number of beads.

3) After stringing each cord, wind the end of the cord around a bobbin or tama.

Bead & cord layout

repeat 26x

repeat 26x

repeat 26x

repeat 26x

repeat 26x

1n 2n
4w   3e
3w   4e
2s 1s

- 8º seed bead, color A
- 8º seed bead, color B
- 3 x 10 mm two-hole crescent bead
- 3 mm magatama bead

Cords 1n and 2n:
Two color A 8ºs, two color B 8ºs
String this pattern a total of 26 times.

Cord 3e:
One crescent, one color B 8º, one magatama, one color A 8º
String this pattern a total of 26 times.

Cord 4e:
One color A 8º, two color B 8ºs, one color A 8º
String this pattern a total of 26 times.

Cord 1s and 2s:
Two color B 8ºs, two color A 8ºs
String this pattern a total of 26 times.

Cord 3w:
One magatama, one color A 8º, one crescent, one color B 8º
String this pattern a total of 26 times.

Cord 4w:
One color B 8º, two color A 8ºs, one color B 8º
String this pattern a total of 26 times.

BRAIDING

1) Work a kongoh gumi with just cords (no beads) for at least ½ in. (1.3 cm). Make sure that you end with all the cords in their original positions, as in the **Bead & cord layout**.

2) Continue working in 2-drop Kongoh, dropping one bead on each cord with each pair of cord movements.

3) When all of the beads have been incorporated into the braid, work at least ½ in. (1.3 cm) with just the cords.

4) Before removing the braid from the marudai or disk, use a hemostat to grasp the cords at the point of braiding. With your other hand, remove the counterweight, and bring the braid down so that the bobbins or tama are resting on your work surface. Use a cord burner to burn off the excess cord. Keep burning the cords to melt and seal the end of the braid.

N O T E The metal jaws of the hemostat act as a heat sink, keeping the heat away from the braid.

ADDING EMBELLISHMENT

1) Center a beading needle on 6 ft. (1.8 m) of Fireline so you are working with doubled thread. Sew through one of the unbeaded braid ends about ¼ in. (6 mm) from the beads, leaving

3-in. (7.6 cm) tails. Tie together the working thread and tails with a square knot, and then tie together the two tails with a square knot.

2) Sew through the braid, working toward the beads, and exit next to the first crescent on this end **(photo, above)**.

3) Pick up three 15º seed beads, and sew through the open hole of the first crescent **(figure, a–b)**.

4) Pick up a 15º, a crescent, a 15º, a crescent, and a 15º, and sew through the open hole of the next crescent in the necklace **(b–c)**.

5) Repeat step 4 until you reach the other end of the necklace.

6) Exiting the last crescent, pick up three 15ºs, and sew into the braid close to the crescent bead so that the 15ºs lay up against the crescent bead. Sew through the unbeaded braid end.

materials
purple/blue necklace 17 in. (43 cm)

- 8º seed beads
  - **6 g** color A (Toho 2635F, semi-glazed turquoise; bottom beads in necklace)
  - **9 g** color B (Toho 90, metallic amethyst gunmetal; top beads in necklace)
- **12 g** 3 x 10 mm CzechMates crescent beads (metallic suede pink)
- **2 g** 3 mm magatamas (Toho 1633F, opaque rainbow frosted blackberry)
- **2 g** 15º seed beads (Toho 90, metallic amethyst gunmetal)
- **1** magnetic clasp with a 4–6 mm opening
- C-Lon or S-Lon Bead Cord (Tex 210, #18)
- beading needle, #12
- Big Eye needle
- Fray Check (optional)
- Fireline, 6 lb. test, or nylon beading thread, size D
- 2-part epoxy adhesive and toothpick
- kumihimo disk with **8** bobbins; or marudai, **8** weighted tama & 30-percent counterweight
- cord burner
- bench block or vise
- third-hand tweezer (optional)

turquoise/gold necklace colors (p. 26)

- 8º seed beads
  - color A (Toho 2604F, semi glazed rainbow turquoise; bottom beads in necklace)
  - color B (Toho 506, higher metallic June bug; top beads in necklace)
- 3 x 10 mm CzechMates crescent beads (matte metallic antique gold)
- 3 mm magatamas (Toho 221, bronze)
- 15º seed beads (Toho 221, bronze)

basics (FacetJewelry.com)
- kongoh gumi on a disk or marudai
- binding or sealing the end of a braid
- square knot

Kits for these necklaces are available at

kumihimoresource.com

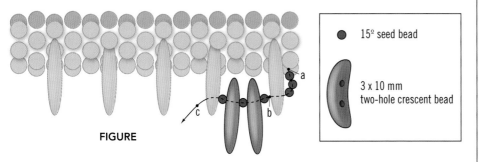

FIGURE

●	15º seed bead
◗	3 x 10 mm two-hole crescent bead

ONE DIRECTION

When stringing the crescents, be sure that each bead is strung in the same direction. If they are strung with the tips facing to the right, there will be more visible color B 8ºs in the finished braid (purple necklace); if they are strung with the tips facing left, there will be more visible color A 8ºs in the finished braid (turquoise necklace).

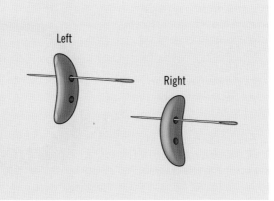

Left

Right

7) Cut off the needle, and tie the tails together with two square knots. Trim the thread close to the knots.

ATTACHING THE CLASP

1) Check that the unbeaded braid ends fit into the openings of the clasp and that the beads butt up against the clasp. If any of the ends are too long, use the cord burner to trim.

2) Stand the clasp on end with the openings pointing upwards. This way gravity will keep the epoxy inside the clasp and not on the beads. If the magnet is flush with the bottom of the clasp, you can place it on a metal bench block. If not, you can secure it in a vise.

3) On a discarded plastic bag, dispense equal amounts of epoxy from each tube, and let it sit for several minutes. Once the epoxy settles, it's easier to see if both amounts are equal. As long as the two parts are not touching or mixed together, the epoxy can sit for a long time. Once mixed, the working time is only a few minutes. Mix both parts together until they are well blended.

4) Use a toothpick to fill the opening about half way with epoxy, and spread epoxy all the way up the sides.

5) Insert one braid end into the clasp opening. If necessary, remove the braid end to either add or remove some of the epoxy. Too little epoxy might not create a secure bond. Too much epoxy will force glue into the beaded braid or onto the clasp. Re-insert the braid end, firmly holding the braid in place while pushing down for several minutes. Immediately wipe off any excess glue.

6) Let dry at least one hour before gluing the other end. If desired, use a third-hand tweezer to hold the braid upright while the epoxy sets. Sometimes it is possible to glue both ends at the same time. However, this is not recommended until you get comfortable with the process.

7) Let the epoxy cure for 24 hours before wearing the necklace. **B&B**

KUMIHIMO Q&A

by Adrienne Gaskell

What type of cord should I use with pearls and gemstones? >>

Working with pearls and gemstones can be challenging because not only are the holes small, the holes often have sharp edges, too. I recommend and use nylon-coated stainless steel beading wire. Sharp edges will not cut through the wire and the beads slide smoothly on it.

All brands of beading wire work well. It is best to use a .014 or .015-in. diameter wire — either will easily fit through most, if not all, pearls and gemstones. I also suggest using 49-strand wire. The more strands within the plastic coating, the more flexible the wire. It is not necessary to match the color of the wire to your beads. I only use black, bronze, or gray.

When using beading wire, I find it easiest to start the braid by cutting double lengths of half the number of cords needed, folding them in half, and tying them at the center to a split ring. This way there are no loose wires on the starting end of the braid to worry about securing later. To begin, load all of the project beads. Braid a small section without beads. This is the portion of the braid that you will use with your closure, so make sure the length will work since you don't want to have to cut it later. When the beaded braid has reached your desired length, braid another small section without beads, making it the same length as the one at the beginning. Without removing the braid from the disk or marudai, tie a square knot with one pair of wires. Secure the wires into the slots of the disk or tape them onto the top of the marudai. Repeat with the remaining wires. Apply a small drop of super glue on the knotted wire. The glue causes a chemical reaction and bonds the nylon coating securely and permanently to itself. Allow the braid to sit undisturbed for at least 15 minutes in order to complete this process.

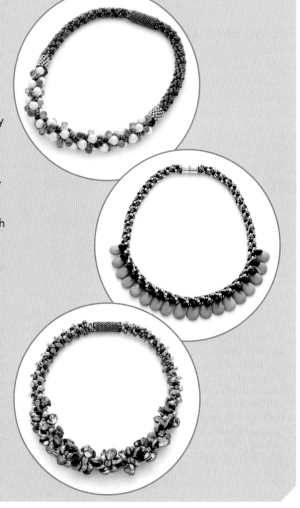

Pinch me necklace

Make this dramatic necklace with daggers set against a backdrop of pinch beads. Because the beads are relatively large, this necklace braids up very quickly!

by Svetlana Chernitsky

SETUP

1) Cut four pieces of nylon cord to 90 in. (2.3 m) each, center them on the 10 mm split ring, and attach them with a square knot.

2) Set up your disk or marudai for kongoh gumi. If desired, apply cord stiffener on the end of each cord and allow it to dry.

3) String each cord with the beads listed in the **Bead & cord layout**. Note that all cords should have 48 beads. If using a disk, attach a stop bead to the end of each cord after you string the entire bead sequence. If using a marudai, wind each cord onto a tama.

BRAID

1) Work in kongoh gumi with just the cords (no beads) for ½ in. (1.3 cm). Make sure you end with all the cords in their original positions, as in the **Bead & cord** layout.

2) Continue in two-drop kongoh, dropping one bead on each cord with each pair of movements. Note that the daggers don't slide on the cord easily, so if you are using a marudai, you may need to move them into position with your fingers rather than letting them slide into place.

3) When all the beads have been incorporated into the braid, work another ½ in. (1.3 cm) with just the cords.

4) Lift the braid from the marudai or disk. Finish the braid, sealing it with a cord burner.

5) Remove the split ring from the other end.

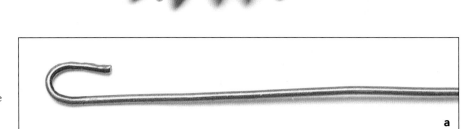

FINISHING

1) Cut the head off of a head pin, and use round-nose pliers to make a small hook at one end **(photo a)**.

2) Slide the hook into one end of the braid, and bend both ends of the wire so they point away from the braid **(photo b)**.

3) Cut 4 in. (10 cm) of 24-gauge wire, and insert one end through the end of the braid, near where you inserted the head pin. Leave one end shorter than the other **(photo c)**.

TIP New laser-etched dagger beads are an exciting option for this necklace. Look for them at your local bead shop or visit knotjustbeads.com or limabeads.com.

Bead & cord layout

◯	4 mm pinch bead, color A
◖	4 mm pinch bead, color B
◗	5 x 16 mm dagger bead

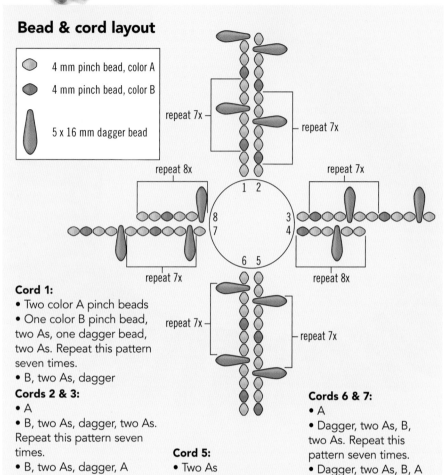

repeat 7x
repeat 7x
repeat 8x
repeat 7x
repeat 7x
repeat 8x
repeat 7x
repeat 7x

1 2
8 3
7 4
6 5

Cord 1:
• Two color A pinch beads
• One color B pinch bead, two As, one dagger bead, two As. Repeat this pattern seven times.
• B, two As, dagger

Cords 2 & 3:
• A
• B, two As, dagger, two As. Repeat this pattern seven times.
• B, two As, dagger, A

Cord 4:
• B, two As, dagger, two As. Repeat this pattern eight times.

Cord 5:
• Two As
• Dagger, two As, B, two As. Repeat this pattern seven times.
• Dagger, two As, B

Cords 6 & 7:
• A
• Dagger, two As, B, two As. Repeat this pattern seven times.
• Dagger, two As, B, A

Cord 8:
• Dagger, two As, B, two As. Repeat this pattern eight times.

DIFFICULTY ●●●○○
kongoh gumi

materials
adjustable necklace 17–19 in. (43–38 cm)

- **64** 5 x 16 mm dagger beads (Czech, turquoise green Picasso)
- 5 x 3 mm pinch beads
  - **256** color A (crystal capri gold)
  - **64** color B (matte blue zircon)
- **8** 8º seed beads (to use as stop beads if using a disk)
- **2** 3–4 mm round accent beads
- **1** 6 mm accent bead
- **2** 12 x 9 mm end caps or cones
- **8 in. (20 cm)** 24-gauge wire
- **3** 2-in. (5 cm) head pins
- **2** 5 mm jump rings
- **1** lobster claw clasp
- **2 in. (5 cm)** chain
- nylon cord, Tex 210 (S-Lon)
- kumihimo disk with 1–2 oz. counter weight or marudai with **8** weighted tama, 150 g counterweight, chopstick, and painter's tape
- **1** 10 mm or larger split ring
- cord burner
- cord stiffener such as Fray Check or super glue (optional)
- chainnose, flatnose, and/or bentnose pliers
- roundnose pliers

basics (FacetJewelry.com)
- square knot
- kongoh gumi on a disk or marudai
- wrapped loop
- plain loop
- opening and closing jump rings

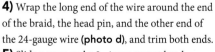
d

e

4) Wrap the long end of the wire around the end of the braid, the head pin, and the other end of the 24-gauge wire **(photo d)**, and trim both ends.
5) Slide a cone and a 3–4 mm accent bead over the head pin wire, and make a wrapped loop **(photo e)**.

6) Use a jump ring to attach the clasp to the wrapped loop.
7) Repeat steps 1–6 at the other end, but substitute the clasp with 2 in. (5 cm) of chain.
8) String a 6 mm accent bead on a head pin, and make a plain loop. Open the loop, and attach it to the end chain link.

BRAIDING AROUND A CORE

Q I've been hearing a lot about using a soft core inside of a beaded braid but I'm unclear — why use a core and how does it work?

A Cores are most often used to prevent a beaded braid from collapsing. A braid may collapse when the inside of the braid forms too large of a hollow space. The core will fill that hollow space and keep the braid round. A two-drop kongoh braid may develop a hollow space if:

• The braid is made up of mostly 6º or larger seed beads. These beads have large holes and the warp cord will fill only a small portion of it. Thus, the beads are pushed to the outside of the braid, leaving a large hollow inside the braid. Sometimes stringing the beads on a heavier warp cord or doubling the warp cord can solve the problem. When this is not possible, a core will do the trick.
• The braid is made with mostly gemstone beads or pearls. Since these usually have tiny holes, a thin warp cord or beading wire is used. The combination of large beads and a thin warp causes a large hollow inside the braid.
• The braid is made with 12 or 16 strands of beads. This will have a larger outside diameter than an eight-strand braid, again causing a large hollow in the center of the braid.

CORE MATERIALS
Many materials can be used as a soft core; rattail, yarn, cording, and t-shirt ribbon, to name a few. Core thickness requirements vary depending on the beads used, and so it may be necessary to test different core materials to determine what works best for your braid.

BRAIDING AROUND A SOFT CORE
If using the split ring start, tie the end of the core to the ring. If using the overhand knot start, tie the end of the core in with the knot. Cut the core at least 6 in. (15 cm) longer than the finished braid length.

There are several ways to manage the core and keep it out of the way while braiding. You can drape it around your neck or clip it to your shirt. It can also be hung above the disk or marudai using a ceiling fan, ceiling hook, or overhead lamp.

If you need to extend the length of the core in order to reach the overhead object, simply tie a long length of CLon/SLon to the end of the core, and wrap the other end of the CLon/SLon onto a plastic bobbin. Hang the bobbin over a fan blade **(photo)**, ceiling hook, or lamp. The weight of the bobbin will keep tension on the core while braiding.

If you're working on a disk, another option is to simply flip the core to the opposite side of the disk from where the warp cords are being worked. Start with the core positioned on the left of the point of braiding, move the upper-right warp cord into position **(figure 1)**. Flip the core from left to right, and move the lower left warp cord into position **(figure 2)**. Rotate the disk, and repeat. **B&B**

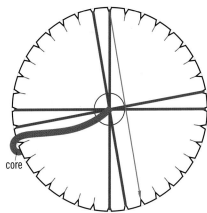

core

FIGURE 1

core

FIGURE 2

Multiple-Stitch Projects

BEAD WEAVING / RIGHT-ANGLE WEAVE

STARLIGHT
necklace

Enclose striking chatons
with a collection of
pearls, Half-Tilas, and
seed beads to create
a stunning necklace.

designed by
Melissa Grakowsky Shippee

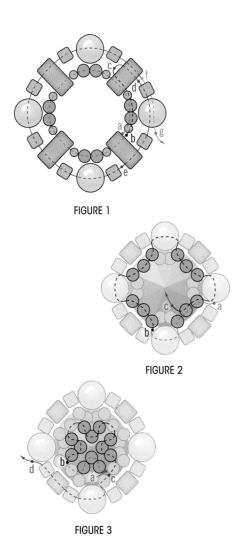

FIGURE 1

FIGURE 2

FIGURE 3

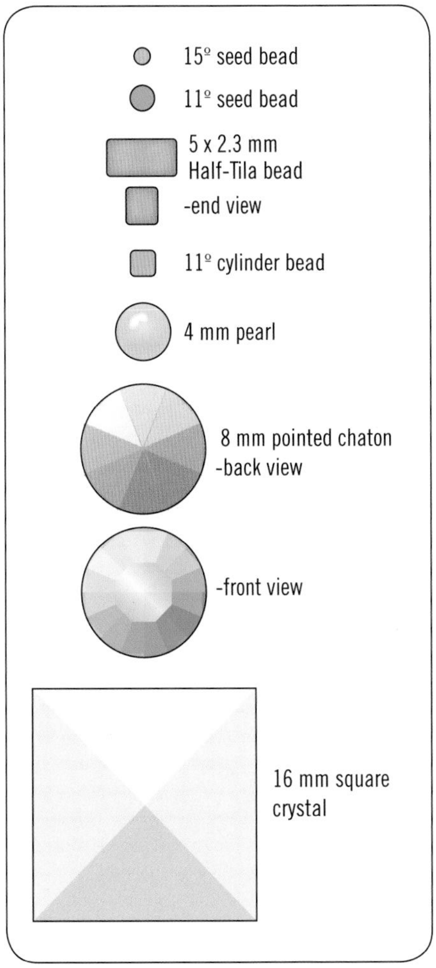

Difficulty rating

Materials

necklace 18½ in. (47 cm)
- **1** 16 mm vision square fancy stone crystal (Swarovski 4481, crystal luminous green)
- **16** pointed 8 mm chatons (Swarovski 1188, crystal luminous green)
- **76** 4 mm pearls (Swarovski, light cream rose)
- **5 g** 5 x 2.3 mm Half-Tila beads (Miyuki, nickel-plated)
- **5 g** 11º seed beads (Miyuki 2028, matte opaque seafoam luster)
- **2 g** 11º cylinder beads (Toho Treasure #1, metallic gold)
- **5 g** 15º seed beads (Toho 465, 24k gold-plated)
- **1** 13 mm round rhinestone filigree clasp (www.beadfx.com)
- Fireline, 6 lb. test
- beading needles, #11 or #12

Basics, p.13
- right-angle weave
- ending and adding thread
- square knot

Beads legend (center):
- 15º seed bead
- 11º seed bead
- 5 x 2.3 mm Half-Tila bead -end view
- 11º cylinder bead
- 4 mm pearl
- 8 mm pointed chaton -back view
- -front view
- 16 mm square crystal

Picking up the Half-Tila beads

The front of the Half-Tila is the side that is smooth. With the holes running horizontally, you will pick up the Half-Tila through the bottom hole.

Necklace
Small components

1 On 4 ft. (1.2 m) of thread, pick up a repeating pattern of one 15º seed bead, two 11º seed beads, one 15º, and one Half-Tila a total of four times. Leaving a 6-in. (15 cm) tail, tie a square knot to form the beads into a ring **(figure 1, a-b)**. Sew through the next five beads in the ring, exiting a Half-Tila **(b-c)**, and continue through the open hole of the same Half-Tila **(c-d)**.

2 Pick up an 11º cylinder bead, a 4 mm pearl, and a cylinder, and sew through the open hole of the next Half-Tila **(d-e)**. Repeat this stitch three times to complete the round **(e-f)**, and step

up through the first cylinder and pearl **(f-g)**. Pull the thread tight. This will dome the beadwork, causing the pearls to sit below the 11ºs in the inner ring.

3 Turn the beadwork over so that the inner ring is facedown, and position a chaton facedown in the center of the beadwork. If needed, pull the thread tight so the pearls are slightly overlapping the back of the chaton.

4 Pick up three 11ºs, and sew through the next pearl **(figure 2, a-b)** to form a picot. Repeat this stitch three times to complete the round, and step up through the first two 11ºs added **(b-c)**.

5 Pick up three 11ºs, and sew through the center 11º in the next picot **(figure 3, a-b)**. Repeat this stitch three times to complete the round **(b-c)**, and continue through the next five beads as shown to exit a cylinder in the outer ring adjacent to a pearl **(c-d)**.

6 Turn the component over to position the chaton faceup. Pick up six 15ºs, skip the next pearl, and sew through the next cylinder, Half-Tila, and cylinder **(figure 4, a–b)** to form a picot. Repeat this stitch three times to complete the round **(b–c)**, and step up through the first three 15ºs added **(c–d)**.

7 Pick up a 15º, and sew through the beadwork as shown to exit the third 15º in the next picot **(figure 5, a–b)**. Repeat this stitch three times to complete the round, and step up through the first 15º added in this round **(b–c)**. End the tail, but not the working thread.

8 Repeat steps 1–7 to make a total of 16 components.

Neck straps

1 Place two components next to each other, with the working threads centered on the right side. With the working thread from the component on the left, pick up an 11º, and sew through the corresponding tip 15º on the next component. Pick up an 11º, and sew

through the 15º your thread just exited **(figure 6)**. Retrace the thread path to reinforce the connection several times, and end this working thread.

2 Work as in step 1 to connect a total of eight small components to create half of the neck strap.

3 Pick up eight 15ºs, and sew through the 15º your thread is exiting, going in the same direction to form a loop. Continue through the first five 15ºs in the loop **(figure 7, a–b)**.

4 Working in right-angle weave (RAW), pick up eight 15ºs, and sew through the last two beads your thread exited in the previous stitch. Continue through the first five beads just added **(b–c)**.

5 Work as in step 4 for a total of 15 RAW stitches to form a chain at the end of the neck strap.

6 To attach half the clasp, work a RAW stitch, but pick up the loop of the clasp after picking up the first four 15ºs. Retrace the thread path of the connection, and

end the working thread.

7 Work as in steps 1–6 to make another neck strap.

Pendant

1 On a comfortable length of thread, pick up a repeating pattern of four 15ºs, a Half-Tila, a 15º, two 11ºs, a 15º, and a Half-Tila a total of four times **(figure 8, a–b)**. Leaving a 6-in. (15 cm) tail, tie a square knot to form the beads into a ring. Retrace the thread path (not shown in the figure for clarity), and sew through the next five beads in the ring **(b–c)**. Continue through the open hole of the same Half-Tila **(c–d)**.

2 Pick up a pearl, a cylinder, and a pearl, and sew through the open hole of the next Half-Tila **(d–e)**. Pick up a cylinder, a pearl, and a cylinder, and sew through the open hole of the following Half-Tila **(e–f)**. Repeat these two stitches three times to complete the round **(f–g)**, and step up through the

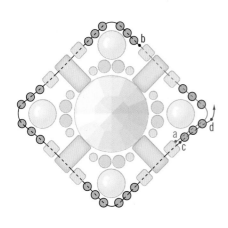

FIGURE 4

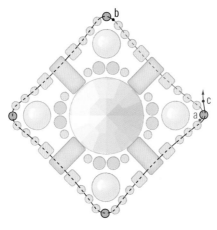

FIGURE 5

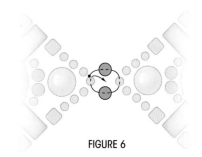

FIGURE 6

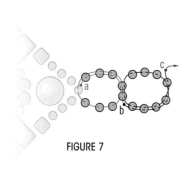

FIGURE 7

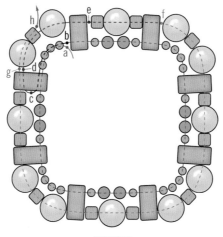

FIGURE 8

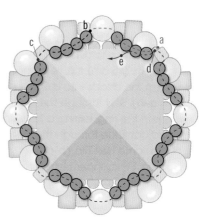

FIGURE 9

next pearl and cylinder **(g–h)**.

3 Turn the beadwork over, and center the square crystal facedown inside the bezel, aligning the corners of the crystal with the corners of the bezel.

4 Pick up four 11ºs, skip the next pearl, and sew through the following pearl **(figure 9, a–b)** to form a picot. Pick up four 11ºs, and sew through the cylinder between the next pair of pearls **(b–c)**. Repeat these two stitches three times to complete the round **(c–d)**, and step up through the first two 11ºs added at the start of this step **(d–e)**.

5 Pick up four 11ºs, and sew through the third and fourth 11ºs in the next picot **(figure 10, a–b)**. Skip the following cylinder, and continue through the first two 11ºs in the next picot **(b–c)**. Repeat this stitch three times to complete the round **(c–d)**. Pull the thread tight. If needed, retrace the thread path of this round to cinch up the beads, and continue through the next two 11ºs, pearl, cylinder, and

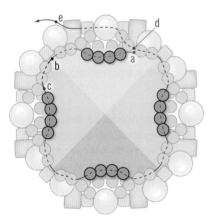

FIGURE 10

Half-Tila as shown **(d–e)**.

6 Turn the bezel faceup. Pick up a cylinder, six 15ºs, and a cylinder, and sew through the corresponding hole of the next Half-Tila to form a picot **(figure 11, a–b)**. Continue through the next cylinder, pearl, cylinder, and Half-Tila **(b–c)**. Repeat this stitch three times to complete the round **(c–d)**, and step up through the first cylinder and three 15ºs added **(d–e)**.

7 Pick up a 15º, and sew through the next three 15ºs and cylinder in the same loop **(figure 12, a–b)** Continue through the beadwork as shown to exit the third 15º in the next picot **(b–c)**. Repeat this stitch three

times to complete the round, and step up through the first 15º added in this round **(c–d)**.

8 To attach the pendant to the neck straps, position the pendant with the working thread centered at the top and a neck strap on each side of the pendant as shown in **figure 13**. Pick up an 11º, and sew through the tip 15º on an end component. Repeat this stitch with the end component on the other strap, and then pick up an 11º, and sew through the 15º your thread exited at the start of this step, going in the same direction **(figure 13)**. Retrace the thread path several times, and end the thread. ●

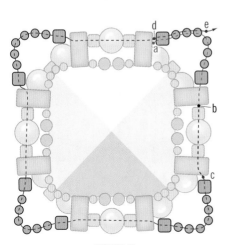

FIGURE 11

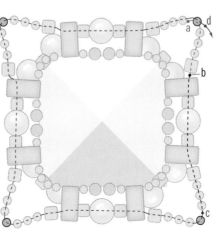

FIGURE 12

FIGURE 13

Floral components, made with multiple stitches, combine for earrings cascading with leaves and flowers — perfect for a summer soirée.

Overview
- Stitch all components (four flowers and six leaves).
- Make cluster pairs.
- Combine clusters.
- Attach ear wires.

⬤	4 mm glass bead or pearl
⬤	8º seed bead, color A
⬤	8º seed bead, color B
⬤	11º seed bead, color C
⬤	11º seed bead, color D
⬤	11º seed bead, color E
◻	11º Delica seed bead, color F
⬤	15º seed bead, color G
⬤	15º seed bead, color H

HERRINGBONE BELL FLOWERS

1) On 20 in. (51 cm) of thread, pick up 10 color H 15º seed beads. Sew through the beads again to form a ring, leaving a 6-in. (15 cm) tail, and continue through the next three Hs **(figure 1)**.

2) Pick up two Hs, skip the next H, and sew through the following H. Repeat this stitch four times to complete the round, and step up through the first H added **(figure 2)**.

3) Pick up two Hs, sew down through the adjacent H and up through the next H in the previous round **(figure 3, a–b)**. Repeat this stitch four times to complete the round,

and step up through the first H added **(b–c)**. Repeat this step once more **(c–d)**.

4) Pick up two Hs, sew down through the next H **(d–e)**. Pick up an H, and sew up through the following H **(e–f)**. Repeat these stitches four times to complete the round, and step up through the first H added **(f–g)**. Tighten your thread to cup the beads. Retrace the thread path of the last round to tighten the tension, and end the threads.

5) Repeat steps 1–4 to make a second bell flower.

FIGURE 1   **FIGURE 2**   **FIGURE 3**

BRIGHT EYES FLOWERS

1) On 20 in. (51 cm) of thread, pick up five color D 11º seed beads. Sew through the beads again to form a ring, leaving a 6-in. (15 cm) tail, and continue through the next two Ds.

2) Pick up three color C 11º seed beads, and sew through the bead your thread is exiting, going in the same direction. Continue through the next two Cs (**figure 4, a–b**). Repeat this step once more (**b–c**).

3) Pick up three Cs, and sew through the C your thread is exiting and the three Cs just added (**figure 5, a–b**).

4) Pick up a C, and sew through the next C (**b–c**). Repeat this stitch once more (**c–d**).

5) Sew through the next D and C (**d–e**), work a stitch with a C, and then pick up a C (**e–f**). Sew though the next seven Cs and two Ds (**f–g**). This completes the first petal.

6) Repeat steps 2–5 four times for a total of five petals.

7) Turn the beadwork over, pick up a color B 8º seed bead, skip the next D, and sew through the following D in the base ring (**figure 6, a–b**). Sew back through the B and the D next to the one your thread exited at the start of this step (**b–c**). End the threads.

8) Repeat steps 1–7 to make a second flower.

materials
purple color earrings 2⅛ in. (5.4 cm)

- **6** 4 mm glass beads or pearls (Swarovski pearl, lavender)
- **8º seed beads**
  - **26** color A (Toho 167, transparent light green AB)
  - **2** color B (Toho 943, light purple-lined crystal)
- **11º seed beads**
  - **1 g** color C (Toho 2224, silver-lined purple)
  - **1 g** color D (Toho 967, crystal/neon rosaline-lined)
  - **1 g** color E (Toho 7B, transparent grass green)
- **2 g** 11º cylinder beads, color F (Myuki Delica DB0152, transparent green AB)
- **15º seed beads**
  - **1 g** color G (Toho 7B, transparent green)
  - **1 g** color H (Toho 2219, silver-lined light grape)
- **1** pair of earring findings
- Fireline, 6 lb. test
- beading needles, #11
- **2** pairs of chainnose, flat-nose, and/or bentnose pliers

basics, p. 13
- ending and adding thread
- peyote stitch, diagonal
- brick stitch
- tubular herringbone
- opening and closing loops

NOTE
For multi-colored petals, shown in blue, pick up two Ds instead of Cs for the vertical center rows.

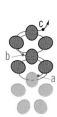

FIGURE 4

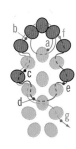

FIGURE 5

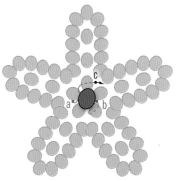

FIGURE 6

DIAGONAL PEYOTE CUPPED LEAF

1) Thread a needle on each end of 30 in. (76 cm) of thread. With one needle, pick up three color G 15º seed beads, and center them on the thread.

2) With one needle, pick up two color F 11º cylinder beads. With the other needle, sew through the first F, and pick up an F **(figure 7, a–b and aa–bb)**. Repeat this step twice **(b–c and bb–cc)**. With both needles together, pick up a color E 11º seed bead **(c–d and cc–dd)**.

3) With one needle, work in diagonal peyote stitch: Pick up an F, and sew through the next F in the previous row. Repeat this stitch twice **(figure 8, a–b)**.

4) Turn by picking up three Gs, and sewing back through the last F picked up **(b–c)**. Work two stitches with Fs **(c–d)**. Pick up an F, an E, and an F, and sew back through the first F picked up in this stitch **(d–e)**.

5) Work two stitches with Fs **(figure 9, a–b)**. Work a turn with three Gs **(b–c)**. Work two stitches with Fs **(c–d)**. Pick up an F, an E, and an F, and sew back through the first F picked up in this stitch **(d–e)**.

6) Repeat step 5 once **(figure 10)**.

7) Repeat step 5 again, but do not pick up the last F, E, and F **(figure 11)**. This completes one half of the leaf. Do not end the thread.

8) With the other needle exiting the first E, work three stitches with Fs on the other side of the original row **(figure 12, a–b)**. Work a turn with three Gs, and then work two stitches with Fs **(b–c)**. Pick up a F, and sew through the next E on the other side of the leaf **(c–d)**. Pinch the beadwork between your forefinger and thumb to keep stitching tight. Pick up a F, and sew back through the F you picked up in the previous stitch **(d–e)**.

9) Stitch the second half of the leaf as a mirror image of the first, but connect the inside edges by sewing through the existing Es instead of adding new ones.

10) Using the first needle, sew through the end E **(figure 13, a–b)**. Pick up an E, and sew through the next E **(b–c)**. Repeat this last stitch twice, and sew through four Fs in the base as shown **(c–d)**. Sew back through all the Es in the leaf **(d–e)**. Pick up three Es and a color A 8º seed bead, skip the A, and sew back through the three Es just added **(e–f)**. End both threads.

11) Repeat steps 1–10 to make a second cupped leaf.

N O T E Steps 1–2 are worked using two needles at the same time. Steps 3–10 are worked with one needle at a time, but both needles are needed to complete the leaf.

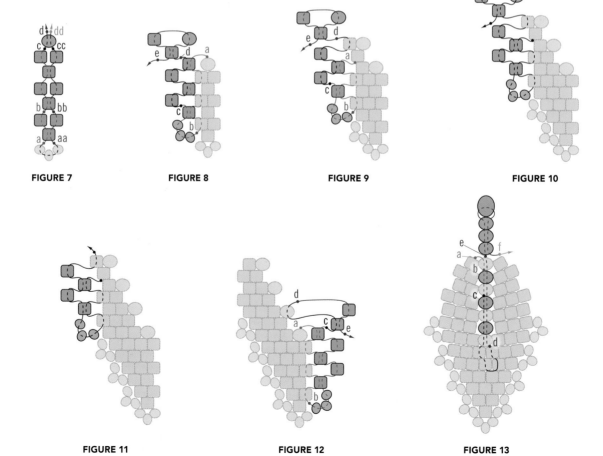

FIGURE 7

FIGURE 8

FIGURE 9

FIGURE 10

FIGURE 11

FIGURE 12

FIGURE 13

BRICK STITCH SMALL LEAVES

1) On 18 in. (46 cm) of thread, pick up four Gs. Sew through the beads again to form two rows, leaving a 6-in. (15 cm) tail **(figure 14, a–b)**. This is rows 1 and 2.

2) Work the rows as follows:

Row 3: Work in brick stitch using three Gs, increasing at each end of the row **(b–c)**.

Rows 4–5: Work in brick stitch using pairs of Gs, increasing at the start and end of the rows for a total of four pairs of Gs **(c–d)**.

Row 6: Work a row in brick stitch with three Gs **(figure 15, a–b)**.

Row 7: Work a stitch with two Gs **(b–c)**.

Row 8: Pick up a G, and sew through the adjacent G **(c–d)**.

3) Sew through the beads along the exterior of the leaf **(figure 16, a–b)**.

4) Pick up two Gs and an E. Skip the E, and sew back through the Gs **(b–c)**. Reinforce the beadwork by sewing through all the edge beads **(c–d)**, and end the working thread. Use the tail thread to sew through the edge beads in the opposite direction, and end the tail.

5) Repeat steps 1–4 to make three more small leaves.

FIGURE 14

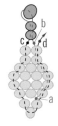

FIGURE 15

FIGURE 16

BERRY CLUSTERS

1) On 24 in. (61 cm) of thread, pick up an A, 12 Es, the 11º at the base of a small leaf, an A, a 4 mm bead, and a H **(figure 17, a–b)**, leaving 6-in. (15 cm) tail. This row will be the main stem.

2) Skip the H, and sew back through the rest of the beads just added **(b–c)**. Skip the A, and sew through the first 10 Es **(c–d)**.

3) Pick up six Es, an A, a bell flower, and an A. Sew back through the bell flower, the A, and the six Es **(figure 18, a–b)**. Sew through the stem E below the E

your thread exited at the start of this step and the next four Es **(b–c)**. Pick up three Es, the 11º at the base of a small leaf, an A, a 4 mm, and a H. Skip the H, and sew back through the beads just added **(c–d)**. Skip the next stem E and sew through the following stem E **(d–e)**. Pick up four Es, an A, a 4 mm, and a H. Skip the H, sew back through the beads just added, and continue through the end three stem Es and the following A **(e–f)**. End the both threads.

4) Repeat steps 1–3 to make a second berry cluster.

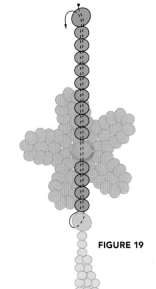

FIGURE 19

FLOWER/LEAF CLUSTER

1) On 24 in. (61 cm) of thread and leaving a 12-in. (30 cm) tail, pick up an A, nine Es, the 8º at the base of a bright-eye flower, four Es, and the 8º at the base of a cupped leaf. Sew back through all the beads just added **(figure 19)**. End the working thread, but not the tail.

2) Repeat to assemble a second flower/leaf cluster.

ASSEMBLY

1) Using the tail from a flower/leaf cluster, sew through the A at the end of a berry cluster **(figure 20, a–b)** and continue through the A at the end of the flower/leaf cluster **(b–c)**. Pick up two As and eight Gs, and sew back through the two As you just picked up **(c–d)**. Retrace the thread path several times to reinforce the connection, and then end the thread.

2) Open the loop of an ear wire, and attach it to the loop of Gs. Repeat to complete the second earring. **B·B**

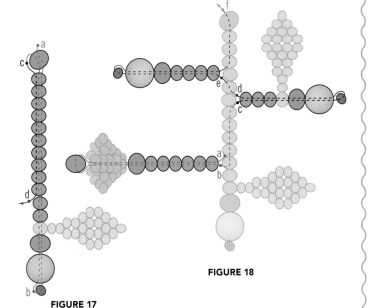

FIGURE 17

FIGURE 18

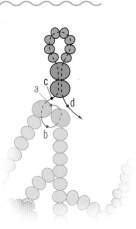

FIGURE 20

SUPER DUPER DONUT

Two layers of SuperDuos, pearls, and seed beads come together with partially hidden crystals along the edge of a sturdy donut pendant.

designed by **Justyna Szlezak**

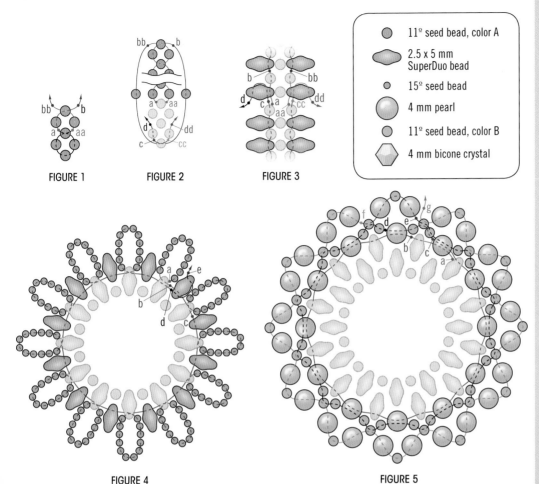

FIGURE 1

FIGURE 2

FIGURE 3

FIGURE 4

FIGURE 5

Legend:
- 11º seed bead, color A
- 2.5 x 5 mm SuperDuo bead
- 15º seed bead
- 4 mm pearl
- 11º seed bead, color B
- 4 mm bicone crystal

Difficulty rating

Materials
pendant 1¾ in. (4.4 cm)

- **48** 2.5 x 5 mm SuperDuo beads (jet metallic suede blue)
- **12** 4 mm bicone crystals (Swarovski, Montana)
- **84** 4 mm glass pearls (aqua grey)
- 11º seed beads
  - **1 g** color A (Toho 705, matte frosted blue iris)
  - **2 g** color B (Toho 512, galvanized blue haze)
- **2 g** 15º seed beads (Toho 706, matte iris teal)
- **1** bail (TierraCast "Legend," silver-plated pewter)
- Fireline, 6 lb. test
- beading needles, #11 or #12
- **2** pairs of chainnose, flatnose, and/or bentnose pliers

Basics, p. 13
- ending and adding thread
- opening and closing jump rings

Pendant

1 Attach a needle to each end of 3 yd. (2.7 m) of thread. With one needle, pick up four color A 11º seed beads. Cross the other needle through the last bead added, and center the beads on the thread **(figure 1, point a and point aa)**.

2 With each needle pick up an A. With one needle, pick up an A, and cross the other needle through it **(a–b and aa–bb)**. Repeat this stitch nine times **(figure 2, a–b and aa–bb)**.

3 With each needle, pick up an A, and sew through the center A on the other end of the strip to form a ring **(b–c and bb–cc)**. With one needle, retrace the thread path of the join (not shown in the figure for clarity). With each needle, continue through the following edge A **(c–d and cc–dd)**.

4 Working with one thread at a time, stitch the front and back surfaces in rounds as follows:

Round 1: With each needle, pick up a SuperDuo bead, and sew through the next edge A **(figure 3, a–b and aa–bb)**. Repeat this stitch to complete the round **(b–c and bb–cc)**, and continue through the following SuperDuo and the open hole of the same SuperDuo **(c–d and cc–dd)**.

Round 2: With each needle, pick up 12 15º seed beads, and sew through the same hole of the SuperDuo, going in the same direction, to form a loop **(figure 4, a–b)**. Only the top layer of the beadwork is shown in **figures 4–6** for clarity. Pick up a SuperDuo, and sew through the open hole of the next SuperDuo **(b–c)**. Repeat these stitches 11 times to complete the round **(c–d)**. As you work the round, position the loops to the outside of the beadwork and the SuperDuos to the inside. When both layers are done, the SuperDuos in each layer should be next to each other and the loops on the outside of the SuperDuos. Continue through the first SuperDuo added in the round and the open hole of the same SuperDuo **(d–e)**.

Round 3: With each needle, pick up a 4 mm pearl, and sew through the open hole of the next SuperDuo **(figure 5, a–b)**. The loops added in the previous step are not shown in this figure for clarity. Repeat this stitch 11 times to complete the round, and

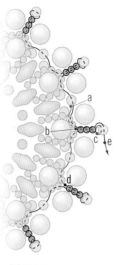

FIGURE 6

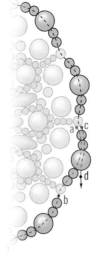

FIGURE 7

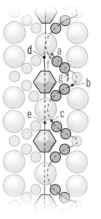

FIGURE 8

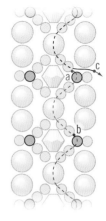

FIGURE 9

continue through the first 4 mm added **(b–c)**. Make sure your loops are still positioned to the outside of the beadwork.

Round 4: With each needle, pick up three color B 11º seed beads, and sew through the next pearl to form a picot **(c–d)**. Repeat this stitch 11 times to complete the round, and continue through the first two Bs added in the first picot **(d–e)**.

Round 5: With each needle, pick up a pearl, a B, and a pearl, and sew through the center B in the next picot

design option
Eliminate the bail and hang the pendant through the center with a ribbon or chain.

(e–f). Repeat this stitch 11 times to complete the round **(f–g)**.

Round 6: With each needle, skip the first four 15ºs in the next loop, and sew through the next two 15ºs **(figure 6, a–b)**. Pick up three 15ºs, and sew through the B between the next two pearls added in the previous round **(b–c)**. Sew back through the three 15ºs just added, and continue through the next two 15ºs in the same loop, the center B in the next picot, and the corresponding two 15ºs in the following loop **(c–d)**. Repeat these stitches 11 times to complete the round, and continue through the first three 15ºs added and the adjacent B **(d–e)**. End and add thread if needed.

5 With one needle, pick up two Bs, a pearl, and two Bs, and sew through the B between the next set of pearls **(figure 7, a–b)**. Repeat this stitch 11 times to complete the round **(b–c)**, and continue through the first two Bs and pearl added in this round **(c–d)**.

6 With the same thread, pick up two Bs, and sew through the B between the next set of pearls on the opposite edge **(figure 8, a–b)**. The edge view of the beadwork is shown for **figures 8 and 9**. Pick up two Bs, and sew through the next pearl along the center edge **(b–c)**. Repeat these stitches 11 times to complete the round, joining the two edges together **(c–d)**.

7 With the other thread exiting at **point d**, pick up a 4 mm bicone crystal, and sew through the next pearl along the edge **(d–e)**. Push the crystal into the opening

of the seed beads so it sits flush with or slightly below the seed beads **(photo)**. The sides of the beadwork expand slightly as the crystals are added. Repeat this stitch 11 times to complete the round **(e–f)**, and continue through the first two Bs added **(f–g)**. End and add thread if needed.

8 With the same thread, pick up a B, skip the next B, and sew through the following two Bs, edge pearl, and two Bs on the same surface **(figure 9, a–b)**. Repeat this stitch 11 times to complete the round **(b–c)**. Sew through the beadwork to the other edge, and repeat the stitch to complete the round on this side.

Bail

Attach a 4 mm jump ring to a bail. With either thread exiting an edge pearl, pick up seven 15ºs and the jump ring with the bail attached, skip over the adjacent crystal, and sew through the next edge pearl. Sew through the beadwork, and retrace the thread path of the bail loop. End the threads. **◗**

Peanut party
bracelet

Brick stitch a diamond pattern of peanut beads, and add an easy embellishment on top for a stunning bracelet.

designed by **Jimmie Boatright**

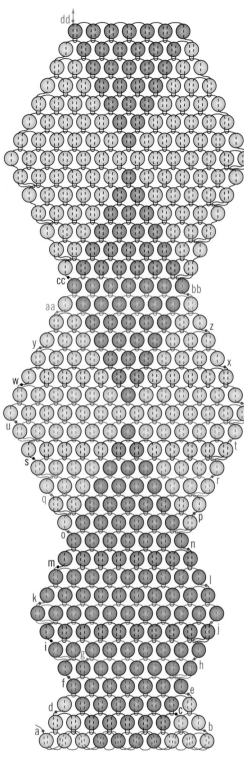

FIGURE 1

Base

1 On a comfortable length of thread and leaving a 6-in. (15 cm) tail, work a 10-bead ladder using three color A peanut beads, four color B peanut beads, and three As **(figure 1, a–b)**. This will be row 1 of the base. End and add thread throughout the pattern as needed.

2 Work row 2 in brick stitch as follows,

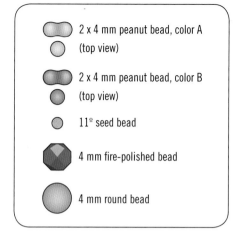

- 2 x 4 mm peanut bead, color A (top view)
- 2 x 4 mm peanut bead, color B (top view)
- 11º seed bead
- 4 mm fire-polished bead
- 4 mm round bead

noting the different terms for each kind of stitch:

Decrease start stitch: Pick up two As, sew under the second-to-last thread bridge in the previous row, and sew back up through the last A just added. Sew through both beads to align them (not shown in the figure for clarity), and exit the last A **(b–c)**.

Regular stitch: Pick up a B, sew under the next thread bridge in the previous row, and sew back up through the B just added. Work four more regular stitches using Bs, and two using As **(c–d)**.

3 Continue to work in rows as follows:

Row 3: Decrease start stitch using an A and a B; five regular stitches using Bs; one regular stitch using an A **(d–e)**.

Row 4: Decrease start stitch using two Bs; five regular stitches using Bs **(e–f)**.

Row 5: Increase start stitch: Pick up two Bs, sew under the last thread bridge in the previous row, and sew back up through the last B just added **(f–g)**; five regular stitches using Bs; **increase end stitch:** pick up a B, sew under the same thread bridge as in the previous stitch, and sew back up through the B just added **(g–h)**.

Row 6: Increase start stitch using two Bs; six regular stitches using Bs; one increase end stitch using a B **(h–i)**.

Row 7: Increase start stitch using two Bs; seven regular stitches using Bs; one increase end stitch using a B **(i–j)**.

Row 8: Increase start stitch using two Bs; eight regular stitches using Bs; one increase end stitch using a B **(j–k)**.

Row 9: Decrease start stitch using two Bs; eight regular stitches using Bs **(k–l)**.

Row 10: Decrease start stitch using two Bs; seven regular stitches using Bs **(l–m)**.

Materials

orange bracelet 1³⁄₈ x 7 in. (3.5 x 18 cm)

- **28** 4 mm fire-polished beads (opaque dark red)
- **28** 4 mm round druk beads (opaque green luster)
- 2 x 4 mm peanut beads
  - **6 g** color A (opaque moss green luster)
  - **6 g** color B (opaque coral luster)
- **1 g** 11º seed bead (Toho 262, crystal gold-lined)
- **1** 5-strand tube clasp
- nylon beading thread, size D
- beading needles, #11 or #12

Information for the alternate colorway is listed at facetjewelry.com/resourceguide

Basics, p. 13

- herringbone stitch: tubular
- ladder stitch: making a ladder, forming a ring
- ending and adding thread

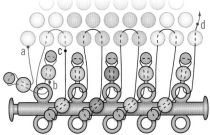

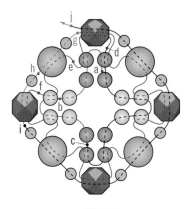

FIGURE 2

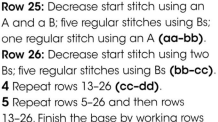

FIGURE 3

FIGURE 4

Row 11: Decrease start stitch using two Bs; six regular stitches using Bs **(m–n)**.
Row 12: Decrease start stitch using two Bs; five regular stitches using Bs **(n–o)**.
Row 13: Increase start stitch using an A and a B; five regular stitches using Bs; one increase end stitch using an A **(o–p)**.
Row 14: Increase start stitch using two As; five regular stitches using Bs and one using an A; one increase end stitch using an A **(p–q)**.
Row 15: Increase start stitch using two As; one regular stitch using an A, four using Bs, and two using As; one increase end stitch using an A **(q–r)**.
Row 16: Increase start stitch using two As; two regular stitches using As, three using Bs, and three using As; one increase end stitch using an A **(r–s)**.
Row 17: Increase start stitch using two As; three regular stitches using As, two using Bs, and four using As; one increase end stitch using an A **(s–t)**.
Row 18: Increase start stitch using two As; four regular stitches using As, one using a B, and five using As; one increase end stitch using an A **(t–u)**.
Row 19: Increase start stitch using two As; eleven regular stitches using As; one increase end stitch using an A **(u–v)**.
Row 20: Decrease start stitch using two As; four regular stitches using As, one using a B, and six using As **(v–w)**.
Row 21: Decrease start stitch using two As; three regular stitches using As, two using Bs, and five using As **(w–x)**.
Row 22: Decrease start stitch using two As; two regular stitches using As, three using Bs, and four using As **(x–y)**.
Row 23: Decrease start stitch using two As; one regular stitch using an A, four using Bs, and three using As **(y–z)**.
Row 24: Decrease start stitch using two As; five regular stitches using Bs, and two using As **(z–aa)**.

Row 25: Decrease start stitch using an A and a B; five regular stitches using Bs; one regular stitch using an A **(aa–bb)**.
Row 26: Decrease start stitch using two Bs; five regular stitches using Bs **(bb–cc)**.
4 Repeat rows 13–26 **(cc–dd)**.
5 Repeat rows 5–26 and then rows 13–26. Finish the base by working rows 5–15 for a 7 in. (18 cm) bracelet. To make the pattern longer, continue working the pattern on both ends. To use a 5-strand clasp, be sure to end with 10 beads in the last row.

Clasp

Pick up an A and an 11º seed bead, sew back through the A just added, and continue down through the end loop of the clasp **(figure 2, a–b)**. Pick up an A and an 11º, sew back through the A just added, and continue up through the same clasp loop, the next end peanut bead, and the following peanut bead **(b–c)**. Repeat these stitches for the remainder of the clasp loops, except use Bs instead of As for the center loop **(c–d)**.

Embellishment ring

1 On 2 ft. (61 cm) of thread, work in ladder stitch using two As, two Bs, two As, and two Bs, and join them into a ring **(figure 3)**.
2 Working in herringbone stitch, pick up two Bs, sew down through the adjacent B, and continue up through the

next A **(figure 4, a–b)**. Pick up two As, sew down through the adjacent A, and continue up through the next B **(b–c)**. Repeat these stitches once more, and sew through the first B added in this round **(c–d)**.
3 Pick up a 4 mm fire-polished bead, and sew down through the adjacent B **(d–e)**. Pick up a 4 mm round bead, and sew up through the next A **(e–f)**. Repeat these stitches three times to complete the round, and sew through the first fire-polished bead added **(f–g)**.
4 Pick up an 11º, and sew through the next round bead **(g–h)**. Pick up an 11º, and sew through the following fire-polished bead **(h–i)**. Repeat these stitches three times to complete the round **(i–j)**, and retrace the thread path. End the tail, but not the working thread.
5 Repeat steps 1–4 to make six more embellishment rings.
6 Position a ring on the base in the center of a diamond, with the fire-polished beads sitting horizontally and vertically on the base. Sew through an adjacent peanut directly below the bead your thread is exiting, and continue through the nearest bead in the ring. Repeat this stitch around the ring to attach it to the base, and end the thread. Repeat to add the remaining embellishment rings to the centers of the diamonds. ●

AFRICAN QUEEN NECKLACE

designed by
Jimmie Boatright

DIFFICULTY ●●●●○

peyote / modified
chenille stitch

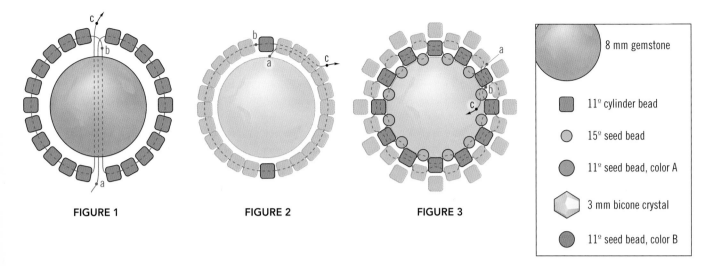

FIGURE 1   FIGURE 2   FIGURE 3

8 mm gemstone

11° cylinder bead

15° seed bead

11° seed bead, color A

3 mm bicone crystal

11° seed bead, color B

Stitch a regal necklace comprised on a bed of seed beads that is embellished with crystals. A perfect project for diving into your personal bead stash.

PENDANT

The pendant is worked as small square components that are then joined together to form one large square.

COMPONENTS

1) On a comfortable length of thread, pick up an 8 mm gemstone and 11 11° cylinder beads, leaving a 12-in. (30 cm) tail. Sew through the 8 mm again in the same direction to form a loop around one side of the 8 mm **(figure 1, a–b)**. Pick up 11 cylinders, and sew through the 8 mm again to form a loop on the other side **(b–c)**.

2) Sew through the first 11 cylinders previously added. Pick up a cylinder, and sew through the next 11 cylinders on the other side of the 8 mm **(figure 2, a–b)**. Pick up a cylinder, and sew through the next three cylinders **(b–c)**. Retrace the thread path through all the beads in the ring. This forms the center of the first square. The ring of cylinders will sit loosely around the gemstone.

3) Work a round of peyote using cylinders, and step up through the first cylinder added in the round **(figure 3, a–b)**.

4) Work a round using 15° seed beads, and step up through the first 15° added **(b–c)**. Pull the thread tightly to dome the beadwork. Sew through the beadwork to exit an up-cylinder in the initial ring **(figure 4, point a)**.

5) Using a combination of herringbone stitch and peyote stitch, work in rounds off the initial ring of cylinders, stepping up at the end of each round and ending and adding thread as needed:

Round 1: Work a corner herringbone stitch:

Pick up two cylinders, and sew through the next cylinder in the previous round **(a–b)**. Work two peyote stitches with color A 11° seed beads **(b–c)**. Repeat these stitches three times to complete the round, and step up through the first cylinder added in this round **(c–d)**. The cylinder beads will become the corners of the component.

Round 2: Work a corner stitch using cylinders, and three peyote stitches using As. Repeat these stitches three times to complete the round **(d–e)**.

Round 3: Work a corner stitch using cylinders, and sew through the next A in the previous round **(figure 5, a–b)**. Work two peyote stitches using As, and continue through the first cylinder in the next corner **(b–c)**. Repeat these stitches three times to complete the round **(c–d)**.

Round 4: Work as in round 2 **(d–e)**, pulling the thread tight after each peyote stitch to make the beadwork dome and making sure the 15°s are positioned on the outside of the component.

Round 5: Pick up a cylinder, and sew through the next cylinder to form the tip. Work four peyote stitches using As. Repeat these stitches three times to complete the round, and step up through the first cylinder added **(e–f)**.

6) Sew through the next cylinder and A in the previous round **(f–g)**. Work three stitches with cylinders **(g–h)**. This edge will be used to join the components. Set the working thread aside.

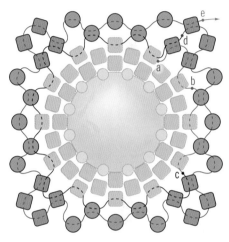

FIGURE 4

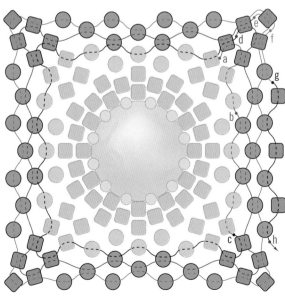

FIGURE 5

7) Using the tail, sew through the beadwork to exit a 15º in the inner ring that is adjacent to a corner 15º, with the needle facing toward the corner 15º (**figure 6, point a**). Add embellishment to the inner ring: Pick up a cylinder, a 15º, a 3 mm bicone crystal, a 15º, and a cylinder, skip the next 15º in the same round, and sew through the following 15º (**a–b**). Pick up a 15º and sew through the next 15º in the round (**b–c**). Repeat these two stitches three times to complete the round (**c–d**). End the tail but not the working thread.

8) Work as in steps 1–7 to make three additional components, then repeat steps 1–4 and round 1 of step 5 to make a smaller fifth component to form the center of the pendant.

JOINING

1) The four identical components will be zipped together. Position the four components into a square shape on your work surface, aligning the cylinder edge on each component with an edge without cylinders on the next component. Be sure to align them correctly so that each component can be zipped to the adjacent component.

2) With the working thread from the cylinder edge of a component, zip up the adjacent component (**figure 7, a–b**). Reverse direction, and zip the edges again to reinforce the connection (**b–c**). End the working thread. Repeat this step to attach the remaining two components and to connect the last component to the first one.

3) Position the small component in the center of the square, aligning its corners with the corresponding corners of the square components. The center component's edges will sit on top of the beadwork. Using the working thread from the center component, sew through the corresponding corner cylinders on the adjacent component to tack it in place (**figure 8**). Retrace the thread path, sew through the beadwork to reach the next corner, and work as before to secure the center in place. End and add thread if needed.

4) With the working thread, work as in step 7 of "Components" to add the top embellishment

to the center component, except sew through the existing bicone crystal of each adjacent component. End the threads.

BAIL

1) Position the pendant on your work surface so it is aligned in a diamond shape. Add a comfortable length of thread to the top component's right-outer edge, exiting the second "up" A bead from the top corner, with the needle facing toward this corner (**figure 9, point a**). Pick up an A, and sew through the next up-A (**a–b**). Pick up a cylinder, and sew through the adjacent tip cylinder. Pick up a cylinder, and sew through the next up-A on this edge (**b–c**).

2) Pick up an A, and sew through the next up-A (**c–d**). Sew through the beadwork as shown to exit the A just added (**d–e**). Pick up an A, and sew through the following cylinder (**e–f**). Pick up a cylinder, a 15º, and a cylinder, and sew through the next cylinder on the opposite edge (**f–g**). Pick up an A, and sew through the next edge A (**g–h**). Sew through the beadwork as shown to exit the topmost edge A on this side (**h–i**).

3) Pick up an A, skip the next cylinder, and sew through the following cylinder (**i–j**). Pick up two cylinders, and sew through the corresponding cylinder on the opposite edge (**j–k**).

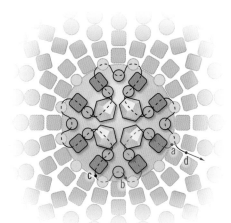

FIGURE 6

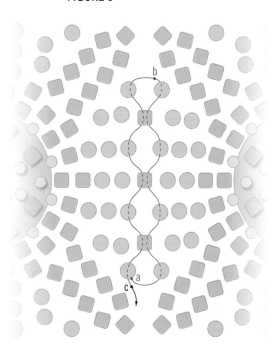

FIGURE 7

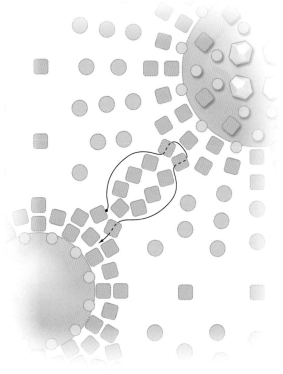

FIGURE 8

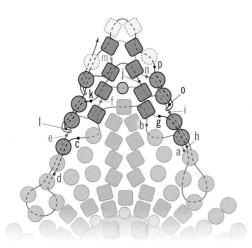

FIGURE 9

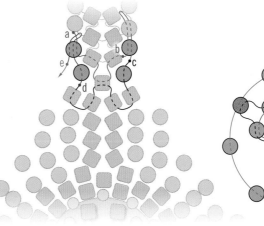

FIGURE 10

FIGURE 11

4) Pick up an A, and sew through the next edge A **(k–l)**. Sew around the closest thread bridge, and continue back through the A your thread is exiting and the following A. Pick up an A, skip the next cylinder, and sew through the following cylinder **(l–m)**.

5) Pick up two cylinders, and sew through the next cylinder on the opposite edge **(m–n)**. Pick up an A, and sew through the next A on this edge **(n–o)**. Sew around the closest thread bridge, and continue back through the A your thread is exiting and the following edge A **(o–p)**.

6) Work as in steps 3–5 until the bail is the desired length. Our bail has 19 repeats.

7) Fold the bail toward the back of the pendant, and align the end with the top tip corner cylinder. With the working thread, pick up an A, and sew through the cylinder adjacent to the tip cylinder on the same edge, the tip cylinder, and the corresponding cylinder on the opposite edge **(figure 10, a–b)**. Pick up an A, sew through the next edge A, around the closest thread bridge, and continue back through the A your thread just exited and the last A just picked up **(b–c)**. Pick up an A, and sew through the next five cylinders as shown **(c–d)**. Pick up an A, sew through the next edge A, around the closest thread bridge, and continue back through the A your thread just exited **(d–e)**. End the thread.

ROPE

1) On a comfortable length of thread, pick up three color B 11⁰ seed beads, and sew through the beads again to form them into a ring, leaving

a 10-in. (25 cm) tail. Sew through the next B in the ring.

2) Pick up two As, and sew through the next B in the ring. Repeat this stitch twice, and step up through the first A added **(figure 11, a–b)**.

3) Pick up a B, and sew through the next A in the previous round, the following B, and the next A in the previous round **(b–c)**. Repeat this stitch twice to complete the round, and step up through the first B added **(c–d)**.

4) Pick up two As, and sew through the next B in the previous round **(d–e)**. Repeat this stitch twice to compete the round, and step up through the first A added **(e–f)**.

5) Repeat steps 3–4 until the rope is the desired length, ending and adding thread as needed. End after adding a round of Bs.

6) To cinch up the end, sew through the three end Bs just added. Pull the thread tight, and retrace the thread path twice.

CLASP

Pick up three As, the loop of a toggle ring, and three As, and sew through the adjacent end B. Sew through the beadwork to retrace the clasp connection several times, and end the working thread. With the tail thread, repeat this step on the opposite end, increasing the number of As if needed for a proper fit. **B•B**

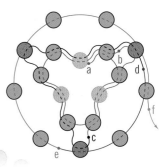

materials
necklace 19 in. (48 cm) with a 2-in. (5 cm) pendant

- **5** 8 mm round African opal gemstones
- **16** 3 mm bicone crystals (Swarovski, sand opal)
- 11⁰ seed beads
  - **8 g** color A (Toho 512F, gray iris metallic matte)
  - **6 g** color B (Miyuki 9457, dark bronze)
- **1 g** 11⁰ Delica cylinder beads (Miyuki 254, bronze metallic)
- **1 g** 15⁰ seed beads (Toho 508, metallic moss green iris)
- **1** toggle clasp
- Fireline, 6 lb. test
- beading needles, #11 or #12

basics, p. 13
- peyote stitch: tubular
- ending and adding thread

Cardinal ornament

Create a seamless band of loomwork that fits an ornament ball perfectly and leaves no warp threads to weave in.

designed by **Deb Moffett-Hall**

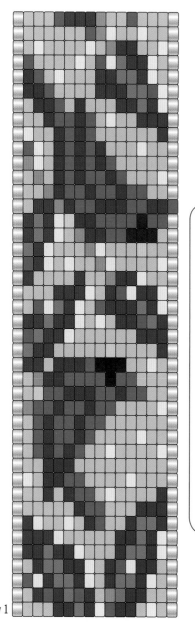

Row 1

PATTERN

11º cylinder beads

- color A
- color B
- color C
- color D
- color E
- color F
- color G
- color H
- color I
- color J

Designed as a versatile loom to make various styles of bracelets, the Endless Loom can also be used to make bands to fit 2⅝-in. (6.7 cm) diameter ornament balls. Fringe at the bottom and decreasing rounds of crystals and seed beads at the top create an heirloom-style ornament cover to be cherished for generations.

Prep the loom

1 Measure your ornament around the widest part. The one in the photos measures 8⁵⁄₁₆ in. (20.8 cm). Due to manufacturing variances, your ornament may differ somewhat.

2 Assemble the loom using the sizing rods marked "Orn." Add easement rod(s) as needed to adjust the loom

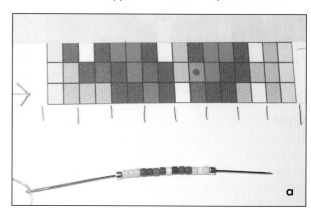

a

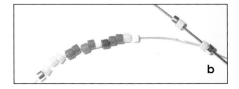

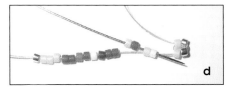

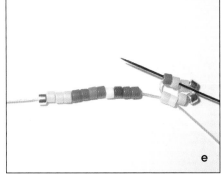

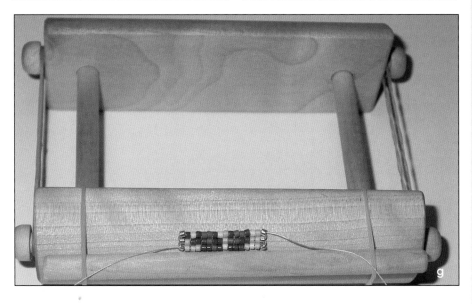

Difficulty rating

◆ ◆ ◇ ◇ ◇

Materials

ornament 2⅝ in. (6.7 cm)

- 11º Miyuki Delica cylinder beads
  - **2 g** color A (DB035, galvanized silver)
  - **4 g** color B (BD879, matte opaque turquoise blue AB)
  - **1 g** color C (DB721, opaque yellow)
  - **1 g** color D (DB653, opaque pumpkin)
  - **2 g** color E (DB727, opaque vermillion red)
  - **2 g** color F (DB654, opaque maroon)
  - **2 g** color G (DB351, matte white)
  - **1 g** color H (DB754, matte opaque green)
  - **2 g** color I (DB656, dyed opaque green)
  - **1 g** color J (DB310, matte black)
- **2 g** 11º seed beads (aqua silver-lined)
- **3 g** 15º seed beads (galvanized silver)
- **54** 6 mm bugle beads (aqua AB)
- **45** 4 mm round beads, color K (red)
- **54** 4 mm round beads, color L (aqua)
- 4 mm Swarovski bicone crystals
  - **54** color M (light emerald)
  - **18** color N (crystal Labrador silver)
- nylon beading thread, size D
- **1** 2⅝-in. (6.7 cm) ornament ball
- Endless Loom
- beading needles, #12
- tape measure

Basics, p. 13

- ending and adding thread
- square knot

◯	11º seed bead
○	15º seed bead
▭	6 mm bugle bead
●	4 mm round bead, color K
●	4 mm round bead, color L
⬡	4 mm bicone crystal, color M
⬡	4 mm bicone crystal, color N

measurement to equal your ornament circumference plus an additional ⅛ in. (3 mm) to accommodate the Delica beads.

3 Wrap your thread 16 times around the loom, and trim. You will use this thread to warp the loom and begin stitching. Attach a needle to one end.

4 Make a square stitch starter strip as follows. Beginning at the lower left-hand corner of the **pattern**, pick up the following 11º cylinder beads for the first row: one A, three Bs, two Is, one H, one I, one G, one E, two Is, one B, one G, one B, and one A **(photo a)**.

5 Reading row 2 of the pattern from right to left, work the next row in square stitch, picking up two beads per stitch: Pick up an A and a B, sew back through the end two beads in row 1 **(photo b)**, and sew through the two new beads

again **(photo c)**. Pick up the next two beads (a B and an I), sew back through the next two beads in row 1 **(photo d)**, and sew through the two new beads again **(photo e)**. Repeat this process across the row, working six more stitches as follows: IH, DB, IE, HI, EI, BA. Sew back through all the beads in row 1 and continue through all the beads in row 2 **(photo f)**.

6 Work row 3 of the pattern from left to right: AE, GI, HH, IG, BI, HH, IG, BA. Sew back through all the beads in row 2 and row 3. This completes the starter strip.

7 Use the starter strip to warp the loom: Position the starter strip so it is resting on the easement rod on the front of the loom with the working thread exiting the upper-right corner **(photo g)**. Wrap the working thread up and around the loom, and sew through the first pair

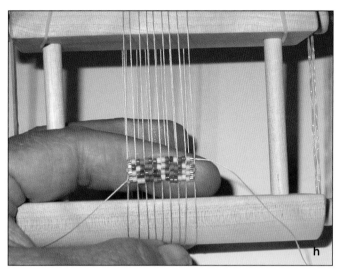

h

i

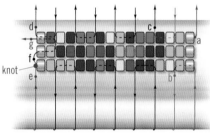

FIGURE 1

of beads on the bottom right of row 1 **(figure 1, a–b)**. Pull snug to form the first warp, but don't worry about keeping tension on the thread just yet.

8 Wrap the thread down and back around the loom, and sew through the second pair of beads from the right in the top row **(b–c)** to create the second warp.

9 Work as in steps 7–8 to add six more warps, each time sewing through the next pair of beads on the opposite side of the starter strip **(c–d)**. For the last warp, wrap the thread up and around the loom **(d–e)**. Pull all the warps snug, and tie the working thread and tail in a square knot. With the working thread, sew through the end two beads in row 2 (starting at the edge), and then sew through the end two beads in row 3 in the opposite direction **(f–g)**.

10 Slide the front easement rod up and over the top edge of the loom, and let it drop into the center bead weaving area. Remove the easement rod. This releases tension on the warps.

11 Rotate the starter strip so it is in the open bead weaving area in the center of the loom. Place a thicker easement rod under the top layer of warps, and

slide it up onto the back end of the loom to place the warps under greater tension. Slide the elastics around the back end of the loom and the easement rod to keep it in place.

Loomwork band

1 Reading the **pattern** from left to right, pick up all the beads for row 4: A, B, I, 2H, 2I, G, B, I, E, G, 2I, B, A. Slide the beads below the top warps, and press them up to position two beads between each set of warps **(photo h)**. Sew back through all the beads in row 4, keeping your needle on top of the warps.

2 Reading each row from left to right, work rows 5–42 following the pattern. As the bead weaving area fills up, drop the back easement rod forward to release the tension, and rotate the beadwork forward to move unbeaded warps into the bead weaving area **(photo i)**. Replace the easement rod. As the beadwork progresses around the loom, you will need to use thinner easement rods to maintain tension.

Row 5: A, 2I, H, 2I, G, 3B, I, 2H, I, G, A
Row 6: A, 3I, G, 5B, 2I, H, I, G, A
Row 7: A, I, G, 2B, G, B, F, E, 2B, I, 2H, I, A
Row 8: A, 5B, F, 2E, 3B, 3I, A
Row 9: A, 2B, F, B, F, 2E, B, G, 4B, I, A
Row 10: A, G, B, 2F, 2E, 4B, G, 3B, A
Row 11: A, 2B, 3F, 9B, A
Row 12: A, B, E, F, E, F, E, 2B, G, 4B, G, A
Row 13: A, B, E, F, 2E, F, E, 4B, G, 2B, A
Row 14: A, B, E, F, 2E, F, 2E, 6B, A
Row 15: A, D, 2E, F, 2E, F, 2E, 4B, G, A
Row 16: A, B, C, 2E, 3F, 2E, F, 2E, 2B, A
Row 17: A, B, D, 2F, 4E, J, 2E, 3B, A
Row 18: A, 2I, B, 3F, E, 3J, 2B, G, B, A

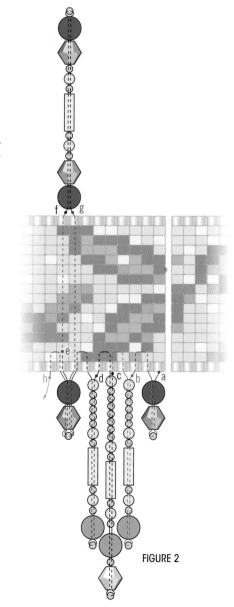

FIGURE 2

154

Row 19: A, H, 2I, 5B, C, 4B, I, A
Row 20: A, E, H, 2I, G, 6B, 3I, A
Row 21: A, 2I, H, 2I, G, B, G, B, 2I, E, H, I, A
Row 22: A, B, E, G, H, I, G, B, E, 3I, H, I, G, A
Row 23: A, 3B, 3I, G, B, I, E, G, 2I, G, A
Row 24: A, I, 4B, I, 2B, D, 2I, G, 2B, A
Row 25: A, E, I, G, B, G, 2B, D, G, 4B, G, A
Row 26: A, H, I, G, 3B, D, G, 3B, C, 2B, A
Row 27: A, I, H, I, G, B, D, 2F, 2E, 3J, B, A
Row 28: A, I, H, I, G, C, 2F, 4E, J, 2E, A
Row 29: A, B, 2I, D, F, 2E, 3F, 2E, 2F, E
Row 30: A, 2B, D, F, 2E, F, 2E, F, 2E, 2B, A
Row 31: A, B, D, B, F, E, F, 2E, F, E, 3B, G, A
Row 32: A, D, G, B, F, E, F, E, F, E, 5B, A
Row 33: A, E, G, B, F, E, F, E, F, 3B, G, 2B, A
Row 34: A, G, 2B, F, E, F, E, 6B, I, A
Row 35: A, 2B, F, 2E, F, E, B, G, 2B, 3I, A
Row 36: A, B, 2F, E, B, F, 3B, 2I, H, I, G, A
Row 37: A, 2F, E, 4B, 3I, 2H, E, G, A
Row 38: A, F, E, B, G, 3B, 2I, 2H, I, G, B, A
Row 39: A, E, 4B, G, B, E, G, H, 2I, G, B, A
Row 40: A, B, G, 4B, G, B, D, 2I, 2B, G, A
Row 41: A, 6B, E, D, G, 2B, G, 2B, A
Row 42: A, 3B, E, 3I, D, 2B, E, 3B, A

3 Repeat rows 1–42 twice for a total of six cardinals. It's OK if there is a small gap left between the first and last row when you're done. Don't tie off the working thread yet. Remove the beadwork from the loom, and allow the band to rest for about an hour. Most (if not all) of the gap will disappear as the thread returns to its starting length. If a small gap remains, gently massage the beads to distribute them evenly along the warps until the gap is gone. End the threads.

Fringe

1 Add a comfortable length of thread to the band, and exit the bottom A in row 1. String a red dangle: Pick up a color K 4 mm round bead, a color M 4 mm bicone crystal, and a 15º. Skip the 15º, sew back through the two new beads and the two bottom beads in the next row, and continue through the two adjacent bottom beads **(figure 2, a–b)**.
2 Add a short dangle: Pick up an 11º, five 15ºs, an 11º, a 15º, a bugle bead, a 15º, an 11º, a 15º, a color L 4 mm round bead, and a 15º. Skip the last 15º, sew back through all the beads just strung and the two bottom beads in the next row, and sew through the bottom two beads in the following row **(b–c)**.
3 Add a long dangle: Pick up an 11º,

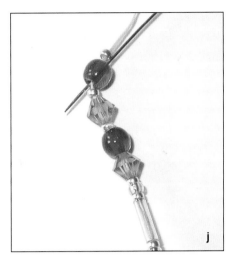

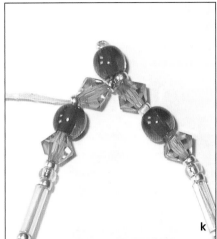

seven 15ºs, an 11º, a 15º, a bugle bead, a 15º, an 11º, a 15º, a color L 4 mm round bead, a 15º, a color N 4 mm bicone crystal, and a 15º. Skip the last 15º, sew back through all the beads just strung and the two bottom beads in the same row your thread exited to start this fringe, and sew through the bottom two beads in the next row **(c–d)**.
4 Add another short dangle and another red dangle **(d–e)**, but don't sew through the next two beads after adding the red dangle. Instead, continue up through all the remaining beads in the row **(e–f)**.
5 Add an upper arm: Pick up a K, an M, a 15º, an 11º, a 15º, a bugle, a 15º, an 11º, a 15º, an M, a K, and a 15º. Skip the last 15º, and sew back through all the beads just strung **(f–g)**. Sew down through the previous row in the band and the corresponding red dangle at the bottom of the band. Skip the bottom 15º, sew back through the red dangle and the two bottom beads in the next row, and continue through the two bottom beads in the following row **(g–h)**.
6 Working as in steps 1–4, add a short dangle, a long dangle, a short dangle, and a red dangle. Do not add an upper arm above this red dangle.

7 Ending and adding thread as needed, work as in steps 1–6 around the band, working in a repeating pattern of short dangle, long dangle, short dangle, red dangle, and adding an upper arm above every other red dangle. You should have a total of nine upper arms. End the thread.

Finishing

1 Add a new thread in the beadwork, and sew through an upper arm, exiting the end 15º.
2 Pick up an M, a 15º, a K, and a 15º. Skip the last 15º, and sew back through the K to create a picot **(photo j)**. Pick up a 15º and an M, and sew through the 15º at the tip of the next arm **(photo k)**. Repeat this stitch eight times to complete the round. Step up through the first M, 15º, K, and 15º added at the start of this step.
3 Place the beadwork on the ornament ball. Pick up six 15ºs, and sew through the 15º at the tip of the next picot **(photo l)**. Repeat this stitch eight times to complete the round. Retrace the thread path through all the 15ºs in the top ring, and end the thread. ●

BEAD WEAVING / | BRICK STITCH

Woodland

Combine a simple collection of crescent beads, round beads, and seed

Earrings

How to pick up the crescent beads: With the tips of the crescent facing down, pick up the bead through the right hole (RH).

1 On 1 yd. (.9 m) of thread, pick up a repeating pattern of a crescent bead (RH) and a color A 15º seed bead six times, and tie the beads into a ring with a square knot, leaving an 8-in. (20 cm) tail. Sew through the first crescent and A **(figure 1)**. The crescents naturally want to from a melon shape; use your fingers to gently fan the beads flat so the crescents lie with their tips facing down.

2 Pick up a 4 mm round bead and an A, sew back through the 4 mm round, and continue through the A in the ring your thread is exiting, going in the same direction **(figure 2, a–b)**. Sew through the next crescent and A **(b–c)**. Repeat these two stitches five times to complete the round, and continue through the first 4 mm round and A added at the start of this step **(c–d)**

3 Pick up three As, and sew through the A your thread is exiting, going in the same direction to form a picot **(figure 3, a–b)**. Pick up two color B 15º seed beads, and sew through the open hole of the next crescent **(b–c)**. Pick up two Bs, and sew

through the A above the next 4 mm round **(c–d)**. Repeat these stitches five times to complete the round, and continue through the

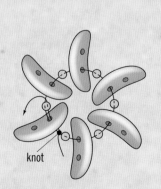

FIGURE 1

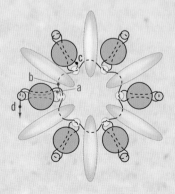

FIGURE 2

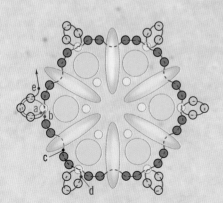

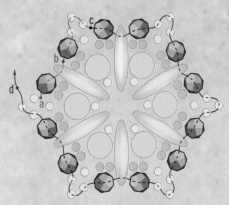

MATERIALS

teal earrings

2⅛ x 1¼ in. (5.4 x 3.2 cm)

- **2** 12 x 16 mm pear drop beads (Czech, milky peridot celsian)
- **12** 3 x 10 mm CzechMates two-hole crescent beads (oxidized bronze clay)
- **12** 4 mm round beads (Czech, sueded gold emerald)
- **2** 4 mm pearls (Swarovski, cream rose)
- **24** 2 mm fire-polished beads (iris purple)
- **15°** seed beads
  - **1 g** color A (Toho 711, nickel)
  - **1 g** color B (Toho 82, metallic nebula)
  - **1 g** color C (Miyuki 4217, Duracoat seafoam)
- **1** pair of earring findings
- Fireline, 6 lb. test
- beading needles, #12

Basics, p. 13

- ending and adding thread
- square knot

earrings

beads to create a playful pair of earrings.

designed by **Lisa Kan**

first three As added in this step **(d–e)**.

4 Pick up a 2 mm fire-polished bead, and sew through the outer hole of the next crescent, positioning it slightly behind the two adjacent Bs **(figure 4, a–b)**. Pick up a 2 mm, position it slightly behind the two adjacent Bs, and sew through the three As in the following picot **(b–c)**. Repeat these two stitches five times to complete the round,

FIGURE 3

FIGURE 4

FIGURE 5

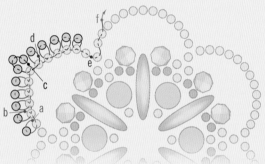

FIGURE 6

FIGURE 7

Legend / Key:

- 3 x 10 mm crescent bead
- – top view
- 15º seed bead, color A
- 4 mm round Czech bead
- 15º seed bead, color B
- 2 mm fire-polished bead
- 15º seed bead, color C
- 12 x 16 mm pear bead
- 4 mm pearl

except on the last stitch sew through only the first two As in the picot **(c–d)**.

5 Pick up 13 As, and sew through the center A of the next picot to form a loop **(figure 5, a–b)**. Repeat this stitch five times to complete the round, and step up through the first two As added in this round **(b–c)**.

6 Work in square stitch to embellish the loop: Pick up a color C 15º seed bead, and sew through the A your thread is exiting, going in the same direction, and the following A in the loop **(figure 6, a–b)**. Repeat this stitch four times **(b–c)**.

7 Pick up three Cs, and sew through the A your thread is exiting, going in the same direction, and the following A in the loop to form a picot

(c–d). Repeat step 6 to complete the loop **(d–e)**, and sew through the center A in the adjacent picot and the next two As in the following loop **(e–f)**.

8 Repeat steps 6–7 five times to complete the round, except sew through only the first A in the following loop after the last stitch to exit **figure 7, point a**.

9 To stabilize the Cs just added, sew through the beadwork as shown to exit the center A in the picot two loops over **(figure 7, a–b)**.

10 Pick up three As, the loop of an ear wire, and three As, and sew through the C your thread is exiting, going in the same direction. Retrace the thread path through the ear wire connection **(b–c)**.

11 Sew through the beadwork as shown to exit the center A in the picot directly opposite **(c–d)**

12 Repeat step 10 once, except pick up a pear drop bead instead of an ear wire **(d–e)**. Sew through the beadwork as shown to stabilize the remaing Cs **(e–f)**. End the working thread.

13 Using the tail, pick up a 4 mm pearl, and sew through the A directly opposite. Continue back through the pearl and the A your thread exited at the start of this step, going in the same direction **(g–h)**. Retrace the thread path, and end the tail.

14 Repeat steps 1–13 to make another earring. ●

materials

blue/purple adjustable bangle inside circumference 2–2¼ in. (5–5.7 cm)

- **2** 14 mm rivolis (Swarovski, satin chrysolite)
- **67** 2 mm pearls (Czech, matte grape pearl)
- **4 g** 11º cylinder beads (Miyuki Delica DB0027, metallic teal iris)
- 11º seed beads
  - **2 g** color A (Miyuki 571, silver-lined mint green)
  - **2 g** color C (Toho 2113, silver-lined milky pomegranate)
- 15º seed beads
  - **2 g** color B (Toho 2113, silver-lined milky pomegranate)
  - **2 g** color D (Miyuki 4217, Duracoat galvanized seafoam)
- **9–12 in. (23–30 cm)** 12-gauge aluminum wire
- Fireline, 6 lb. test
- beading needles, #12
- **1** pair of wire cutters

basics, p. 13

- right-angle weave: flat strip, adding rows, forming a strip into a ring
- peyote stitch: tubular
- ending and adding thread
- square knot

Combine colorful seed beads and pretty rivolis to create a bangle with adorable flowers that burst from each end.

BANGLE

1) On a comfortable length of thread, pick up four color A 11º seed beads, and sew through the beads again to form a ring, leaving a 6-in. (15 cm) tail. Continue through the first three As added (**figure 1, a–b**). This forms the first right-angle weave (RAW) stitch.

2) Working in (RAW), pick up three As, and sew through the A your thread exited at the start of this step. Continue through the first two As just added (**b–c**), and tighten. Work one more RAW stitch to form the first row (**c–d**), and then sew through the bottom edge bead of the last stitch (**d–e**) to get into position to start row 2.

3) Continue using As to work a strip of RAW that is three stitches wide until the beadwork is 3 in. (7.6 cm) longer than your actual wrist size. End and add thread as needed. Our strip is 8 in. (20 cm).

4) To form the strip into a tube, fold the strip lengthwise. Pick up an A, and sew through the corresponding A on the opposite edge (**figure 2, a–b**). Pick up an A, sew through the A your thread exited at the start of this step, going in the same direction, and continue through the first A added and the next A on the opposite edge (**b–c**).

5) Pick up an A, and sew through the corresponding A on the opposite edge (**c–d**). Continue through the A added in the previous stitch,

the A your thread exited at the start of this step, the A just added, and the following A on the opposite edge (**d–e**). Repeat this stitch to complete the connection.

6) Cut a piece of aluminum wire 1 in. (2.5 cm) longer than the tube, and center it inside the beadwork. Form the tube into an oval with the ends overlapping by about 1 in. (2.5 cm), and trim each end flush.

7) Gently spread the ends apart. With the working thread, sew through the four end As to enclose the wire inside the tube, retrace the thread path twice, exiting an end A in the inner curve of the band.

8) Sew through the adjacent A in the end stitch (**figure 3, a–b**). Only the top view of the inner curve is shown for clarity in **figure 3**. Embellish the inner curve of the band: Pick up a color B 15º seed bead, and sew through the next A (**b–c**). Repeat this last stitch for the remainder of the row (**c–d**).

9) Repeat steps 7–8 to close up this end and embellish the opposite edge of the same row (**d–e**). Sew through the next end A (**e–f**).

10) Work as in steps 8–9 using color C 11º seed beads to embellish the outside curve of the bangle. End the threads, and set the bangle aside.

FLOWERS
Bezel

1) On a comfortable length of thread, pick up 36 cylinder beads.

Leaving a 6-in. (15 cm) tail, tie the beads into a ring with a square knot, and sew through first few beads again. These beads will shift to form the first two rounds as the next round is added.

2) Work a round of peyote stitch using cylinders, and step up through the first cylinder added (**figure 4, a–b**).

3) Work two rounds using color D 15º seed beads, stepping up at the end of each round (**b–c**). Pull snug so the beadwork begins to cup.

4) Sew through the beadwork to exit a cylinder in the first round. Place a rivoli faceup into the beadwork. Stepping up at the end of each round, work a round using Ds

⬤	11º seed bead, color A
⬤	15º seed bead, color B
⬤	11º seed bead, color C
⬤	15º seed bead, color D
⬜	11º cylinder bead

14 mm rivoli

-back surface

⬤	2 mm pearl

FIGURE 1

FIGURE 2

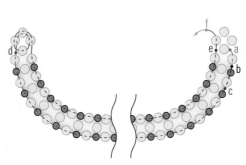

FIGURE 3

FIGURE 4

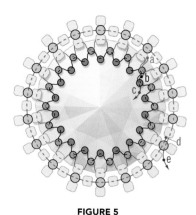

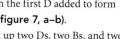

FIGURE 5

FIGURE 6

FIGURE 7

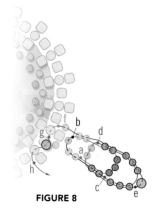

FIGURE 8

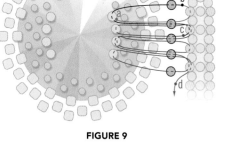

FIGURE 9

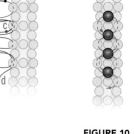

FIGURE 10

(figure 5, a–b), and another round using Bs **(b–c)**.

5) Sew through the beadwork to exit a cylinder in the middle round of cylinder beads **(point d)**. Work a round of stitch-in-the-ditch using As, stepping up at the end of the round **(d–e)**. These As will sit on top of the beadwork.

6) With the tail, sew through the beadwork to exit a 15º in the inner round on the back of the rivoli. Use As to work four stitches **(figure 6, a–b)**. Sew through the next five Ds in the previous round without adding any beads **(b–c)**. Repeat these stitches **(c–d)** to form two sets of connector beads on the back surface of the bezel. End the tail.

Petals

1) With the working thread of the bezel exiting an A in the last round added, pick up a D, a B, and a D, and sew through the same A, going in the same direction, and continue

through the first D added to form a loop **(figure 7, a–b)**.

2) Pick up two Ds, two Bs, and two Ds, skip the B in the first loop, and sew through the following D to form a second loop **(b–c)**. Continue through the adjacent A, the next D in the first loop and the first two Ds added in the second loop **(c–d)**.

3) Pick up two Ds, three Bs, and two Ds, skip the two Bs in the second loop, and sew through the following two Ds to form a third loop **(figure 8, a–b)**. Continue through the next B in the first loop, the following two Ds in the second loop, and the first two Ds added in the new loop **(b–c)**.

4) Pick up six Ds, skip the three Bs in the previous loop, and sew through the following two Ds to form a fourth loop **(c–d)**. Continue through the two Bs in the second loop, the two Ds in the previous loop, and the first three Ds just added **(d–e)**.

5) Pick up a C, and sew through the next eight Ds on the outer edge of the petal as shown **(e–f)**. Continue through the adjacent A in the bezel **(f–g)**. Pick up a C, and sew through the next A in the bezel **(g–h)**.

6) Work as in steps 1–5 17 times to make a total of 18 petals, and then sew through the ring of As and Cs at the base of the petals to reinforce the connection and stiffen the petals. Do not end the working thread.

7) Work as in steps 1–6 to make a second flower.

Connection

1) With the working thread of a flower, sew through the beadwork to exit an end A connector bead on the back of the bezel, with the needle facing toward the next connector bead **(figure 9, point a)**.

2) Center the flower on one end of the bangle. The flower will be attached to the bangle using a RAW thread path. With the working thread of the flower, pick up a C, and sew through the corresponding

end C on the outside curve of the bangle **(figure 9, a–b)**. Pick up a C, sew through the C your thread exited at the start of this step, going in the same direction, and continue through the first C added, and the next C on the bangle **(b–c)**.

3) Using Cs, work three more RAW stitches to connect the end of the bangle to the connector beads on the back of the bezel **(c–d)**.

4) Work as in steps 1–3 to attach the remaining flower to the opposite end of the bangle, but don't end the working thread.

5) Embellish the center row of the outer curve of the bangle: Sew through the bangle to exit an edge C along the outer curve of the bangle two stitches away from the base of the attached flower. Using the Cs in each stitch as the base, work a RAW thread path to attach 2 mm pearls between the rows of Cs **(figure 10)**. Only the top view of the outer curve of the bangle is shown in the figure for clarity. The pearls will sit on top of the beadwork. End the thread. **B&B**

ENDLESS DIAMOND BANGLES

designed by Regina Payne

DIFFICULTY ●●●○○

peyote / crossweave

Peyote diamonds form a base that supports a continuous pattern of crystal and pearl clusters.

base

1) On a comfortable length of thread, pick up a repeating pattern of five color A 11° cylinder beads and a color B 11° cylinder bead 26 times for a 3-in. (7.6 cm) diameter bangle.

T I P Test the fit to see if the strand will fit around the widest part of your hand. Adjust the number of repeats by an even number to adjust the size.

Center the beads on the thread, and wrap the tail on a thread bobbin or piece of cardboard. These beads will shift to form rows 1 and 2 as the next row is added. End and add thread throughout the beadwork as needed.

2) Work row 3 in flat even-count peyote stitch, following a repeating pattern of one stitch using a B and two stitches using As **(figure 1, a–b)**. Keep your tension even, and make sure the beadwork is not twisted.

3) Join the ends together by sewing through the first B added in row 3 on the opposite end as shown **(b–c)**, making sure the beadwork is not twisted. Unwind the tail, and attach a needle. With the tail thread, repeat the join, but sew through the B adjacent to the one your working thread is exiting.

4) With each needle, work in tubular peyote stitch as follows, and step up at the end of each round:

Rounds 4 and 5: Work three stitches using a B, an A, and a B. Repeat these stitches to complete the round **(figure 2, a–b and aa–bb)**.

Rounds 6 and 7: Work two stitches using one B per stitch and one using a color C 11° cylinder bead. Repeat these stitches to complete the round **(b–c and bb–cc)**.

Rounds 8 and 9: Work one stitch using a B and two using Cs. Repeat these stitches to complete the round **(c–d and cc–dd)**.

materials
purple bangle 3-in. (7.6 cm) diameter

- **52** 4 mm crystal pearls (Swarovski, cream)
- **52** 4 mm crystal bicones (Swarovski, tanzanite)
- **13** 3 mm crystal bicones (Swarovski, purple velvet)
- **26** 2 mm glass pearls (white)
- 11° cylinder beads
  - **2 g** color A (Miyuki Delica DB0284, sparkle purple-lined aqua luster)
  - **3 g** color B (Miyuki Delica DB0042, silver-lined gold)
  - **2 g** color C (Miyuki Delica DB0221, gilt-lined white opal)
- **2 g** 15° seed beads (Toho PF557, galvanized starlight)
- Fireline, 8 or 6 lb. test
- beading needles, #11 or #12
- thread bobbin or piece of cardboard

basics, p. 13
- peyote stitch: flat even count, forming a strip into a ring, tubular
- ending and adding thread

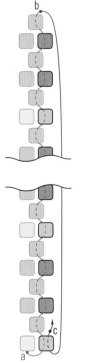

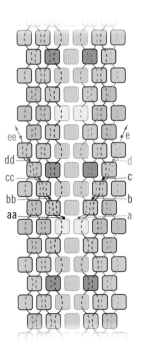

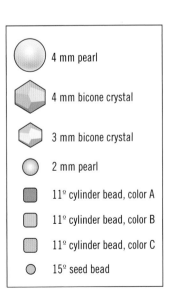

4 mm pearl

4 mm bicone crystal

3 mm bicone crystal

2 mm pearl

11° cylinder bead, color A

11° cylinder bead, color B

11° cylinder bead, color C

15° seed bead

FIGURE 1

FIGURE 2

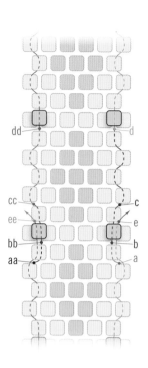

FIGURE 3

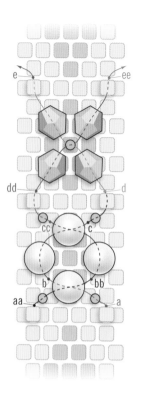

FIGURE 4

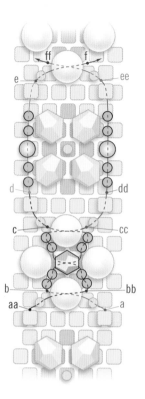

FIGURE 5

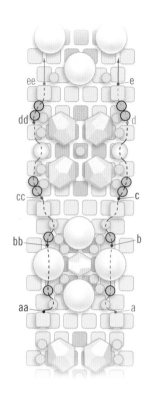

FIGURE 6

Rounds 10 and 11: Work three stitches using a B, a C, and a B. Repeat these stitches to complete the round (**d–e and dd–ee**), and sew through the next C (**figure 3, a–b and aa–bb**).

5) With each needle, pick up a B, skip the next C, and sew through the following C so the B sits on top of the base (**b–c and bb–cc**). Continue through the next four beads (**c–d and cc–dd**). Repeat these stitches to complete the round, and sew through the first raised B added in this round (**d–e and dd–ee**).

Embellishment

1) With one needle, pick up a 15º seed bead and a 4 mm pearl (**figure 4, a–b**). With the other needle, pick up a 15º, and cross through the 4 mm pearl just added (**aa–bb**). With one needle, pick up two 4 mm pearls (**b–c**). With the other needle, pick up a 4 mm pearl, and cross through the last 4 mm pearl added (**bb–cc**). With each needle, pick up a 15º, and sew through the next raised B added on the base (**c–d and cc–dd**).

2) With one needle, pick up a 4 mm bicone crystal, a 15º, and a 4 mm crystal, cross to the other side of the base, and sew through the next raised B (**d–e**). With the other needle, pick up 4 mm crystal, sew through the center 15º added in the previous stitch, pick up a 4 mm crystal, and sew through the following raised B on the opposite side of the base (**dd–ee**).

3) Repeat steps 1–2 for the remainder of the base. With each thread, sew through the next 15º, and cross through the first 4 mm pearl

(figure 5, a–b and aa–bb).

4) With one needle, pick up two 15°s, a 3 mm bicone crystal, and two 15°s, cross the pearl embellishment diagonally, and sew through the opposite 4 mm pearl, going in the same direction **(b–c)**. With the other needle, pick up two 15°s, sew through the 3 mm crystal, pick up two 15°s, and cross through the opposite 4 mm pearl, going in the same direction **(bb–cc)**. With each needle, sew through the next 15° and raised B **(c–d and cc–dd)**.

5) With each needle, pick up two 15°s, a 2 mm pearl, and two 15°s, skip the next two 4 mm crystals, and sew through the following raised B **(d–e and dd–ee)**. With each needle, sew through the next 15°, and cross through the 4 mm pearl **(e–f and ee–ff)**.

6) Repeat steps 4–5 for the remainder of the base, but after the last stitch, do not sew through the next 15° and pearl.

7) With each needle, sew through the adjacent 15°, pick up a 15°, and sew through the next edge 4 mm pearl **(figure 6, a–b and aa–bb)**. Pick

up a 15°, and sew through the following 15° and raised B **(b–c and bb–cc)**.

8) With each needle, pick up two 15°s, skip the next C in the base, and sew through the following B on the outside edge of the base, the 2 mm pearl in the embellishment, and the next B on the outside edge of the base **(c–d and cc–dd)**. Pick up two 15°s, and sew through the following raised B **(d–e and dd–ee)**.

9) Repeat steps 7–8 for the remainder of the base using an even tension, and end the threads. **B&B**

LOTUS BLOSSOM PENDANT

designed by **Lisa Kan**

DIFFICULTY ●●●●○

tubular peyote / CRAW / square stitch

materials
turquoise pendant 3 in. (7.6 cm)

- **1** 14 mm crystal rivoli (Swarovski, crystal purple haze)
- **27** 3 x 6 mm CzechMates two-hole crescent beads (matte metallic bronze iris)
- **9** 2 mm fire-polished beads (transparent pink topaz luster)
- 11º seed beads
  - **15 g** color A (Toho 2634F, semi-glazed rainbow turquoise)
  - **1 g** color D (Toho 221, bronze)
  - **1 g** color E (Toho 85, purple iris)
- 15º seed beads
  - **1 g** color B (Toho 221, bronze)
  - **1 g** color C (Toho 85, purple iris)
  - **1 g** color F (Toho 2634F, semi-glazed rainbow turquoise)
- **1 g** 15º Charlotte beads (24k gold AB)
- Fireline, 6 lb. test
- beading needles, #12

Kits for all colors available at ariadesignstudio.com

basics, p. 13
- cubic right-angle weave
- peyote stitch: tubular
- ending and adding thread
- square stitch

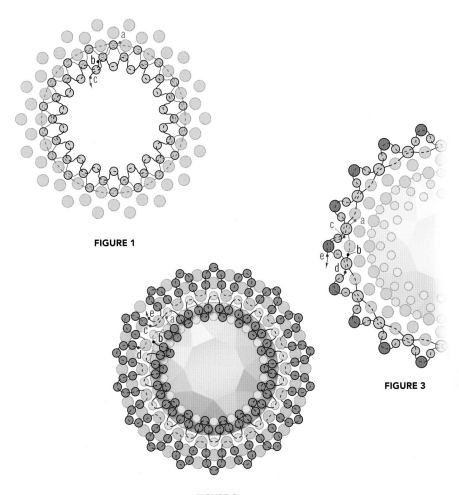

FIGURE 1

FIGURE 2

FIGURE 3

Embrace summer with this stunning flower pendant with cupped seed bead petals.

BEZEL

How to pick up the crescent beads: With the tips of the crescent pointing toward you on your bead mat, pick up the crescent through the left hole (LH) or the right hole (RH).

1) On comfortable length of thread, work a cubic right-angle weave unit using 12 color A 11º seed beads, and leaving a 6-in. (15 cm) tail. Continue to work CRAW units to form a tube of 17 units. End and add thread throughout the beadwork as needed.

2) Using As, connect the ends of the CRAW tube to form a ring with a total of 18 CRAW units, making sure the tube is not twisted.

3) Sew through the beadwork to exit an inside-edge A with the needle pointing in a counter-clockwise direction **(figure 1, point a)**. For clarity, only one side of the CRAW base is shown in the following figures.

4) Work in tubular peyote stitch as follows, stepping up at the end of each round:

Round 1–2: Work two rounds using color B 15º seed beads, **(a–b)**.

Round 3: Work a round using 15º Charlottes **(b–c)**.

5) Sew through the beadwork to exit the corresponding A on the opposite inside edge of the CRAW base. Flip the beadwork over so the rows of peyote you just completed are on the bottom, and insert the rivoli faceup into the beadwork. Repeat step 4 to work the front of the bezel, and continue through the beadwork to exit a B in round 1 on the front of the bezel **(figure 2, point a)**. End the tail thread.

6) Pick up three Cs, skip the next inside edge A, and sew through the next B in the same round **(a–b)**. Repeat this stitch 17 times to complete the round, and sew through the following A on the top inside edge of the CRAW bezel **(b–c)**.

7) Pick up five Cs, and sew through the next A on the same inside edge **(c–d)**. Repeat this stitch 17 times to complete the round **(d–e)**. Sew through the beadwork to exit an A on the top outside edge of the CRAW bezel **(figure 3, point a)**. For clarity, the top bezel embellishment is not shown in the figure.

8) Pick up a color D 11º seed bead, and sew through the next A on the top outside edge **(a–b)**. Repeat this stitch 17 times to complete the round, and step up through the first D added **(b–c)**.

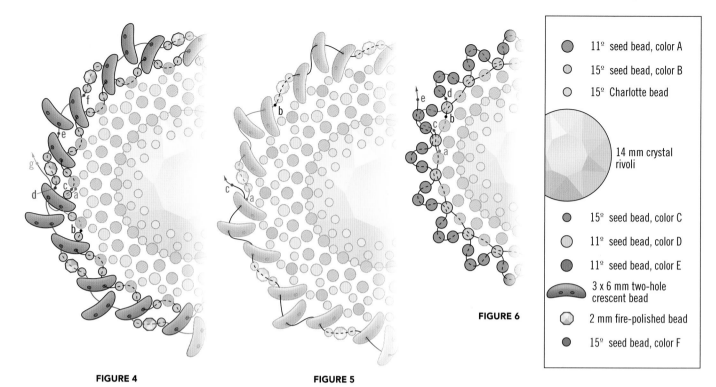

FIGURE 4

FIGURE 5

FIGURE 6

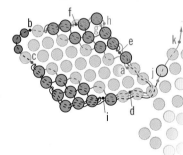

FIGURE 7

FIGURE 8

9) Pick up a B, a color E 11º seed bead, and a B, and sew through the next D to form a picot (**c–d**). Repeat this stitch 17 times to complete the round, and step up through the first B and E added (**d–e**).

10) Pick up B, a crescent bead (RH), and a B, and sew through the center E in the next picot (**figure 4, a–b**). Repeat this stitch 17 times to complete the round (**b–c**), retrace the thread path (not shown in the figure for clarity), sew through the first B and crescent added, and continue through the open hole of the same crescent (**c–d**). The crescents should curve inward toward the bezel with the open hole on top.

11) Pick up B, a 2 mm fire-polished bead, and a B, and sew through the open hole of the next crescent (**d–e**). Pick up a crescent (LH), and sew through the open hole of the following crescent (**e–f**). Repeat these stitches eight times to complete the round (**f–g**). The tips of the crescents just added should face up and the open hole should be on the outside.

12) Sew through the next B, 2 mm, B, adjacent top hole of the next crescent, open outside hole of the following crescent, and adjacent top hole of the next crescent (**figure 5,**

a–b). Repeat this stitch eight times to complete the round (**b–c**), and end the thread.

SMALL PETAL

1) Flip the beadwork over so the bottom of the bezel is facing up, and add a comfortable length of thread, exiting an A in the bottom outer edge of the CRAW bezel going clockwise (**figure 6, point a**).

2) Pick up a D, and sew through the next A on the bottom outside edge (**a–b**). Repeat this stitch 17 times to complete the round, and step up through the first D added (**b–c**).

3) Pick up three As, and sew through the next D to form a bezel picot (**c–d**). Repeat this stitch 17 times to complete the round, and sew through the first two As added (**d–e**).

4) Pick up 11 As, skip the last three beads added to form a picot, and sew back through the next A (**figure 7, a–b**). Working in peyote stitch, work four stitches using As, sewing through the center A in the bezel picot for the last stitch (**b–c**). Step up through the first A added in this step (**c–d**).

5) Work four peyote stitches with

As (**d–e**). Pick up an A, and sew through the center A of the end picot (**e–f**). Work five more stitches using As, sewing through the center A in the bezel picot after the last stitch, and step up through the first A added in this step (**f–g**).

6) Work four peyote stitches with As (**figure 8, a–b**). Pick up three color F 15º seed beads, skip the next end A, and sew through the following end A (**b–c**). Work four more stitches using As (**c–d**), and sew through the next five beads as shown to step up through the first A added (**d–e**).

7) Work three stitches using As, sew under the thread bridge between the next two As, and sew back through the A your thread just exited and the last A added (**e–f**). Tighten the thread slightly so the beadwork begins to cup toward the front of the bezel.

TIP When stitching the small and large petals, use an even tension so beadwork only cups slightly and the edges are not over-curled.

8) Work two stitches using As, sew under the thread bridge between the next two As, and sew back through

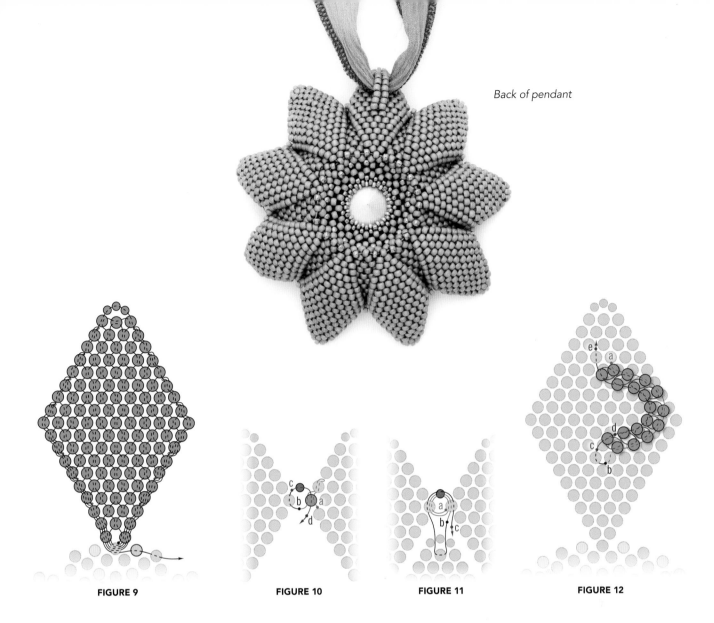

Back of pendant

FIGURE 9

FIGURE 10

FIGURE 11

FIGURE 12

the A your thread just exited and the last A added **(f–g)**.

9) Work one stitch using an A, sew under the thread bridge between the next two As, and sew back through the A your thread just exited and the last A added **(g–h)**. Continue through the next nine beads as shown to exit the corresponding A on other side of the petal **(h–i)**.

10) Work as in steps 7–9 to complete this side of the petal, and sew through the beadwork to exit the A in the bezel picot at the base of this petal **(i–j)**. Pick up a D, and sew through the center A in the next bezel picot **(j–k)**.

LARGE PETAL

Work as in "Small petal," but start with 19 As instead of 11 and work

additional rows on each side to complete the decreases **(figure 9)**. For clarity, the small petal is not shown in the figure.

ADDITIONAL PETALS

1) Work another small petal, but in step 9 on the second side, exit the last A added (edge point) after securing it **(figure 10, a–b)**. Position the small petals in front of the large petal. The large petal is not shown in the figure for clarity.

2) Sew through the corresponding edge point on the previous small petal **(b–c)**, pick up an F, and sew through the A your thread exited at the start of this step, going in the same direction **(c–d)**. Retrace the thread path several times, sew through the beadwork to exit the center A in the bezel picot, add the

D as before, and continue through the next bezel picot.

3) Work another large petal, but exit the last A added (edge point) on the second side after securing it. Make sure the large petals are positioned behind the small petals, and connect the two large petals in the same way as the small petals, retracing the thread path twice **(figure 11, a–b)**. Sew through the end center A on the adjacent small petal, and continue through the side A on the first large petal, the new F, and the side A on the second large petal **(b–c)**. Retrace this connection.

4) Sew through the beadwork to exit the center A in this bezel picot, pick up a D, and sew through the center A in the next bezel picot.

5) Continue adding and joining petals as before to complete the

round, and connect the last small and large petals to the first small and large petals as before.

BAIL

1) Sew through the beadwork to exit at **figure 12, point a** on a large petal.

2) Pick up nine As, skip the next three As in the peyote row, and sew down through the next A **(a–b)**. Sew up through the adjacent bead **(b–c)**.

3) Working in square stitch, pick up an A, sew through the last A added in the loop, and continue through the new A **(c–d)**. Add eight more beads in square stitch, then sew through the A adjacent to the one the first loop of the bail is attached to **(d–e)**. Retrace the thread path of the bail, and end the thread. **B&B**

SASSY SCALLOPED BRACELET

**designed by
Debora Hodoyer**

DIFFICULTY ●●●○○

right-angle weave /
bead weaving

materials
pink bracelet 7¼ x 1⅜ in. (18.4 x 3.5 cm)

- **16** 5 x 10 mm Arcos par Puca beads (light rose ceramic look)
- **7 g** 2.5 x 5 mm SuperDuo beads (chalk lilac luster)
- **14** 4 mm fire-polished beads (matte metallic Aztec gold)
- **17** 4 mm round glass beads (opaque topaz pink luster)
- **6 g** 3.8 mm O-beads (matte metallic brass gold)
- **30** 2.5 x 3 mm Minos par Puca beads (light rose ceramic look)
- **1 g** 11º seed beads (Toho PF565, permanent finish galvanized blue slate)
- **1 g** 15º seed beads (Toho 617, matte dark olive)
- **6** 6 mm jump rings (gold)
- **1** 30 x 20 mm flower toggle clasp (beadcorp.com)
- beading thread, size D, or Fireline, 6 lb. test
- beading needles, #12
- **2** pairs of chainnose, flatnose, and/or bentnose pliers

basics, p. 13
- right-angle weave: flat strip
- ending and adding thread
- opening and closing loops and jump rings

Use Arcos beads to create a fresh and playful edging on this stylish bracelet.

How to pick up the Arcos beads: Place the Arcos on your bead mat with the tips facing you, and sew through the right or left side hole as indicated, entering from the inside edge or the outside edge. The center holes will not be used for this pattern.

Bracelet

1) On a comfortable length of thread, pick up a repeating pattern of two O-beads, two SuperDuo beads, two O-beads, and a 4 mm round bead twice. Leaving a 6-in. (15 cm) tail, sew through all the beads again (not shown in the figure for clarity) to form a ring, and continue through the first seven beads to exit a 4 mm round (**figure 1, a–b**). End and add thread throughout the project as needed.

2) Working in right-angle weave, pick up two O-beads, two SuperDuos, two O-beads, a 4 mm round, two O-beads, two SuperDuos, and two O-beads, and sew through the 4 mm round your thread exited at the start of this step (**b–c**). Continue through the next seven beads to exit the newly added 4 mm round (**c–d**). Repeat this stitch 14 times using tight tension for a total of 17 4 mm round beads. This will make a 7¼-in. (18.4 cm) bracelet, including about 2 in. (5 cm) for the clasp and jump rings.

Do not sew through the end 4 mm bead in the last stitch (**figure 2, point a**).

N O T E If using a smaller toggle clasp, you may need to add more right-angle weave (RAW) units to achieve the same length bracelet but always make sure you end with an odd number of 4 mm round beads in the initial row. Each RAW unit adds ⅜ in. (1 cm) to the length.

3) Pick up an 11º seed bead, eight 15º seed beads, and an 11º, skip the next 4 mm round, and sew through the following two O-beads to add a clasp loop (**a–b**). Retrace the thread path through the last unit and the clasp loop, and sew through the next two O-beads and the open hole of the following SuperDuo (**b–c**).

4) Pick up an O-bead, a SuperDuo, and an O-bead, and sew through the open hole of the next SuperDuo (**c–d**). Pick up an 11º, and sew through the open hole of the following SuperDuo (**d–e**). Repeat these stitches for the remainder of the row, and work one more stitch to add a final O-bead, SuperDuo, and O-bead. Continue through the next two O-beads.

5) Repeat step 3 to add a clasp loop on this end, and then repeat step 4 on the other edge.

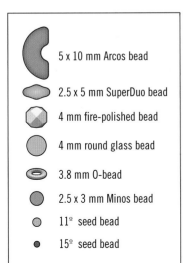

5 x 10 mm Arcos bead

2.5 x 5 mm SuperDuo bead

4 mm fire-polished bead

4 mm round glass bead

3.8 mm O-bead

2.5 x 3 mm Minos bead

11º seed bead

15º seed bead

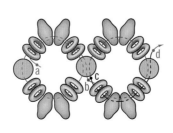

FIGURE 1

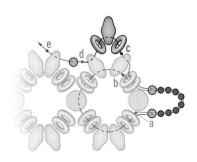

FIGURE 2

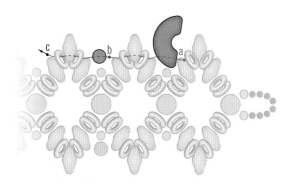

FIGURE 3

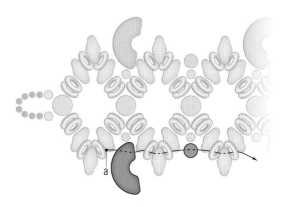

FIGURE 4

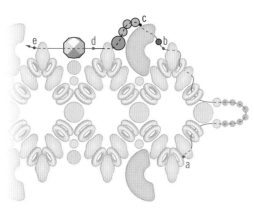

FIGURE 5

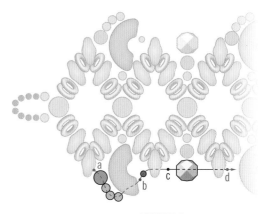

FIGURE 6

Sew through the clasp connection on the first end, and continue through the beadwork to exit the second O-bead added on the first edge (**figure 3, point a**).

6) Pick up an Arcos bead (left side, inside edge), and sew through the next O-bead, SuperDuo, and O-bead (**figure 3, a–b**). Pick up a Minos bead, and sew through the following O-bead, SuperDuo, and O-bead (**b–c**). Repeat these stitches to add a total of eight Arcos and seven Minos on this edge, and sew through the bead-work and clasp loop to exit the second O-bead on the opposite outside edge (**figure 4, point a**).

N O T E If the beads in the clasp loop are getting too filled with thread to sew through, skip them and sew through the 4 mm round instead.

7) Work as in step 6 to add Arcos and Minos along this edge, but pick up the Arcos through the right side, outside edge so they are a mirror image of the first row of Arcos (**figure 4**). Continue through the beadwork and clasp loop as shown to exit the open hole of the first SuperDuo on the opposite edge (**figure 5, a–b**).

8) Pick up a 15º, and sew through the open hole of the next Arcos (**b–c**). Pick up three 11ºs and a Minos, and sew through the open hole of the following SuperDuo (**c–d**). Pick up a 4 mm fire-polished bead, and sew through the open hole of the next SuperDuo (**d–e**). Repeat these stitches for the remainder of this edge, ending after adding the 11ºs and Minos on the last repeat. Sew through the beadwork to exit the end SuperDuo on the opposite edge (**figure 6, point a**).

9) Pick up a Minos and three 11ºs, and sew through the open hole of the next Arcos (**a–b**). Pick up a 15º, and sew through the open hole of the following SuperDuo (**b–c**). Pick up a 4 mm fire-polished bead, and sew through the open hole of the next SuperDuo (**c–d**). Repeat these stitches for the remainder of this edge, ending after adding the final 15º. End the threads.

10) Open two 6 mm jump rings, and attach them to an end clasp loop. Open one jump ring, and attach half of the clasp to the two jump rings. Repeat for the other clasp loop. **B&B**

materials
blue pendant 2 in. (5 cm)

- **1** 18 x 13 mm oval crystal stone (Swarovski 4120, light turquoise)
- **5 g** 2.5 x 5 mm SuperDuo beads (pastel emerald)
- Swarovski bicone crystals
  - **14** 4 mm (white opal AB)
  - **2** 3 mm (light turquoise AB)
- **2 g** 11º seed beads (Miyuki 4201, Duracoat galvanized silver)
- **1 g** 15º seed beads (Miyuki 4201, Duracoat galvanized silver)
- **1** lobster claw clasp
- **17 in. (43 cm)** small-link chain
- **1** 8 mm jump ring
- **3** 6 mm jump rings
- Fireline, 6 lb. test
- beading needles, #12
- **2** pairs of chainnose, flat-nose, and/or bentnose pliers
- wire cutters

basics, p. 13

- peyote stitch: tubular
- ending and adding thread
- opening and closing jump rings

FIGURE 1

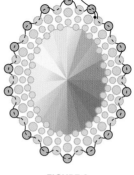

FIGURE 2

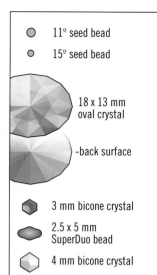

A clever combination of SuperDuos and seed beads creates a fluttering pendant that is sure to signify summer is on the way.

BUTTERFLY
Bezel

1) On a comfortable length of thread, pick up 36 11º seed beads, and sew through the first three beads again to form a ring, leaving a 6-in. (15 cm) tail. These beads will shift to form rounds 1 and 2 as the next round is added.

2) Work rounds of tubular peyote stitch for the front of the bezel as follows, and step up at the end of each round.

Round 3: Work a round using 11ºs.

Rounds 4–6: Work three rounds using 15º seed beads **(figure 1)**.

3) Sew through the beadwork to exit an 11º in round 1 of the outer ring. Place the oval stone facedown into the beadwork. Sewing through the 11ºs in round 1, repeat rounds 3–6 to work the back of the bezel. End and add thread as needed.

4) With the bezel still facedown, sew through the beadwork to exit an 11º in the center round of 11ºs on the edge (round 1). Using 11ºs, work a round of "stitch-in-the-ditch" to make a base for attaching the antennae and wings **(figure 2)**. Be sure to step up through the first 11º added in this round.

Antennae and wings

1) Position the bezel vertically on your work surface with the front of the bezel facing up. Sew through the beadwork, if needed, to exit the 11º that is left of the top center bead in the round just added **(figure 3, point a)**.

2) To form the antennae, pick up a 15º, nine 11ºs, a 3 mm bicone crystal, and a 15º. Sew back through the 3 mm and nine 11ºs. Pick up a 15º and sew through the next 11º in the previous round **(a–b)**. Repeat these stitches once more to form the other antenna **(b–c)**. Pick up an 11º and sew through the next 11º in the previous round **(c–d)**.

3) Pick up five SuperDuos, skip the next 11º in the previous round, and sew through the following 11º **(d–e)**. Using 11ºs, work two peyote stitches **(e–f)**. Repeat these three stitches three times, except on final repeat, work only one peyote stitch after adding the SuperDuos **(f–g)**.

N O T E Use medium tension when stitching the wings as a tight tension may make them pucker.

4) Sew through the beadwork to exit the 11º before the first set of SuperDuos **(figure 4, point a)**.

N O T E This is the perfect opportunity to retrace the thread path through the antennae, which will help stiffen them.

basics, p. 13

FIGURE 3

FIGURE 4

FIGURE 5

5) Pick up a 15º, and sew through the open hole of the next SuperDuo (**a–b**). Pick up a SuperDuo, and sew through the open hole of the following SuperDuo. Repeat this last stitch three times (**b–c**). Pick up a 15º, and sew through the next three 11ºs in the bezel (**c–d**). Repeat these stitches three times, except on the last repeat, sew through only two 11ºs after adding the SuperDuos (**d–e**). Sew through the beadwork to exit the first 15º picked up at the start of this step (**figure 5, point a**).

6) Pick up three 15ºs, and sew through the open hole of the next SuperDuo (**a–b**). Pick up two SuperDuos, and sew through the open hole of the following SuperDuo. Repeat this last stitch twice (**b–c**). Pick up three 15ºs, and sew through the next 15º (**c–d**).

7) Pick up two 11ºs, and sew through the next 15º (**d–e**). Pick up three 15ºs, and sew through the open hole of the following SuperDuo (**e–f**). Pick up a 4 mm bicone crystal, and sew through the open hole of the next SuperDuo. Repeat this last stitch twice (**f–g**). Pick up three 15ºs, and sew through the following 11º in the bezel (**g–h**).

8) Pick up three 15ºs, and sew through the next 11º in the round to form a small picot (**h–i**).

9) Add beads following the same pattern to create a mirror image on the opposite side of the butterfly (**i–j**). Sew through the beadwork to exit the third 15º added at the start of this round (**figure 6, point a**).

10) Pick up three 15ºs, skip the next SuperDuo, and sew through the open hole of the following SuperDuo added in the last round (**a–b**). Work five stitches using a 4 mm, a 15º, a SuperDuo, a 15º, and a 4 mm in this sequence (**b–c**).

11) Pick up three 15ºs, and sew through the next three 15ºs, two 11ºs, and three 15ºs on the adjacent wing (**c–d**).

12) Pick up three 15ºs, and sew through the next 4 mm. Repeat this stitch twice (**d–e**). Pick up four 15ºs, and sew through the next three 15ºs on this edge of the wing (**e–f**).

13) Pick up a 15ºs and sew through the center 15º of the adjacent picot (**f–g**).

14) Add beads following the same pattern to create a mirror image on the opposite side of the butterfly (**g–h**). Sew through the beadwork to exit the third 15º added at the start of this round (**figure 7, point a**).

15) Pick up three 15ºs, and sew through the next 4 mm (**a–b**). Pick up a 15º, a 4 mm, and a 15º, and sew through the open hole of the next SuperDuo in the last round (**b–c**). Pick up seven 15ºs, and sew through the SuperDuo your thread is exiting, going in the same direction to form a loop for adding the chain (**c–d**). Retrace the thread path through the loop twice (not shown in the figure for clarity). Add the same pattern of beads on the opposite side of the loop (**d–e**).

16) Sew through the beadwork to reach the wing on the other side (**e–f**), and add beads to create a mirror image on the opposite wing (**f–g**). End the thread.

ASSEMBLY

1) Cut two 8½-in. (21.6 cm) pieces of chain. Attach a 6 mm jump ring to the end link of a chain and a loop on the wing of the butterfly. Repeat this step on the opposite side of the butterfly.

2) At the end of one chain, attach an 8 mm jump ring. On the other chain, use a 6 mm jump ring to attach a lobster claw clasp. **B** · **B**

FIGURE 6

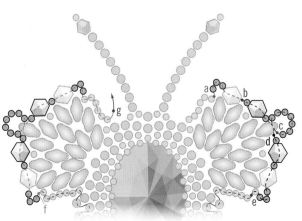

FIGURE 7

PEARL PASSION BRACELET

designed by Natalija Bekic

DIFFICULTY ●●●○○

herringbone stitch /
bead weaving

Revel in your passion for pearls with this classically-styled bracelet that has a sprinkling of crystals for added sparkle.

END COMPONENTS

1) On 1½ yd. (1.4 m) of thread, pick up 12 color A 15º seed beads, and tie the beads into a ring with a square knot, leaving a 6-in. (15 cm) tail. Sew through the first A.

2) Pick up two 11º seed beads, and sew through the next three As in the ring (**figure 1, a–b**). Repeat this stitch three times to complete the round, and step up through the first 11º added (**b–c**).

3) Working in herringbone stitch, pick up two 11ºs, and sew down through the adjacent 11º in the same stack (**c–d**). Pick up an A, and sew up through the following 11º in the next stack (**d–e**). Repeat these stitches three times to complete the round, and step up through the first 11º added in the first stack (**e–f**).

4) Working in herringbone stitch, pick up an 11º, an A, and an 11º,

and sew through the next two 11ºs in the same stack, the following A, and the next two 11ºs in the following stack (**figure 2, a–b**). Repeat this stitch three times to complete the round, and step up through the first 11º and A added (**b–c**).

5) Pick up a 10 mm pearl, and sew through the A at the tip of the opposite stack (**figure 3, a–b**). Sew back through the pearl and A your thread exited at the start of this step, going in the same direction (**b–c**).

6) Pick up two 11ºs, two MiniDuo beads, and two 11ºs, and sew through the A at the tip of the next stack (**c–d**). Repeat this stitch three times to complete the round (**d–e**).

7) Pick three color B 15º seed beads, an A, and three Bs, and sew through the A at the tip of the next stack (**figure 4, a–b**). Position these beads on top of

the previous round of beads and close to the pearl. Repeat this stitch three times to complete the round (**b–c**), and sew through the first three Bs, A, and two Bs added in this round (**c–d**).

8) Pick up a 3 mm bicone crystal, skip the next B, A, and B, and sew through the following two Bs, A,

materials
purple bracelet 7½ in. (19.1 cm)

- crystal pearls (Swarovski, burgundy)
  - **6** 10 mm
  - **7** 8 mm
- bicone crystals
  - **24** 4 mm color C (Preciosa, crystal AB)
  - **12** 4 mm color D (Swarovski, light peach)
  - **50** 3 mm (Preciosa, crystal AB)
- **3 g** 2 x 4 mm MiniDuo beads (metallic pink suede)
- **2 g** 11º seed beads (Miyuki 4202, Duracoat galvanized gold)
- 15º seed beads
  - **2 g** color A (Toho PF551, permanent finish galvanized rose gold)
  - **1 g** color B (Toho PF558, permanent finish galvanized aluminum)
- **1** box clasp
- **2** 4 mm jump rings
- Fireline, 6 lb. test
- beading needles, #12

basics, p. 13
- herringbone stitch: tubular
- ending and adding thread
- square knot

○	15º seed bead, color A
○	11º seed bead
●	10 mm pearl
⬭	2 x 4 mm MiniDuo bead
○	15º seed bead, color B
⬡	3 mm bicone crystal
⬡	4 mm bicone crystal, color C
●	8 mm pearl
⬡	4 mm bicone crystal, color D

TIP Since the pearls are a bit bulky, you need to make the bracelet a bit longer than a normal flat bracelet would be.

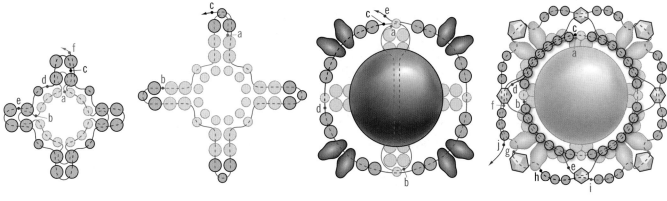

FIGURE 1   **FIGURE 2**   **FIGURE 3**   **FIGURE 4**

and two Bs (d–e). Repeat this stitch three times to complete the round, and sew through the first 3 mm added (e–f).

9) Pick up three Bs, and sew through the open hole of the next MiniDuo (f–g). Pick up a color C 4 mm bicone crystal, and sew through the open hole of the following MiniDuo (g–h). Pick up three Bs, and sew through next 3 mm (h–i). Repeat these stitches three times to complete the round, and continue through the first three Bs added (i–j).

10) Pick up three As, an 8 mm pearl, and three As, and sew through the previous three Bs, 3 mm, and three Bs your thread exited at the start of this step so the pearl sits next to the 3 mm

(figure 5, a–b). Continue through the following MiniDuo, C 4 mm, and MiniDuo (b–c).

11) Pick up a 3 mm, a color D 4 mm bicone, and a 3 mm, and sew through the next MiniDuo, C 4 mm, MiniDuo, three Bs, 3 mm, and three Bs (c–d).

12) Pick up three As, an 8 mm, and three As, and sew through the three Bs, 3 mm, and three Bs your thread just exited and the first three As just added (d–e).

13) Pick up three As, three Bs, a 3 mm, three Bs, and three As, and sew through the 8 mm to form a loop (e–f). Continue through the next three As, MiniDuo, C 4 mm, and MiniDuo (f–g).

14) Pick up a 3 mm, a D 4 mm, and a 3 mm, and sew through the

next MiniDuo and C 4 mm (g–h).

15) Pick up two As, and sew through the next three Bs, 3 mm, and three Bs (figure 6, a–b). Pick up two As, and sew through the following C 4 mm (b–c).

16) Pick up two As, and sew through the next 3 mm, D 4 mm, and 3 mm (c–d). Pick up two As, and sew through the following C 4 mm (d–e).

17) Pick up two As, and sew through the next three As (e–f). Pick up an 11º, and sew through the following 13 beads (f–g). Pick up an 11º, and sew through the next 21 beads as shown to exit the end 3 mm (g–h).

18) Attach a 4 mm jump ring to the clasp loop. Pick up two 11ºs, the jump ring with the loop attached,

and two 11ºs, and sew through the 3 mm your thread exited at the start of this step (h–i). Retrace the thread path (not shown in the figure for clarity), and sew through the next seven beads (i–j).

19) Pick up three Bs, and sew through the 11º your thread is exiting, going in the same direction (figure 7, a–b). Sew through the next 14 beads as shown to exit the 11º on the opposite side of the 8 mm (b–c). Add three Bs as before, and sew through the beadwork as shown to exit the third A after the 11º on the opposite side (c–d).

20) Pick up two As, and sew through the next C 4 mm (d–e). Pick up two As, and sew through the following 3 mm, D 4 mm, and 3 mm (e–f). Pick up two As, and

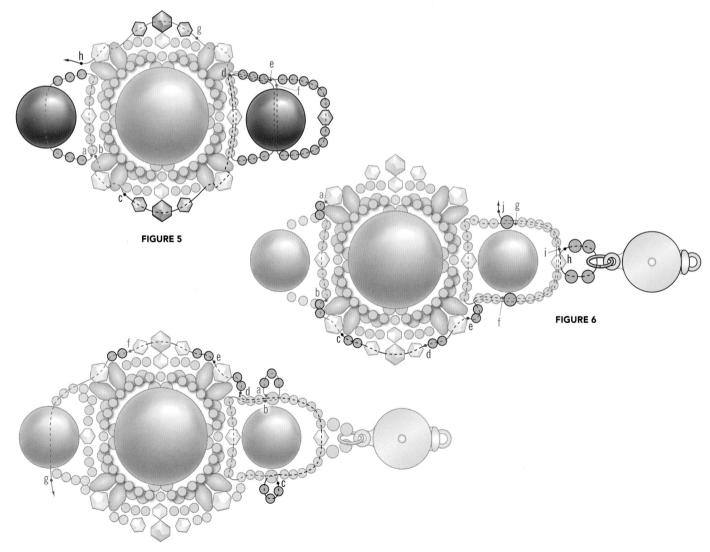

FIGURE 5

FIGURE 6

FIGURE 7

sew through the next C 4 mm, three As, and 8 mm (f–g). End the tail but not the working thread, and set the component aside.

21) Repeat steps 1–20 to make another end component, attaching the other half of the clasp.

CENTER COMPONENTS WITH A SIDE PEARL

1) Repeat steps 1–10 of "End components."

2) Repeat step 11 of "End components" **(figure 8, a–b)**, and then continue through the next MiniDuo, C 4 mm, and MiniDuo **(b–c)**. Pick up 3 mm, D 4 mm, and 3 mm, and sew through next MiniDuo and C 4 mm **(c–d)**.

3) Repeat steps 15–16 of "End components" twice **(d–e)**, and then

sew through the next three As and 8 mm **(e–f)**. End the tail but not the working thread, and set this component aside.

4) Repeats steps 1–3 to make two more components.

CENTER COMPONENT WITHOUT A SIDE PEARL

1) Repeat steps 1–9 of "End components," and continue through the next MiniDuo, C 4 mm, and MiniDuo.

2) Repeat step 11 of "End components," and then continue through the next MiniDuo, C 4 mm, and MiniDuo. Pick up 3 mm, D 4 mm, and 3 mm, and sew through next MiniDuo and C 4 mm to complete a component without a side 8 mm pearl.

3) Repeat steps 15–16 of "End components" twice, then sew through the next two As, three Bs, 3 mm, and three Bs. End the tail but not the working thread, and set this component aside.

JOINING COMPONENTS

1) Position an end component on your bead mat with the clasp on the right side and a center component with a side pearl to the left of it with the pearl on the left side.

2) With the working thread from the end component, pick up an 11º and three As, and sew through the end three Bs, 3 mm, and three Bs on the other component **(figure 9, a–b)**. Pick up three As and an 11º, and sew through the pearl your thread exited at the start of this

step and the adjacent 11º **(b–c)**.

3) Pick up three Bs, and sew through the 11º your thread is exiting to add a picot **(figure 10, a–b)**. Sew back through the 8 mm and the adjacent 11º **(b–c)**. Work a picot off of this 11º **(c–d)**. Retrace the thread path through the join as shown using a tight tension **(d–e)** and end this working thread.

4) Work as in steps 2–3 to add the remaining center components with the attached side pearls.

5) Work as before to add the remaining center component (without the side pearl) between the last center component added and the remaining end component. End the remaining threads. **B&B**

FIGURE 8

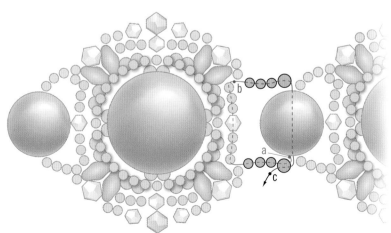

FIGURE 9

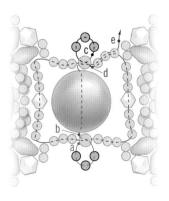

FIGURE 10

BRILLIANT SPLENDOR NECKLACE

designed by
Norma Jean Dell

DIFFICULTY ●●●●○

right-angle weave / peyote stitch

The diamond-shaped clasp blends seamlessly into the overall design

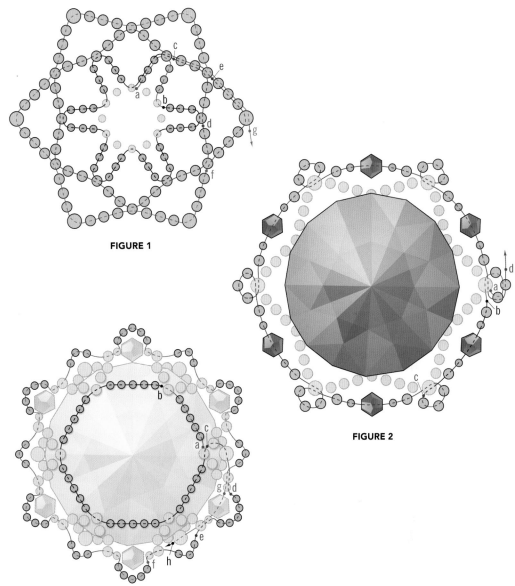

FIGURE 1

FIGURE 2

FIGURE 3

Seed beads and crystals come together to form a show-stopping necklace.

materials
blue necklace 17½ in. (44.5 cm)

- rivolis (Swarovski, green sphinx)
  - **1** 18 mm
  - **3** 12 mm
- **1** 18 mm spike crystal (Swarovski 6480, Bermuda blue)
- bicone crystals (Swarovski)
  - **2** 6 mm (Jet AB2X)
  - **46** 4 mm (Jet AB2X)
  - **18** 3 mm (Olivine AB2X)
- **24** 4 mm fire-polished beads (blue zircon)
- **2 g** 8° seed beads (Miyuki 4203, Duracoat galvanized yellow gold)
- **5 g** 11° seed beads (Miyuki 4203, Duracoat galvanized yellow gold)
- 15° seed beads
  - **6 g** color A (Miyuki 4203, Duracoat galvanized yellow gold)
  - **2 g** color B (Toho 506, higher metallic June bug)
- Fireline, 6 lb. test
- beading needles, #11 or #12

basics, p. 13
- peyote stitch
- right-angle weave
- ladder stitch
- ending and adding thread
- square knot

LARGE COMPONENT

1) On 5 ft. (1.5 m) of thread, pick up 12 color A 15° seed beads, and sew through the beads again to form a ring, leaving a 6-in. (15 cm) tail. Tie the working thread and tail together with a square knot, and continue through the next 15°.

2) Pick up three As, an 11° seed bead, and three As, skip the next A in the ring, and sew through the following A (**figure 1, a–b**). Repeat this stitch five times to complete the round, and sew through the first three As and 11° added (**b–c**). End the tail.

3) Pick up five 11°s, and sew through the next 11° to form a picot (**c–d**). Repeat this stitch five times to complete the round, and sew through the first three 11°s added (**d–e**).

4) Pick up three 11°s, an 8° seed bead, and three 11°s, and sew through the center 11° in the next picot (**e–f**). Repeat this stitch five times to complete the round, and sew through the first three 11°s and 8° added (**f–g**).

5) Pick up three 11°s, and sew through the 8° your thread is exiting, going in the same direction, to

form a picot (**figure 2, a–b**). Pick up an 11°, an A, a 4 mm bicone crystal, an A, and an 11°, and sew through the next 8° (**b–c**). Repeat these stitches five times using a tight tension to complete the round, allowing the beadwork to cup upward, and continue through the first two 11°s added (**c–d**).

6) Place the 18 mm rivoli faceup in the beadwork. Pick up five color B 15°s, and sew through the center 11° in the next picot (**figure 3, a–b**). Repeat this stitch five times to complete the round and enclose the rivoli (**b–c**), retrace the thread path

181

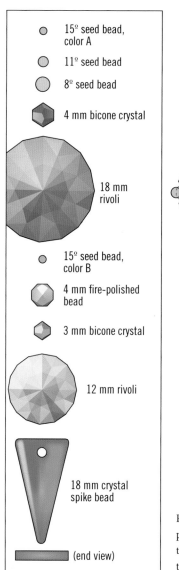

- 15º seed bead, color A
- 11º seed bead
- 8º seed bead
- 4 mm bicone crystal
- 18 mm rivoli
- 15º seed bead, color B
- 4 mm fire-polished bead
- 3 mm bicone crystal
- 12 mm rivoli
- 18 mm crystal spike bead (end view)

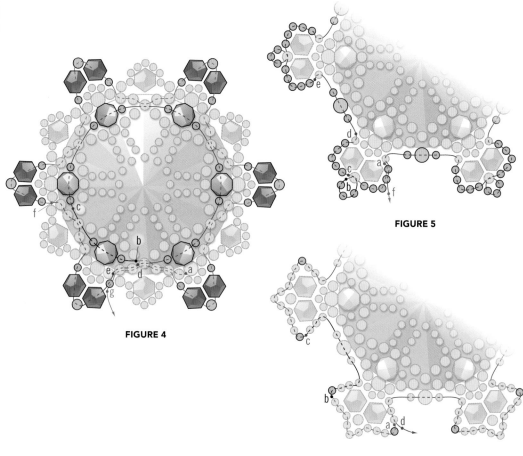

FIGURE 4

FIGURE 5

FIGURE 6

(not shown in the figure for clarity), and continue through the adjacent 11º, 8º, 11º, and A as shown (**c–d**).

7) Pick up five As, skip the next 4 mm bicone, and go through the following A and 11º (**d–e**). Pick up three Bs, and sew through the next 11º and A (**e–f**). Repeat these stitches five times to complete the round (**f–g**), and sew through the next 4 mm bicone, A, 11º, and 8º (**g–h**). On the back of the beadwork, continue through the next four 11ºs as shown (**figure 4, a–b**). The back of the beadwork is shown in **figures 4–6**.

8) Pick up an A, a 4 mm fire-polished bead, and an A, and sew through the corresponding center 11º behind the next bicone (**b–c**).

Repeat this stitch five times to complete the round (**c–d**), and continue through the next two 11ºs toward the edge on the back of the beadwork (**d–e**).

9) Pick up an A, a 4 mm bicone, an 11º, a 4 mm bicone, and an A, skip the next 11º, 8º, and 11º, and sew through the next five 11ºs as shown to form a crystal picot (**e–f**). Repeat this stitch five times to complete the round, and continue through the first A added in this round (**f–g**).

10) Pick up five As, skip the next 4 mm bicone, and sew through the following 11º (**figure 5, a–b**). (The crystal embellishment between the crystal picots is not shown in the figure for clarity.) Pick up three Bs, and sew through the 11º your thread is exiting (**b–c**). Pick up five As, skip the next 4 mm bicone, and sew through the following A (**c–d**). Pick up an A, an 8º, and an A, and sew through the first A in the following crystal picot (**d–e**). Repeat these

stitches five times to complete the round, and continue through the first two As added (**e–f**).

11) Pick up an A, and sew through the next three As, three Bs, and three As (**figure 6, a–b**). Pick up an A, and sew through the next four As, 8º, and four As (**b–c**). Repeat these stitches five times to complete the round (**c–d**), and end the thread.

SMALL COMPONENT

1) On 4 ft. (1.2 m) of thread, pick up a repeating pattern of a fire-polished bead and 8º six times, and sew through the beads again to form a ring, leaving a 6-in. (15 cm) tail. Tie the working thread and tail together with a square knot, and continue through the next fire-polished bead and 8º.

2) Pick up two As, an 11º, and two As, and sew through the next 8º (**figure 7, a–b**). Repeat this stitch five times to complete the round,

and continue through the first two As and 11º (**b–c**). End the tail.

3) Pick up three Bs, and sew through the 11º your thread is exiting, going in the same direction, to form a picot (**c–d**). Pick up an A, a 3 mm bicone crystal, and an A, and sew through the next 11º (**d–e**). Repeat these stitches five times to complete the round using a tight tension to make the beadwork cup upward (**e–f**).

4) Place the 12 mm rivoli faceup in the beadwork. Pick up three As, sew through the 11º your thread is exiting, going in the same direction so this picot sits in front of the previous picot and is positioned toward the center of the rivoli, and then continue through the following A (**figure 8, a–b**). Pick up four As, and sew through the next A and 11º to form a loop (**b–c**). Repeat these stitches five times to complete the round (**c–d**), and sew through the first two As in the first picot (**d–e**).

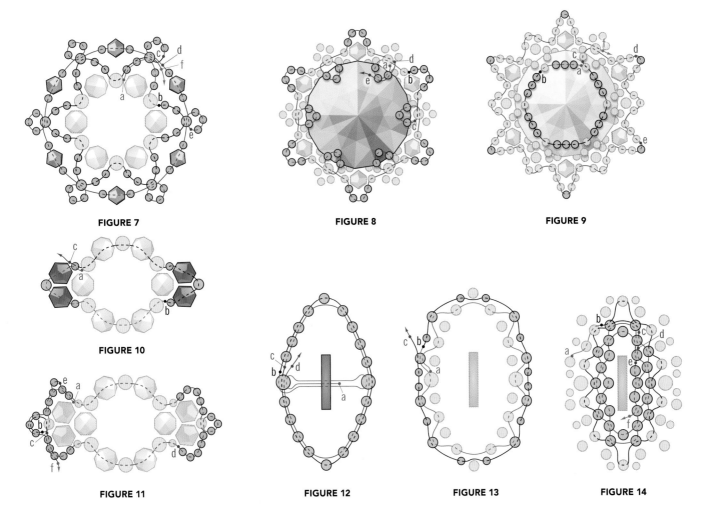

FIGURE 7

FIGURE 8

FIGURE 9

FIGURE 10

FIGURE 11

FIGURE 12

FIGURE 13

FIGURE 14

5) Pick up three Bs, and sew through the center A in the next picot (**figure 9, a–b**). Repeat this stitch five times to complete the round (**b–c**), retrace the thread path using a tight tension (not shown in the figure for clarity), and continue through the next A, 11º, and three As as shown to exit the second A in the loop around the adjacent 3 mm (**c–d**).

6) Pick up a B, and sew through the next three As, three Bs, and three As (**d–e**). Repeat this stitch five times to complete the round except after adding the last B, sew through only the next three As and 11º, with the needle exiting toward the back of the component (**e–f**). Flip the component over so the back is facing up, and continue through the following two As and 8º in the center ring on the back of the component.

7) Pick up an A, a 4 mm bicone, an 11º, a 4 mm bicone, and an A,

skip the next fire-polished bead, and sew through the following five beads (**figure 10, a–b**). Just the ring of beads on the back of the component is shown in the figure for clarity. Repeat this stitch, and continue through the first A added (**b–c**).

8) Pick up five As, skip the next 4 mm bicone, and sew through the following 11º (**figure 11, a–b**). Pick up three Bs, and sew through the 11º again, going in the same direction to add a picot (**b–c**). Pick up five As, skip the next 4 mm bicone, and sew through the following seven beads (**c–d**). Repeat these stitches once more, and continue through the next two As (**d–e**).

9) Pick up an A, and sew through the next three As, three Bs, and three As (**e–f**). Work as in the previous stitch to add an A to the center of this set of six As. Sew through the beadwork to exit in

the center of the next set of As at the other end of the component.

10) Repeat step 9 at this end of the component, and continue through the beadwork to exit the center B in the next picot. Do not end the working thread.

11) Repeat steps 1–10 to make two more small components.

SPIKE COMPONENT

1) On 1 yd. (.9 m) of thread, pick up a crystal spike and an 8º, and sew back through the spike bead, leaving a 6-in. (15 cm) tail. Repeat this stitch to add an 8º on the other side of the spike, and continue through the first 8º added (**figure 12, a–b**).

2) Pick up nine 11ºs, and sew through the other 8º. Repeat this stitch to form a loop on the other side of the spike (**b–c**). Retrace the thread path, skipping the center 11º in each loop and using a tight tension (**c–d**). These beads will shift

to form rounds 1 and 2 as the next round is added.

3) Work in rounds of modified tubular peyote stitch as follows:

Round 3: Using 11ºs, work eight stitches, but sew through two beads instead of one on stitches two and six (**figure 13, a–b**).

Round 4: Using a tight tension, work a stitch with a B and then a stitch with two Bs. Repeat these two stitches three times (**b–c**).

Round 5: Sew through the next two 11ºs to exit an up bead in round 1 (**figure 14, a–b**). Work 10 stitches using 11ºs, and step up through the first two 11ºs added in this round, skipping the tip bead (**b–c**).

Round 6: Using 11ºs, work four regular stitches, sewing through two 11ºs for the fourth stitch. Repeat these stitches to add four more stitches, and step up through the first 11º added in this round (**c–d**).

Round 7: Work eight stitches using 11ºs, and step up (**d–e**).

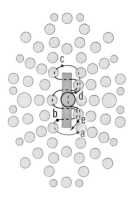

FIGURE 15

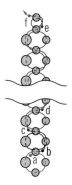

FIGURE 16

TIP To lengthen the necklace, add more neck chain units to each side to reach the desired length.

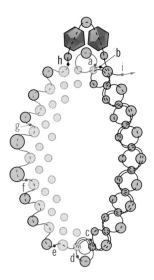

FIGURE 17

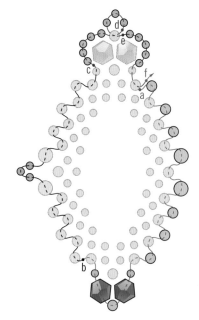

FIGURE 18

4) Using 11⁰s and a tight tension, work two regular stitches (e–f). Skip the next up-bead, and sew through the following up-bead in the previous round (**figure 15 a–b**).

5) Zip up the opening (**b–c**), and then sew through the opposite 11⁰ and the following 11⁰ (**c–d**).

6) Pick up an 8⁰, and sew through the next 11⁰ in the same row (**d–e**). Sew through the beadwork and back through the 8⁰ just added to reinforce the connection, exiting the 8⁰.

7) End the tail but not the working thread, sewing through the spike and 8⁰s again if necessary, using a tight tension.

DIAMOND COMPONENT

1) On 1 yd. (.9 m) of thread, pick up three As and an 11⁰. Leaving a 6-in. (15 cm) tail, sew through the beads again (not shown in the figure for clarity) and continue through the first A (**figure 16, a–b**).

2) Working in right-angle weave (RAW), pick up two As and an 11⁰, sew through the A your thread is exiting, and continue through the next two As (**b–c**).

3) Pick up an 11⁰ and two As, and sew through the A your thread is exiting and the next 11⁰ and A (**c–d**).

4) Repeat step 2–3 three more times for a total of nine units (d–e), using a tight tension.

5) Work a turn stitch: Work one ladder stitch with an A (e–f). Pick up an 11⁰, and sew through the previous A and the A just added (**figure 17, a–b**).

6) Work nine RAW stitches to make the other side of the component as a mirror image of the first side (**b–c**).

7) Join the RAW ends with a ladder stitch (**c–d**). Pick up an 11⁰, sew through the As just joined, and continue through the next 11⁰ on the first unit (**d–e**).

8) Using 11⁰s, work three peyote stitches between the 11⁰s on the edge (e–f), work two stitches using 8⁰s (f–g), and three stitches using 11⁰s (g–h).

9) Pick up an A, a 4 mm bicone, an 11⁰, a 4 mm bicone, and an A, skip the next 11⁰, and sew through the following 11⁰ (**h–i**).

10) Repeat steps 8–9 (**figure 18, a–b**).

11) Sew through six 11⁰s and an 8⁰, pick up three Bs, and sew through the next 8⁰, seven 11⁰s, and an A (**b–c**). Keep an even tension so the beadwork remains

flat for the remainder of the diamond.

12) Pick up five As, skip the next 4 mm bicone, and sew through the following 11⁰ (**c–d**). Pick up three Bs, and sew through the same 11⁰ (**d–e**). Pick up five As, skip the next 4 mm bicone, and sew through the following A and 11⁰ (**e–f**).

13) Repeat steps 11–12.

14) Sew through the edge of the beadwork to the opposite end, exiting the first two As in the loop around the bicone. Pick up an A, and sew through the next three As, three Bs, and three As (**figure 19**). Repeat this last stitch to add an A on this side in the corresponding position. Repeat these stitches at the other end of the beadwork, and sew through the beadwork to exit a center B on an end picot. End the tail but not the working thread.

15) Repeat steps 1–14 to make three more components.

NECK CHAIN

1) On a comfortable length of thread, pick up an 11⁰, four As, an 11⁰, and four As. Leaving a 10-in. (25 cm) tail, sew through the first eight beads again to form a ring (**figure 20, a–b**).

2) Pick up a B, and sew through the next two As, 11⁰, and two As. Pick up a B, and sew through the following two As and 11⁰ (**b–c**).

3) Pick up four As, an 11⁰, and four As, and sew through the 11⁰ your thread is exiting and the next seven beads.

4) Repeat steps 2–3 13 times and step 2 once more for a neck chain that has a total of 14 units.

5) Pick up an 11⁰, a 6 mm bicone crystal, and three Bs, and sew back through the 6 mm bicone, 11⁰, and the 11⁰ your thread exited at the start of this step, going in the same direction. Retrace the thread path several times, and end the working thread but not the tail.

6) Make another neck chain.

CONNECTIONS
Spike to the small component

With the working thread from the spike, pick up a B and an 11⁰, and sew through the tip B on a small component, opposite where the working thread is exiting. Pick up an 11⁰ and a B, and sew through the 8⁰ your thread exited at the start of the connection (**figure 21**). Retrace the thread path several times, and end the thread from the spike.

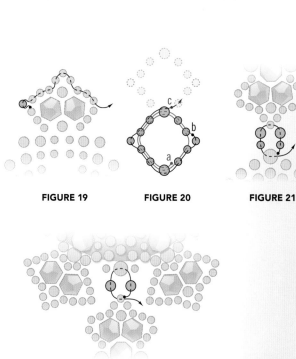

FIGURE 19   **FIGURE 20**   **FIGURE 21**

FIGURE 22

Small component to the large component

With the working thread from the small component and the back of the component facing up, pick up an 11º, and sew through the 8º that sits between a pair of 4 mm bicones on the back of the large component. Pick up an 11º, and sew through the B your thread exited at the start of the connection (figure 22). Retrace the thread path several times, and end the thread from the small component.

Diamond component to the large component

Identify the two 8ºs on the back of the large component that are opposite the existing connection but just off center. With the working thread from a diamond component and the back of the large component facing up, connect the diamond component to one of the 8ºs, using the same method you used to attach the small and large components. Repeat to connect another diamond component to the other 8º. End this working thread.

Small components to the diamond components

With the working thread from

the small component, work as in "Connections: Small component to the large component," but sew through the tip B on the diamond component instead of an 8º. Attach the remaining diamond to the other end of the small component, and end this working thread.

Neck chain to diamond component

With the tail thread on the diamond component, work as in "Connections: Small components to the diamond components" to connect the chain to the end tip of the diamond component. End this tail thread.

CLOSURE

1) Repeat steps 1–8 of "Diamond component," and then work one more peyote stitch using an 11º.

2) Pick up an A, an 11º, and an A, and sew through the 11º your thread is exiting.

3) Using 11ºs, work four peyote stitches, two stitches using 8ºs, and four stitches using 11ºs. Repeat step 2.

4) Work one peyote stitch using an 11º, and step up through the next 11º. Sew through the beadwork to the next 8º, pick up three Bs, and

sew through the next 8º. Continue through the beadwork to exit the next A and 11º on the tip of the component.

5) Pick up 18 Bs, sew through the 11º your thread is exiting, going in the same direction to add a clasp loop. Check the fit of the loop over the 6 mm bicone on the neck

chain, and add or remove Bs if necessary. Retrace the thread path several times.

6) Sew through the beadwork to add three Bs between the 8ºs on the next side and then add the clasp loop on the other end as before. End the threads. **B&B**

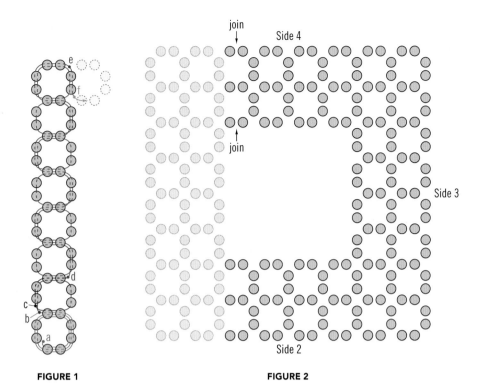

FIGURE 1

FIGURE 2

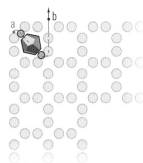

FIGURE 3

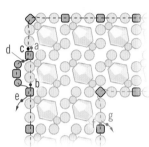

FIGURE 4

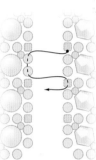

FIGURE 5

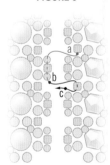

FIGURE 6

This reversible pendant is embellished with crystals and pearls for two looks that are both stylish and wearable.

BASE LAYERS

1) On a comfortable length of thread, pick up eight 11° seed beads, and sew through all the beads again to form a ring, leaving a 10-in. (25 cm) tail. Continue through the first four 11°s again (**figure 1, a–b**).

2) Work in modified right-angle weave (RAW): Pick up six 11°s, sew through the last two 11°s your thread exited at the start of this step (**b–c**), and continue through the next four 11°s (**c–d**). Repeat this stitch to work a total of eight units using a tight tension (**d–e**), and then sew through the next two 11°s (**e–f**).

3) Working off the previous row, stitch a second row of eight modified right-angle weave units using 11°s to complete side 1.

4) Work in modified right-angle weave using 11°s to add the remaining sides as follows, ending and adding thread as needed (**figure 2**):

• **Sides 2–3:** add two rows of six units off the last two units of the previous side.

• **Side 4:** add two rows of three units off of side 3.

• **Join side 4 to side 1:** Pick up two 11°s, sew through the correspond-

ing two 11°s on side 1, pick up two 11°s, and sew through the two 11°s your thread exited on side 4. Sew through the beadwork to the unfinished unit, and add two 11°s to complete the join.

5) Sew through the beadwork to exit the upper left corner edge 11°s as shown (**figure 3, point a**). Pick up a 15° seed bead, a 4 mm bicone crystal, and a 15°, cross the opening diagonally, and sew through the corresponding two 11°s going in the same direction (**a–b**). Work as in the previous stitch to embellish the remainder of the base, making sure all the crystals are positioned in the same direction. Sew through the beadwork to exit two outside edge corner 11°s with the needle pointing toward the opposite edge of the base (**figure 4, point a**).

6) Pick up an 11° cylinder bead, and sew through the next two edge 11°s (**a–b**). Repeat this stitch for the remainder of the outside edge including the corners (**b–c**). Continue through the first cylinder added (**c–d**).

7) Pick up a 15°, a cylinder, and a 15°, and sew through the next

cylinder (**d–e**). Repeat this stitch around the outer edge. End and add thread if needed.

8) With the tail thread, sew through the beadwork to exit an inner edge pair of 11°s, and work as in step 6 to add cylinders to the inside edge, including in the corners (**f–g**). Continue through the next cylinder.

9) Work as in steps 1–8 to make another base, but substitute 4 mm pearls for the crystals. End the threads on the pearl base.

JOINING THE LAYERS

1) Place the crystal base on top of the pearl base, with the embellished sides facing outward, and the inside edge 11°s on both bases directly across from each other. With the tail thread remaining from the crystal base, sew through the next two corresponding 11°s on the pearl base, and continue through the following cylinder on the crystal base (**figure 5**). The edge view of the beadwork is shown in **figures 5–6**. Repeat this stitch to join the remaining inside edges, and end this thread.

2) Tear off a piece of plastic wrap

that is 6 in. (15 cm) long, and fold it into a strip that is approximately ¼ in. (6 mm) wide. Fold the strip in half. Starting at one corner, lay the plastic wrap around the inside edge between the two bases (**photo**).

3) With the working thread remaining from the crystal base, sew through the next 15°, cylinder, and 15° on the pearl base (**figure 6, a–b**), and continue through the next cylinder in the same row of

FIGURE 7

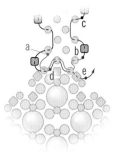

FIGURE 8

FIGURE 9

FIGURE 10

the crystal base (b–c). Repeat this stitch to join the remainder of the outside edge, making sure to keep the plastic wrap tucked inside. If necessary, trim any excess plastic wrap before completing the join. Sew through the beadwork to exit an outside-edge 15º nearest to a corner on the crystal side of the pendant (figure 7, point a).

BAIL

1) Pick up a 15º, and sew through the corresponding 15º on the opposite edge (a–b). Pick up a 15º and sew back through the 15º just added. Pick up a 15º, and sew through the 15º your thread exited at the start of this step (b–c). Using 15ºs, continue working rows of two stitches each in flat even-count peyote for a total of 28 rows or the desired length.

2) Fold the bail toward the pearl side of the pendant, and zip the end row of the bail to the corresponding two corner 15ºs on the pearl side (figure 8, a–b).

3) Pick up a cylinder, and sew through the next two edge 15ºs (b–c). Repeat this stitch for the remainder of the edge, sew through the beadwork to the opposite edge, and repeat this stitch for this edge (c–d). Continue through the beadwork as shown to exit the nearest edge cylinder on the pearl base (d–e).

4) Pick up two 15ºs, and sew through the next edge cylinder on the bail (figure 9, a–b). Repeat this stitch to embellish both edges of the bail (b–c), and end this thread.

DANGLE

Add 12 in. (30 cm) of thread to the beadwork, and exit the center cylinder of the corner on the crystal side, opposite the bail. Pick up two 15ºs, a 5 mm pearl, two 15ºs, an 8 mm bicone crystal, two 15ºs, a 4 mm pearl, and three 15ºs. Skip the last three 15ºs, and sew back through the remaining beads picked up and the cylinder your thread exited at the start of the step, going in the same direction. Retrace the thread path, and end the thread.

NECK CHAIN

1) On a comfortable length of thread, pick up 14 15ºs, and sew through the beads again to form a ring, leaving a 12-in. (30 cm) tail.

2) Pick up three 15ºs, and sew through the last three 15ºs your thread exited and the three 15ºs just picked up (figure 10, a–b).

3) Pick up 11 15ºs, and sew through the three 15ºs your thread just exited to form a loop, and continue through the next seven 15ºs (b–c).

4) Repeat steps 2–3 for the desired length, ending and adding thread as needed.

5) With the working thread, pick up three 15ºs, an 8 mm crystal, a 15º, a 5 mm pearl, and a 15º. Skip the last 15º added, and sew back through the pearl, 15º, crystal, and 15º. Pick up two 15ºs, and sew through the three 15ºs your thread exited at the start of this step to form a dangle at the end of the chain. Retrace the thread path, and end the working thread.

6) With the tail, repeat step 2 twice, and step 3 once. Pick up 25 15ºs, and sew through the last three 15ºs your thread is exiting, going in the same direction. Test the fit of the loop over the 8 mm crystal, and add or remove 15ºs if necessary. End the tail. B&B

Legend:

- ⬤ 11º seed bead
- ● 15º seed bead
- ⬡ 4 mm bicone crystal
- ▢ 11º cylinder bead
- ◯ 4 mm pearl

materials

gray pendant 3¼ x 2 in. (8.3 x 5 cm) with a 30-in. (76 cm) beaded chain

- bicone crystals (Swarovski, silver night)
  - **2** 8 mm
  - **48** 4 mm
- crystal pearls (Swarovski, dark gray)
  - **2** 5 mm
  - **49** 4 mm
- **3 g** 11º seed beads (Miyuki 152, transparent gray)
- **1 g** 11º cylinder beads (Miyuki Delica DB1818, dyed rustic gray silk satin)
- **7 g** 15º seed beads (Toho 9B, transparent smoky gray)
- Fireline, 4 or 6 lb. test
- beading needles, #11 or #12
- 11 x 6 in. (28 x 15 cm) plastic wrap

Find info for the alternate colorway at FacetJewelry.com/ resourceguide

basics, p. 13

- right-angle weave
- peyote stitch: flat even-count, zipping up or joining
- ending and adding thread

materials

blue and ecru cuff
6½ x 1⅛ in. (16.5 cm x 2.9 cm)

- 11º seed beads
  - **3 g** color A (Toho 618, mudbrick)
  - **1 g** color B (Toho 8DF, transparent frosted cobalt)
  - **4 g** color C (Toho 2110, silver-lined milky light topaz)
  - **3 g** color D (Toho 332, gold luster raspberry)
  - **3 g** color E (Toho 2606F, semi-glazed soft blue)
- **1 g** 11º hex-cut cylinder beads, color F (Miyuki Delica DB12, metallic dark raspberry)
- 11º Demi seed beads
  - **2 g** color G (Toho 711, nickel)
  - **2 g** color H (Toho 82, metallic nebula)
- **1 g** 15º seed beads color I (Miyuki 190F, matte nickel plated)
- ⅜ in. (10 mm) button with shank
- 3½ ft. (1.1 m) 1.5 mm round leather (metallic bronze) [small looms use less leather]
- Fireline, 6 lb. test
- KO thread (dark purple)
- beading needles, #12
- beeswax
- chainnose pliers
- hypo cement
- bead loom and masking tape

basics, p. 13

- conditioning thread
- loomwork: warping the loom, weaving the pattern
- overhand knot
- half-hitch knot

Demi beads provide twice the design possibilities in this updated Southwestern bracelet, while metallic leather provides a modern touch.

Warping the loom

1) To warp the loom, tie Fireline to one end of the loom (front end) and wind it around a peg. Guide the Fireline back and forth across the loom, going through five adjacent grooves on the loom bars. Skip the next five grooves on the loom bars, and then string the Fireline through the next five adjacent grooves.

2) Tie off your Fireline on the same end of the loom where you started (the front end), leaving a 2-ft. (61 cm) tail. Wrap the tail around your loom or tape it to the side.

3) Fold the leather in half, slide the button shank to the center, and then tie an overhand knot to secure the button. Position the button at the front end of the loom, with the two leather cords straddling a screw or peg, if applicable to your loom, or tape it to the loom.

4) Place the two strands of leather down the middle of the loom in grooves six and 10. Tie or tape the ends of the leather to the other end of your loom, similar to the button end. You now have a total of 12 warp threads, including the leather strands (**figure 1**).

Weave the pattern

1) For the "weft," condition 1 yd. (.9 m) of KO thread, and tie an overhand knot near the loom's front

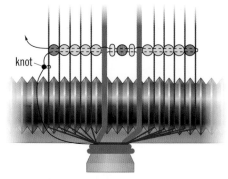

knot

FIGURE 2

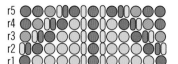

r5
r4
r3
r2
r1

FIGURE 3

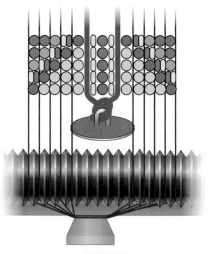

FIGURE 4

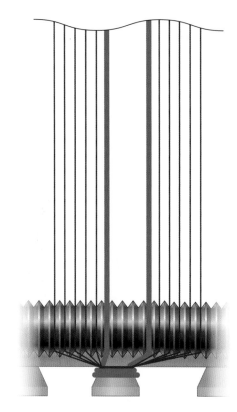

FIGURE 1

r3
r2
r1

FIGURE 5

end on Warp 1. (If left-handed, tie to Warp 12.) Leave an 8-in. (20 cm) tail, and tape it near your Fireline knots. Slide the knot towards the front of the loom.

2) Pick up beads in the following pattern: 1A, 4C, 1G, 1D, 1G, 4C, 1A (for a total of 13 beads). Pass the beading weft thread under the warp threads. With the index finger of your non dominant hand, gently push the beads up between the warp threads. The three center beads (1G, 1D, 1G) will lie between the leather warp strands. While holding the beads in place, sew back through the beads, making sure your needle passes over the

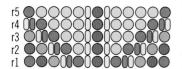

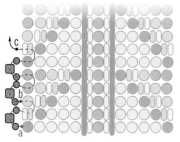

FIGURE 6

FIGURE 7

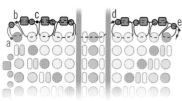

FIGURE 8

⬤	11º seed bead, color A
⬤	11º seed bead, color B
⚪	11º seed bead, color C
◍	11º seed bead, color D
⬤	11º seed bead, color E
⬛	11º hex-cut cylinder bead, color F
⬚	11º Demi bead, color G
▮	11º Demi bead, color H
⬤	15º seed bead, color I

warp threads **(figure 2)**. If you are left-handed, sew through the beads left to right.

3) Complete the first half of the cuff pattern **(figure 3)** as follows:
Row 2: 1G, 1H, 1A, 3C, 1G, 1D, 1G, 3C, 1A, 1H, 1G
Row 3: 1E, 1G, 1H, 1A, 2C, 1G, 1D, 1G, 2C, 1A, 1H, 1G, 1E
Row 4: 1D, 1E, 1G, 1H, 1A, 1C, 1G, 1D, 1G, 1C, 1A, 1H, 1G, 1E, 1D
Row 5: 1B, 1D, 1E, 1G, 1H, 1A, 1G, 1D, 1G, 1A, 1H, 1G, 1E, 1D, 1B.

NOTE Every time there are two Demi beads together (Gs and Hs), they will share one warp space.

4) After weaving five rows of the pattern, detach the knotted leather at both ends of the loom. Gently slide the leather until the button sits at the end of the beadwork **(figure 4)**. Re-tie the two loose leather ends to the back of the loom.
5) Repeat the pattern in rows 1–5 until you have a total of 35 rows.

NOTE The five-row pattern is about ³⁄₈ in. (1 cm) long. To adjust the bracelet length, work more or fewer repeats, making sure you weave the same number of rows on the second half of the bracelet. Seven repeats (35 rows) makes a 6½-in. (16.5 cm) bracelet. For a 7¼ in. (18.4 cm) bracelet, work the pattern eight times.

6) Work the center three rows:
Row 1: 4B, 1C, 1G, 1D, 1G, 1C, 4B
Row 2: 3A, 1C, 1B, 1G, 1D, 1G, 1B, 1C, 3A
Row 3: 4B, 1C, 1G, 1D, 1G, 1C, 4B **(figure 5)**.
7) The second half of the cuff pattern is the reverse of the first half:
Row 1: 1B, 1D, 1E, 1G, 1H, 1A, 1G, 1D, 1G, 1A, 1H, 1G, 1E, 1D, 1B
Row 2: 1D, 1E, 1G, 1H, 1A, 1C, 1G, 1D, 1G, 1C, 1A, 1H, 1G, 1E, 1D
Row 3: 1E, 1G, 1H, 1A, 2C, 1G, 1D, 1G, 2C, 1A, 1H, 1G, 1E
Row 4: 1G, 1H, 1A, 3C, 1G, 1D, 1G, 3C, 1A, 1H, 1G

Row 5: 1A, 4C, 1G, 1D, 1G, 4C, 1A **(figure 6)**.
8) Repeat the five-row sequence in step 7 six times. End and add thread as needed.

Finishing

1) Remove your beadwork from the loom, leaving your warp threads as long as possible. End all Fireline within the beadwork, except for the last 2-ft. (61 cm) tail. Avoid knotting along the edges since edging will be added. Leave the leather ends long until completion.
2) With the 2-ft. (61 cm) tail exiting the edge bead in row 1, pick up an I, an F, and an I, and sew through the next two Demis and 11º **(figure 7, a–b)**, treating the Demis the same as a single 11º seed bead. Repeat this stitch along the entire edge **(b–c)**, sewing through each single 11º or pair or Demis along the edge.
3) At the end of the band, pick up an I, and sew through the A you just exited and the new I **(figure 8, a–b)**. Pick up an F and an I, sew through the next C in the row below, and continue through the new F and I **(b–c)**. Repeat, picking

up Fs and Is until you reach the leather warps. Sew under the leather, through the middle three beads, and under the second leather warp **(c–d)**. Continue adding Is and Fs along the edge to mirror the other side **(d–e)**. Work as before to add the edging along the remaining side. When you reach the other end, add Fs and Is as you did on the first end.
4) With one leather strand, make a loop just big enough to fit over the button. With the other leather strand, tie an overhand knot around the base of the loop to secure the loop. Check the loop size by hooking it over the button. Adjust if needed, and then make a second overhand knot. Tighten the knot with your pliers, and glue the knot with hypo cement. When dry, trim the leather ends. **B✦B**

To tie off your thread, pass your needle under an adjacent weft thread. Bring your needle around the weft thread, make a half-hitch knot, and then pull to tighten. Sew through the rest of the row, and trim your thread. To start thread, use the same process, but tie a half-hitch knot over a weft thread, and then sew to your starting place.

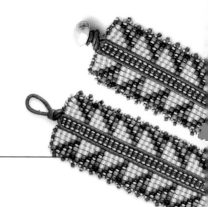

TIPS »

- This project requires Japanese seed beads. Do not substitute Czech beads since the width will not match the Demi beads.
- To help you get started, go to FacetJewelry.com and search "loomwork." Plus, most manufacturers offer basic videos specific to their looms.
- If you don't like working with KO thread and beeswax, use Fireline for the entire project. I like the hint of color on the leather warp threads that the KO provides.
- If you have a hard time separating the warp threads for the first few rows, take a piece of yarn and go through the warp threads, over and under, and slide it to the bottom of the loom. This will keep them separated until your weaving establishes the spacing. Discard when finished.

TUBULAR PEYOTE /
RIGHT-ANGLE WEAVE /
BEAD WEAVING

Rosette

pendant

Bezel a rivoli with seed beads, and enhance
it with a delightful combination of fire-polished
beads, crescents, and triangle beads.

designed by **Patrick Duggan**

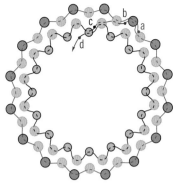

FIGURE 1

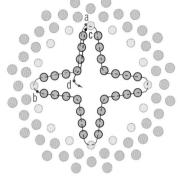

FIGURE 2

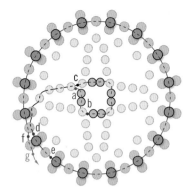

FIGURE 3

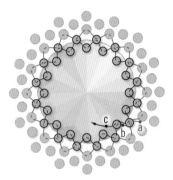

FIGURE 4

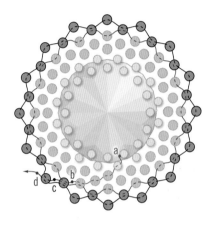

FIGURE 5

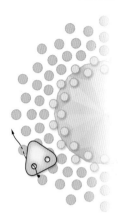

FIGURE 6

- 11º seed bead
- 15º seed bead, color A
- 14 mm rivoli
- 6 mm two-hole triangle bead - top view
- 3 x 10 mm crescent bead - top view
- 4 mm fire-polished bead
- 15º seed bead, color B
- 2 mm fire-polished bead
- 6º seed bead
- 15º seed bead, color C

Pendant

How to pick up triangle beads: With the point of the triangle with no hole facing away from you, pick up the bead through the left hole (LH). How to pick up crescent beads: With the tips of the crescent facing down, pick up the bead through the left hole (LH).

1 On a comfortable length of thread, pick up 32 11º seed beads, and sew through the beads again. Continue through the next two 11ºs to form a ring, leaving a 6-in. (15 cm) tail. These beads will shift to form rounds 1 and 2 as the next round is added.

2 Work a round of tubular peyote stitch using 11ºs, and step up through the first 11º added in the round **(figure 1, a–b)**.

3 Sew through the beadwork to exit an 11º in round 1 **(b–c)**. Work a round using color A 15º seed beads, and step up through the first A added in the round **(c–d)**.

4 Pick up seven As, skip the next three As in the previous round, and sew through the following A to form a loop **(figure 2, a–b)**. Repeat this stitch three times to complete the round **(b–c)**, and step up through the first four As added in this round **(c–d)**. Pick up two As, and sew through the center A in the next loop **(figure 3, a–b)**. Repeat this stitch three times to complete the round **(b–c)**, and retrace the thread path (not shown in the figure for clarity). This is now the back of the bezel.

5 Sew through the beadwork as shown to exit a "down" 11º in the outer ring **(c–d)**. Stitch in the ditch: Pick up an 11º, and sew through the next 11º in the same round **(d–e)**. Repeat this stitch 15 times to complete the round **(e–f)**, and sew through the adjacent 11º in the outer round **(f–g)**. Flip the beadwork over, and place the rivoli faceup inside the bezel setting.

6 Work a round using As, and step up through the first A added in this round **(figure 4, a–b)**. Repeat this step once **(b–c)**, and retrace the thread path. Sew through the beadwork as shown to exit an 11º stitch-in-the-ditch bead added in step 5 **(figure 5, a–b)**.

7 Using a firm but not tight tension, work a round using 11ºs, and step up at the end of the round **(b–c)**. Retrace the thread path (not shown in the figure for clarity). Any exposed thread will be

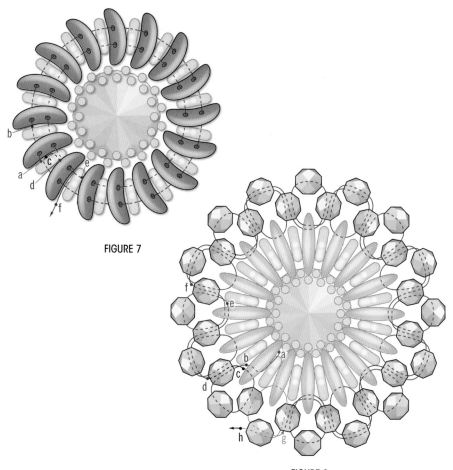

FIGURE 7

FIGURE 8

Difficulty rating

     ◇ ◇

Materials
green pendant 2 in. (5 cm)
- **1** 14 mm rivoli (Swarovski, volcano)
- **16** 3 x 10 mm CzechMates two-hole crescent beads (matte metallic antique gold)
- **16** 6 mm CzechMates two-hole triangle beads (opaque luster Picasso)
- **32** 4 mm fire-polished beads (opaque turquoise Picasso)
- **32** 2 mm fire-polished beads (turquoise bronze Picasso)
- **1 g** 6º seed beads (Toho 221, bronze)
- **1 g** 11º seed beads (Toho 221, bronze)
- 15º seed beads
  - **2 g** color A (Toho 221, bronze)
  - **1 g** color B (Miyuki 412, opaque light teal)
  - **1 g** color C (Miyuki 403, opaque bone)
- **1** 12 mm bail (gold)
- **1** 6 mm jump ring
- Fireline, 6 lb. test
- beading needles, #11 or #12
- **2** pairs of chainnose, flatnose, and/or bentnose pliers

Basics, p. 13
- peyote stitch: tubular
- right-angle weave: tubular
- ending and adding thread
- opening and closing jump rings

cinched up in future rounds. Repeat this step once **(c–d)**.

8 Pick up a triangle bead (LH) from front to back, and sew through the next 11º in the previous round **(figure 6)**. The triangle will sit on top of the beadwork with the open hole facing toward the rivoli. Repeat this stitch 15 times to complete the round. Retrace the thread path, and sew through the first triangle added **(figure 7, point a)**.

9 Pick up a crescent bead (LH) from front to back, and sew through the next triangle (LH) **(a–b)**. The crescent will sit on top of the beadwork with the open hole facing toward the rivoli. Repeat this stitch 15 times to complete the round, and retrace the thread path (not shown in the figure for clarity), exiting the last triangle **(b–c)**. Continue through the open hole of the triangle your thread is exiting **(c–d)**.

10 Sew through the open hole of the next crescent and triangle **(d–e)**. Repeat this stitch 15 times to complete the round, retrace the thread path (not shown in figure for clarity), and continue

through the next crescent **(e–f)**. Sew through the other hole of the crescent your thread is exiting **(figure 8, a–b)**.

11 Pick up three 4 mm fire-polished beads, and sew through the crescent your thread is exiting, going in the same direction **(b–c)**. Retrace the thread path (not shown in the figure for clarity), and continue through the first 4 mm added **(c–d)**.

12 Working in right-angle weave (RAW), pick up two 4 mms, and sew through the next crescent, the adjacent 4 mm in the previous stitch, and the two 4 mms just added. Retrace the thread path (not shown in the figure for clarity), and continue through the following crescent in the ring **(d–e)**. Pick up two 4 mms, and sew through the adjacent 4 mm in the previous stitch, the crescent your thread just exited, and the first 4 mm added in this stitch **(e–f)**. Retrace the thread path (not shown in the figure for clarity).

13 Repeat step 12 six times **(f–g)**. To complete the round, pick up a 4 mm, sew through the adjacent 4 mm in the

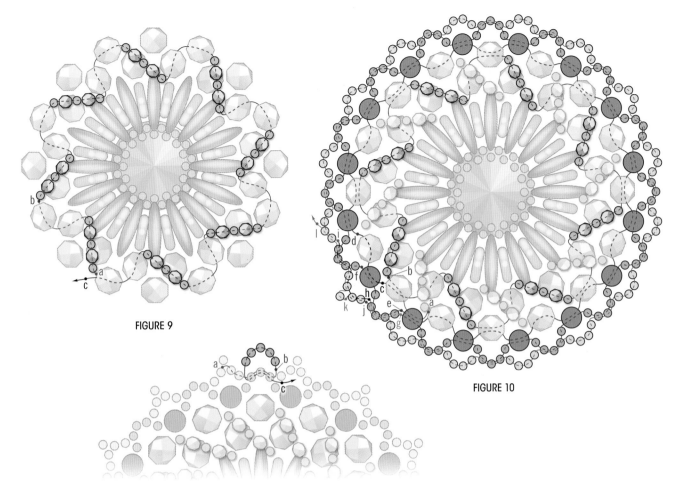

FIGURE 9

FIGURE 10

FIGURE 11

first stitch, the next crescent, the 4 mm your thread exited at the start of this step, and the 4 mm just added **(g–h)**.
14 Pick up a color B 15º seed bead, a 2 mm fire-polished bead, a B, a 2 mm, and a B, skip the next two 4 mms, and sew through the following two 4 mms **(figure 9, a–b)**. Repeat this stitch seven times to complete the round **(b–c)**.
15 Pick up a 6º seed bead, and sew through the next 4 mm in the outer ring **(figure 10, a–b)**. Repeat step 14 to add eight more bead sets between the previous sets, making sure to sew under the sets previously added **(b–c)**.
16 Pick up a 6º, and sew through the next 4 mm in the outer ring **(c–d)**. Repeat this stitch 14 times to complete the round. Retrace the thread path (not shown in the figure for clarity), and step up through the next 6º **(d–e)**.
17 Pick up five As, and sew through the next 6º to form a loop **(e–f)**. Repeat this stitch 15 times to compete the round **(f–g)**, and step up through the first four As added in this round **(g–h)**.

18 Pick up four color C 15º seed beads, skip the next A, 6º, and A, and sew through the center three As in the following loop to form a picot **(h–i)**. Repeat this stitch 15 times to complete the round **(i–j)**, and step up through the first two Cs added in this round **(j–k)**.
19 Pick up a C, and sew through the next seven beads as shown to exit the second C in the following picot **(k–l)**. This will form the tip of the picot. Repeat this stitch 15 times to complete the round. Retrace the thread path, but skip the C just added in each picot to make each tip C form a point.

Bail

1 Sew through the next five beads as shown **(figure 11, a–b)**. Pick up five As, and sew through the last three As your thread exited, going in the same direction to form the loop for the bail **(b–c)**. Retrace the thread path several times, and end the threads.
2 Open a jump ring, and attach the bail to the pendant loop. ●

change it up

If desired, alternate a second color of 11ºs in the bezel ring for a cool checkered pattern on the back of the pendant.

materials

canyon red necklace
13½ in. (34.3 cm)

- **1** 14 mm crystal rivoli (Swarovski, light topaz)
- **1** 12 x 14 mm gemstone nugget (white coral, white turquoise, or howlite; etsy.com)
- **10** 4 x 8 mm Trinity beads (gold luster)
- **6** 8 mm Dobble beads (matte metallic red)
- **43** 3 mm fire-polished beads (champagne opaque luster)
- **10** 3 mm round pearls (Swarovski, dark brown)
- **5 g** 8º seed (Miyuki 4452, Duracoat opaque banana)
- **11 g** 11º seed beads (Toho PF2113, permanent ruby opal silver-lined)
- **1** toggle clasp
- **2** 6 mm jump rings
- beading needles, #12
- Fireline, 6 lb. test
- thread burner (optional)
- **2** pairs of chainnose, flatnose, and/or bentnose pliers

basics, p. 13

- ending and adding thread
- ladder stitch
- tubular herringbone
- opening and closing loops and jump rings

Talise derives from an Iroquoian expression meaning "beautiful water." Spectacular sunken pools in the Grand Canyon inspired the creation of this pendant, which nestles a sparkling rivoli within walls of Trinity, Dobble, and seed beads.

Bezel

How to pick up the Trinity and Dobble beads: Place the Trinity beads on your bead mat with one hole pointing toward you. Pick up each bead through the left hole (LH), right hole (RH), or bottom hole (BH), per the instructions. Pick up Dobble beads through the left hole (LH) or right hole (RH). When using two- and three-hole beads, check first to ensure that all holes are open.

1) On a comfortable length of thread, pick up a repeating pattern of a size 11º seed bead and a size 8º seed bead 10 times. Leaving a 6-in. (15 cm) tail, sew through the beads again to form a ring, and continue through the first 11º and 8º picked up. Pick up an 11º, and sew through the next 8º **(figure 1, a–b)**. Repeat this stitch nine times to complete the round, and step up through the first 11º added **(b–c)**.

2) Pick up a 3 mm pearl, and sew through the next 11º. Repeat this stitch nine times to complete the round, and step up through the first pearl added **(c–d)**.

3) Pick up a 3 mm fire-polished bead, and sew through the next pearl. Repeat this stitch nine times to complete the round, but do not step up **(d–e)**.

4) Pick up three 11ºs, and sew through the next pearl to form a picot. Repeat this stitch nine times to complete the round, and step up through the first two 11ºs added **(e–f)**.

5) Insert the rivoli face down into the beadwork. Pick up one 11º, and sew through the center 11º in the next picot **(figure 2, a–b)**. Using tight tension, repeat this stitch nine times to complete the round, sewing through the first 11º added **(b–c)**. Work another round using 11ºs to secure the rivoli, and sew through the beadwork to exit a fire-polished bead.

6) Pick up a Trinity bead (BH), and sew through next fire-polished bead **(figure 3, a–b)**. Repeat this stitch nine times to complete the

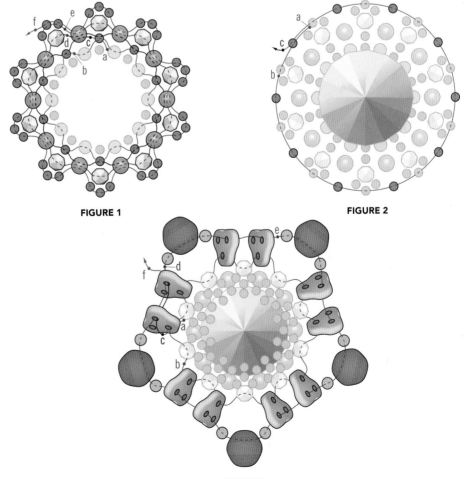

FIGURE 1

FIGURE 2

FIGURE 3

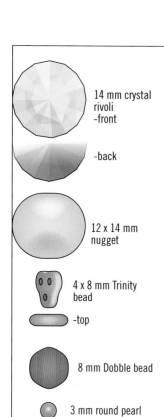

14 mm crystal rivoli
-front

-back

12 x 14 mm nugget

4 x 8 mm Trinity bead

-top

8 mm Dobble bead

3 mm round pearl

3 mm fire-polished bead

8º seed bead

11º seed bead

round, and step up through the first Trinity (BH) added **(b–c)**. Sew through the (RH) of same Trinity just exited, and continue through the next Trinity (RH) **(c–d)**.

7) Pick up an 8º, a Dobble bead, and an 8º, and sew through the next two Trinities (RH) **(d–e)**. Repeat this stitch four times to complete the round **(e–f)**.

NOTE Make sure the Trinity beads' holes are aligned, since it is easy to twist them. When you flip the beadwork, the thread that once went through a (RH) will now appears to go through a (LH).

8) Flip the beadwork over so the rivoli is face up. Sew through the open hole (RH) of the Trinity just exited, and sew through the open hole of the next Trinity. Pick up an 11º and an 8º, and sew through the open hole of the next Dobble. Pick

up an 8º and an 11º **(figure 4, a–b)**. Repeat this stitch four times to complete the round **(b–c)**. Retrace the thread path through the last round **(c–d)**, and then continue through one Trinity (RH) and the adjacent fire-polished bead **(d–e)**.

9) Pick up two 11ºs and sew through the next fire-polished bead **(e–f)**. Repeat this stitch nine times to complete the round, and step up through the next Trinity's inner hole (RH) **(f–g)**.

10) Pick up two 11ºs, and sew through the adjacent outer hole of the same Trinity (RH) and the corresponding hole of the next Trinity **(figure 5, a–b)**. Pick up two 11ºs, and sew through the adjacent hole of the same Trinity (RH) and the corresponding hole of the previous Trinity **(b–c)**. Continue through the first two 11ºs added in this step **(c–d)**.

11) Pick up an 11º, a fire-polished bead, and an 11º, and sew through

the next two 11ºs **(figure 6, a–b)**. Pick up an 11º, a fire-polished bead, and an 11º, and then sew through the next two 11ºs **(b–c)**, ending where you started. Sew through the next 11º, fire-polished bead, and four 11ºs, exiting the front side of pendant **(c–d)**.

12) Pick up an 11º, a Dobble, an 11º, the nugget bead, and three 11ºs, and sew back through the nugget **(d–e)**. Pick up an 11º, and sew through the open hole of the Dobble **(e–f)**. Pick up an 11º, and sew through the next three 11ºs **(f–g)**. Pull the thread and tighten the beads. Retrace the thread path, and end both threads.

Herringbone neck strap

1) On 5 ft. (1.5 m) of thread, pick up four 11ºs, leaving a 10-in. (25 cm) tail. Sew through all four beads again **(figure 7)** so you have two stacks of two beads,

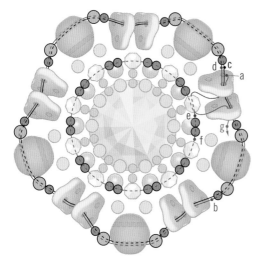

FIGURE 4

FIGURE 5

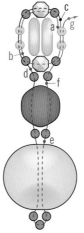

FIGURE 6

THE CHOICE IS YOURS

The turquoise necklace is made with Fireline, 6 lb. test, while the red necklace is made with One-G thread in a matching color. Fireline gives a firm feel and the pendant appears slightly smaller. The thread makes the red rope softer and the pendant slightly larger.

and tighten. Working in ladder stitch, pick up two beads per stitch to make a strip of four two-bead stacks of 11ºs. Form a ring by sewing through the first stack and then the last stack again **(figure 8)**. These two-bead stacks will form the first two rounds of your rope.

2) Working in tubular herringbone stitch, work in rounds as follows:

Round 3: Pick up two 11ºs, and sew through the next two top end 11ºs in the ring **(figure 9)**. Repeat once, and step up through the first bead added in this round.

Rounds 4–15: Continue using 11ºs until you have a total of 15 rounds.

Rounds 16–17: Work two rounds using 8ºs.

Round 18: Work one round with two fire-polished beads per stitch.

Rounds 19–20: Work two rounds using 8ºs.

Rounds 21–50: Work 30 rounds with 11ºs.

3) Repeat rounds 16–50 three times.

4) To form a beaded loop at the end of the rope, pick up eight 11ºs, and sew through the opposite 11º in the end round **(figure 10)**. Sew through the adjacent end 11º, and the sew back through the loop and the 11º next to the one you exited at the start of this step. Retrace the thread path several times to reinforce the loop. End the working thread but not the tail.

5) Repeat steps 1–4 to make another neck strap.

Assembly

1) Attach a needle to the tail of a neck strap. Pick up a fire-polished bead, and sew through two Trinities (RH) at the top of the pendant **(figure 11, a–b)**. Pick up a fire-polished bead, and sew through the end two 11ºs in the adjacent stack at the end on the neck strap **(b–c)**. Sew through the end two 11ºs on the next stack at the end of the strap.

N O T E As you attach the ropes to the pendant, make sure they are not twisted.

2) Pick up a fire-polished bead, and sew through the other outer holes of the two Trinities this rope is attached to. Pick up a fire-polished bead, and sew through the end two 11ºs in the remaining open stack in the neck strap.

3) Retrace the thread path several times to reinforce the connection, and end the thread.

4) Repeat steps 1–3 to attach the other neck strap to the adjacent set of Trinities at the top of the pendant.

5) Open a jump ring, and attach it to the loop of a toggle clasp and the beaded loop at the end of a neck strap. Repeat at the end of the other neck strap. **B&B**

Back of pendant

FIGURE 7

FIGURE 8

FIGURE 9

FIGURE 10

FIGURE 11

Other
Techniques

Botanical bling
necklace

Combine dangles and a filigree bezel finding to make a playful necklace.

designed by **Irina Miech**

Necklace

1 Place the rivoli in the bezel setting and use flat-nose pliers to press the filigree side inward around the perimeter of the bezel.

2 Cut a 1-in. (2.5 cm) piece of chain, and attach a 6 mm jump ring to the crystal drop bead and an end link of the chain.

3 Cut a ½-in. (1.3 cm) piece of chain. On a head pin, string a 6 mm bicone crystal, make the first half of a wrapped loop, attach the loop to an end link of the chain, and complete the wrap.

4 Cut a ½-in. (1.3 cm) piece of chain. Attach a 5 mm jump ring to the flower charm and an end link of the chain.

5 Use a 5 mm jump ring to attach the three chains, and then use two 5 mm jump rings to attach the group of chains and the bezel loop to a 12 mm soldered ring.

6 For each side of the necklace, use 3.5 mm jump rings to alternate three 1-in. (2.5 cm) pieces of chain with three connector links. End with a 5-in. (13 cm) piece of chain.

7 Use 3.5 mm jump rings to attach a clasp on one end and an extender chain on the other end. Attach a 5 mm bicone crystal dangle to the end of the extender chain. ●

Materials
necklace 20½ in. (52.1 cm) plus extender chain
- 1 14 x 12 mm crystal drop bead (Swarovski, violet)
- 1 12 mm rivoli (Swarovski, light sapphire)
- 1 6 mm bicone crystal (Swarovski, violet)
- 1 5 mm bicone crystal (Swarovski, light sapphire)
- 1 10 mm flower charm (silver)
- 6 13 x 4 mm two-hole connector links
- 1 12 mm filigree bezel setting
- 1 lobster claw clasp
- **20 in. (51 cm)** 2 mm rolo chain
- **2 in. (5 cm)** extender chain
- **2** 2-in. (5 cm) ball-end head pins
- 1 12 mm soldered jump ring
- 1 6 mm jump ring
- 5 5 mm jump rings
- 16 3.5 mm jump rings
- 2 pairs of chainnose, flatnose, and/or bentnose pliers

Basics, p.13
- opening and closing jump rings
- wrapped loops

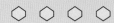

materials
pendant 2 x 2¼ in. (5–5.7 cm)

- **34** 12 x 7.6 mm aluminum scales (frost, theringlord.com)
- **1** ¾ in. (large), 16-gauge SWG jump ring (aluminum, candtdesigns.com)
- **104** ⁷⁄₆₄ in. (small), 20-gauge jump rings (black ice, theringlord.com)
- **2** pairs of chainnose, flat-nose, and/or bentnose pliers
- tape

basics, p. 13
- opening and closing jump rings

Suggesting dragons, fish, or birds, this light-as-air pendant is a great introduction to chain mail built on a micro scale.

You will start making this pendant at the bottom point and work your way up.

NOTE In the step-by-step photos, the jump rings being added are shown in several colors for visibility. In the project the rings are all the same color.

1) Open all the jump rings.
2) Use two small jump rings to connect three scales together, making sure the concave side of each scale is facing up (**photo a**).
3) Use tape to position the three scales and jump rings as shown in **photo b**. You have just created the first two rows. The first row consists of one scale and the second row consists of two scales. As you add rows, each new row will have one more scale than the previous row, expanding the width of the piece.
4) Weave rows as follows:
Row 3: Use two jump rings to attach a scale above and between the scales in the previous row (**photo c, red rings**). Be sure the new scale is positioned underneath rows 1 and 2. Use two more jump rings to attach a scale on the right and a scale on the left (**photo d, turquoise rings**).
Row 4: Using two jump rings each, attach two scales to the previous row (**photo e, red rings**). Complete the row by adding a jump ring and scale on each end of the row (**photo f, turquoise rings**).

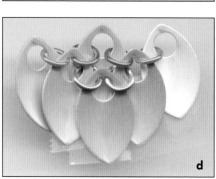

a

b

c

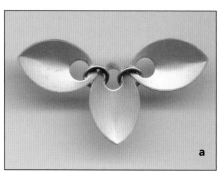

d

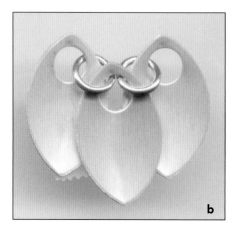

e

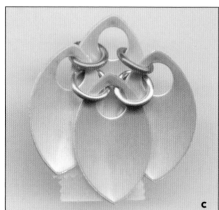

f

5) Continue adding rows as in step 4 until you have seven rows (this last row has seven scales).

6) Begin to work one more row, but add only six scales instead of eight — omit the end scales.

7) One at a time, add one small jump ring to the outer edge of the left scale in the second row from the top, and one small jump ring to the outer edge of the right scale in the second row from the top **(photo g, red rings)**. These two jump rings become the first and last jump ring of the top row of jump rings (14 jump rings in total).

8) One at a time, weave a small open jump ring through each pair of jump rings in the previous row to add a total of seven rings **(photo h, orange rings)**.

9) One at a time, weave two small jump rings through each of the small jump rings added in step 4, connecting them to the scales in the top row **(photo i, green rings)**.

The outer jump rings added keep the outer edges of the pendant even. Make sure you add a total of 14 jump rings in this step.

10) One at a time, add a row of 13 small jump rings, weaving them through the jump rings added in the previous row **(photo j, pink rings)**.

11) One at a time, add a row of 14 small jump rings through the rings added in the previous row **(photo k, yellow rings)**.

12) Following the weaving path shown in **photo l**, weave the large open jump ring through each of the small rings added in the previous row **(photo m)**. Close the large jump ring.

13) String your pendant as desired.
B&B

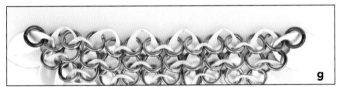

g

h

i

j

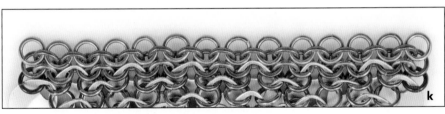

k

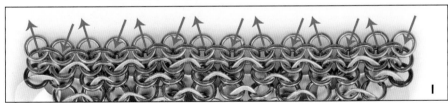

l

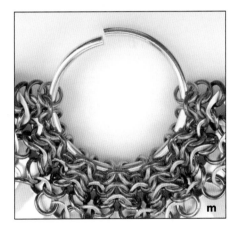

m

YOU'VE GOT CHAIN MAIL TIPS >>

• The jump rings used in this project are tiny. It's helpful to use magnification while making this.

• Always have more jump rings handy, in case a ring gets bent or is otherwise unusable for a project.

• Keep in mind that scales have a front and back. Unless otherwise told in directions, the front is convex, and the back is concave.

• Have an awl or toothpick on hand for positioning the scales and jump rings as you work.

• Choose pliers with small, thin jaws.

• When making your own jump rings, always smooth and polish the rings with a file to eliminate sharp edges.

Leather chevron bracelets

by Becky Guzman

The key to making this bracelet work is using beads, rings, and leather cording in the correct proportions.

this simple design has been shared online and in classes for several years. It's a great example of a design that hearkens back to days at summer camp but has been updated and up-scaled to reflect a more sophisticated sensibility. The many choices of bead styles, colors, leather cords, and rings make it a design that appeals to many tastes.

A single wrap bracelet requires about 30 in. (76 cm) of leather; a double wrap requires 45 in. (1.1 m); and a triple wrap uses 60 in. (1.5 m). To make this easy bracelet, center a button on a length of leather, and tie an overhand knot with both cords to secure it. Slide a bead on one strand of leather, and then slide a ring over both strands. Switch to the other strand, and do it again. Alternate beads and rings until you reach the desired length. Tie two knots to make an opening to fasten the button, and then stack on your newest bracelet!

BEADS

A wide range of beads work well with this bracelet style. The most important factor is to use beads with large (1.5–2.5 mm), consistent-sized holes so that the beads fit on the leather and the design flows smoothly. This design comes together best when the leather fits the bead holes without excessive wiggle room. Avoid any bead holes with rough edges — they can cut through leather over time.

LEATHER

When using leather, it's important to make sure it is strong and will hold up over time. The quality of the hide, the tanning process, and oil content determine the strength and softness of leather cord. Test that your leather is suited to this purpose by running it through your fingers, feeling for

COMBINATIONS THAT WORK WELL TOGETHER:

BEAD TYPE	HOLE SIZE	LEATHER SIZE	RING SIZE (OUT-SIDE DIAMETER)	APPROX. # OF BEADS NEEDED FOR A 6½-IN. (16.5 CM) WRIST
4 mm or size 6º seed bead	1.5–1.6 mm	1–1.5 mm	6 mm	56
5 mm or size 5º seed bead	2 mm	1.5–2 mm	7–8 mm	48
6 mm round	1.2–1.5 mm	1–1.5 mm	7–8 mm	40
8 mm round	2.5 mm	1.5–2 mm	8 mm	28
8 mm rondelle	2.5 mm	1.5–2 mm	8 mm	36–44

bumps, thin spots, or splices that indicate that the leather has been joined at that point. Higher-quality leathers will be knotted where two pieces are joined. If you can break your leather by simply pulling firmly, it isn't the quality you want to use for this type of bracelet.

The thinnest leather available is .5 mm in diameter and it will fit through lots of bead holes, but it isn't a good choice for this type of bracelet, as even high-quality .5 mm leather can be easily torn.

Keep in mind that there is an industry tolerance of +/- .3 mm for leather cording. For example, 1.5 mm leather can range in size from 1.2–1.8 mm, so if you are working with $6^{\underline{o}}$ seed beads, you may find your 1.5 mm leather to be too thick and then you either need to choose beads with larger holes or find a thinner leather.

RINGS

Rings should fit over two strands of leather such that the ring separates the bead on each strand and isn't so large that it slides over the bead or so small that it pulls it too tightly and prevents a nice zig-zag flow. A heavier gauge ring (18–19 gauge) works best. Soldered rings, twisted jump rings and split rings all work well and each gives a unique look.

VARIATIONS

• Feature more leather and fewer beads by positioning the beads in a 1½–3 in. (3.8–7.6 cm) segment at the center of the bracelet. Tie a knot at each end of the beaded segment to keep the beads in place.
• Make a necklace by positioning a 5–8-in. (13–20 cm) segment of beads in the center of a necklace-length (48–60 in./1.2–1.5 m) piece of leather.
• Add large-hole focal beads. This is a great way to feature handmade glass or clay beads.
• Your beads don't all have to be the same size and shape — try an asymmetrical, organic look.
• Use leather ends with a traditional lobster or toggle clasp to take this look from bohemian to sophisticated. Gel Control Super Glue is a great choice for bonding leather to metal ends.
• For a more elegant look, string bicone crystals and glass pearls on beading wire and use 4–6 mm closed rings. **B**B

Diakonos Designs offers a variety of chevron bracelet kits at their retail bead store in downtown Stoughton, Wisconsin, and online at DiakonosDesigns.com.

TIPS

 Twist a tight bead onto the leather and pull it through carefully. A close but not too snug fit is best. If the leather tip gets blunted, pinch and pull it out to compress and elongate it, and snip it to a sharp point.

• If you start with one of the cords just a slight bit longer than the other (to differentiate them as you work), it's easy to load three or four beads and rings at a time, then slide them down the leather to the end and gently press them into place.

• Check for size before stringing more beads than you need. The leather loop at the end functions like a toggle, so it becomes part of the overall bracelet length.

PUSSY WILLOW BOUQUET

by Svetlana Sapegina

DIFFICULTY ●●●○○

French beaded flowers

Stretch your beading skills with this stunning bouquet. Though it uses just one technique, it poses a big challenge — do you have the stamina to complete the whole thing?

materials
one branch 27 in. (69 cm)

- 10^0 two-cut seed beads
  - **15–20 g** color A (white, gray, or yellow-green)*
  - **3 g** color B (brown)
  - **3 g** color C (light green)
- 26-gauge craft wire, **1** spool each of silver and brown
- **27 in. (69 cm)** 12-gauge wire (for main stem)
- **20 in. (51 cm)** 14-gauge wire (for offshoot branch)
- brown floral tape
- roundnose pliers
- wire cutters

* The pussy willow bouquet is made up of 33 branches, each of which features colors A, B, and C two-cut beads. There are nine different shades of color A beads, but each individual branch uses color A beads in a single hue.

a

b

c

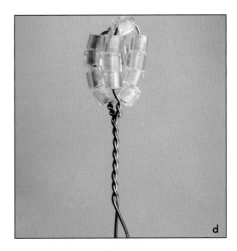

d

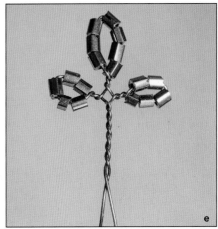

e

CONTINUOUS LOOPS TECHNIQUE

Use this technique throughout this project, using the wire and beads indicated for each component.

1) String beads as indicated in your pattern onto a spool of wire. Slide the beads that will make up the first loop toward the end of the wire. The directions for the project will indicate either a specific number of beads or a specific length of beaded wire to use for each loop.

2) Leaving a 1–2-in. (2.5–5 cm) tail of bare wire, make a loop with the beads, grasp the loop, and twist it several times below the loop of beads (**photo a**). Leave a small amount of bare wire, and then make another loop with the next group of beads (**photo b**). Repeat until you've made all the loops needed for the component you're making.

3) Leaving about 1–2 in. (2.5–5 cm) of bare wire after the last loop, trim the wire, and then twist the two wire tails together (**photo c**).

BUD

For each bud, string 1 in. (2.5 cm) of color B 10^0 two-cut beads on brown wire, and make two loops with ½ in (1.3 cm) of beads each. Repeat this step to make a total of eight buds.

SMALL WILLOW CATKIN

1) Make willow fluff: On silver wire, string 1 in. (2.5 cm) of color A 10^0 two-cut beads, and make two loops with ½ in. (1.3 cm) of beads each (**photo d**).

2) Make sepals: On brown wire, string 17 Bs, and make three loops — one with five beads, one with seven beads, and one with five beads. Twist the ends together — there should be a small hole in the center (**photo e**).

3) Insert the willow fluff through the hole in the center of the sepal, twist the wires together (**photo f**).

4) Repeat steps 1–3 to make a total of six small catkins.

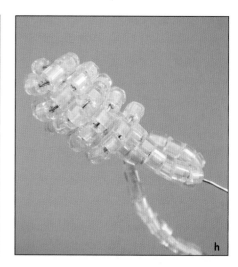

MEDIUM WILLOW CATKIN

1) Work as in "Small willow catkin" with the following changes:

- For the willow fluff, string 3 in. (7.6 cm) of As and make four loops, each with ¾ in. (1.9 cm) of beads.
- For the sepals, string 15 Bs, and make three loops of five beads each.

2) Repeat to make a total of 10 medium catkins.

LARGE WILLOW CATKIN

1) Work as in "Small willow catkin" with the following changes:

- For the willow fluff, string 4 in. (10 cm) of As, and make four loops with 1 in. (2.5 cm) of beads each.
- For the sepals, string 20 color C 10º two-cut beads, and make a loop of six, a loop of eight, and a loop of six.

2) Repeat to make a total of 10 large catkins.

BLOSSOMING BUD

1) String about 2¼ in. (5.7 cm) of As. With the end 1½ in. (3.8 cm) of beads, make a loop. Bring the working wire up toward the end of the loop, and slide the remaining beads to the base of the loop. The beads should fill the space inside the loop.

2) Cut the wire about 10 in. (25 cm) from the last bead strung, and fix the wire in place by making one wrap around the wire at the end of the loop **(photo g)**.

3) String 7½ in. (19.1 cm) of As, and make a small loop at the end of the wire to prevent the beads from slipping off the wire in the next step.

4) Wrap the strand of As around the loop from top to bottom **(photo h)**. Twist the wire ends together.

5) Make sepals: String 20 color C 10º two-cut beads, and make a loop of six, a loop of eight, and a loop of six.

6) Attach the fluff to the sepals as before.

7) Repeat steps 1–6 to make a total of four blossoming buds.

ASSEMBLY

1) Each branch is actually made up of one main stem and one offshoot branch. Separate the components into two groups **(photo i)**.

Main stem:	Offshoot branch:
6 buds	2 buds
3 small catkins	3 small catkins
7 medium catkins	3 medium catkins
7 large catkins	3 large catkins
3 blossoming buds	1 blossoming bud

2) Stick the end of the brown floral tape to the end of the main stem wire. Stretching the tape as you work, wrap the tape around the stem wire, attaching components as you go, distributing them in pairs or in a staggered arrangement. Repeat this step with the other stem wire and the components for the offshoot branch **(photo j)**.

3) Attach the two stems together, and make small bends to give the brand a natural-looking shape **(photo k)**.

4) For a full bouquet, make a total of 33 branches, varying the color A beads as desired. **B&B**

Alternate faceted round beads with gemstone rondelles to create an upscale bracelet that showcases a stunning amethyst link.

ROTATING RONDELLE BRACELET

designed by Sarah Caligiuri

DIFFICULTY ● ○ ○ ○ ○

Stringing

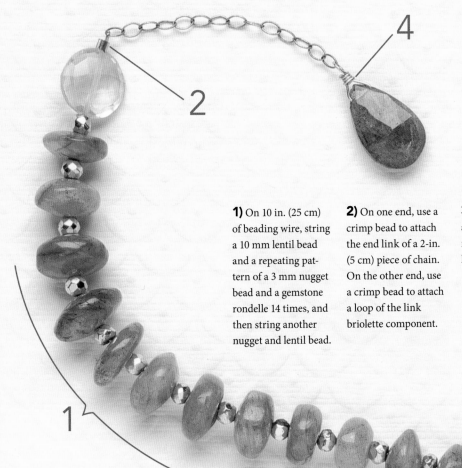

1) On 10 in. (25 cm) of beading wire, string a 10 mm lentil bead and a repeating pattern of a 3 mm nugget bead and a gemstone rondelle 14 times, and then string another nugget and lentil bead.

2) On one end, use a crimp bead to attach the end link of a 2-in. (5 cm) piece of chain. On the other end, use a crimp bead to attach a loop of the link briolette component.

3) Use a jump ring to attach the clasp to the remaining loop on the link component.

4) On a 3-in. (7.6 cm) piece of wire, center a 12 x 8 mm briolette, and cross the ends to form an X above the briolette. Using chain-nose pliers, make a small bend in each end so they form a right angle. Wrap the horizontal wire around the vertical wire. Trim the excess wrapping wire. Make a wrapped loop with the vertical wire, but slide the loop onto the end link of the chain before completing the wrap. B&B

materials
adjustable bracelet
6½–8 in. (16.5–20 cm)

- **1** 12 x 8 mm briolette (labradorite)
- **2** 10 mm lentil or oval beads (green amethyst or quartz)
- **14** 6–8 mm gemstone rondelles (labradorite)
- **15** 3 mm faceted nugget beads (22k gold-plated metal)
- **1** 12 x 18 mm briolette stone link component (amethyst with gold bezel; beadaholique.com)
- **1** spring ring clasp (gold)
- **3 in. (7.6 cm)** 22-gauge wire (gold)

- **2 in. (5 cm)** small-link chain (gold)
- **1** 5 mm jump ring (gold)
- **2** crimp beads
- **10 in. (25 cm)** flexible beading wire (.014)
- chainnose pliers
- crimping pliers
- roundnose pliers
- wire cutters

basics, p. 13

- crimping
- opening and closing jump rings
- wrapped loop

Sunset harbor
earrings

Create clever tassels and incorporate them into a whimsical pair of framed earrings.

designed by **Jamie Van**

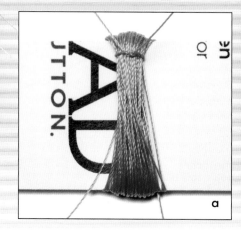

a

b

c

d

Tassels

1 Determine the desired length of your tassel, allowing an additional ³⁄₁₆ in. (5 mm) for the end cap. Our tassels measure between 1⁵⁄₁₆–1⁷⁄₁₆ in. (3.3–3.7 cm). Trim a business card or scrap piece of card stock to the desired size. Working with the free end of the spool of S-Lon nylon cord, complete 60 wraps around the card, wrapping the cord within a ¼ in. (6 mm) section on the card. Trim the cord so the tails extend about ½ in. (1.3 cm) beyond the edge of the card.

2 Cut a 12-in. (30 cm) piece of cord, and pass it under the wrapped cords just below the top edge, center it, and make a square knot around the wrapped cords **(photo a)**. Do not trim the tails.

tip It may help to use a needle to get the 12-in. (30 cm) cord under the wrapped cords.

3 Gently slide the wrapped cord off the card. Using a tail from the knotted cord from step 2, make five wraps around the cords to cover the knotted section, make a square knot **(photo b)**, and trim the tails to the same length as the other tassel cords.

4 With a toothpick, apply a small dab of E6000 adhesive inside a 6 mm end cap. Squeeze the sides of the wrapped cords together near the knotted section, and insert the cord inside the end cap **(photo c)**. Set the tassel aside to dry for an hour.

5 Use a pair of scissors to cut the bottom end of the loop **(photo d)**, and trim any uneven cords.

6 If desired, hold the ends of the tassel over a candle flame or lighter for a few seconds to seal and prevent the ends from fraying.

7 Work as in steps 1–6 to make a matching tassel.

Assembly

1 Cut a 3-in. (7.6 cm) piece of 24-gauge wire. On one end, make a small wrapped loop. String one hole of a bead frame, a spacer bead, a 12 mm pearl, and a spacer bead, and thread the wire through the open hole of the bead frame. Make a wrapped loop on the other end of the wire **(photo e)**.

2 Use a 6 mm jump ring to attach the tassel's end cap to a wrapped loop on the bead frame **(photo f)**.

3 Open the loop of an ear wire, and attach the remaining wrapped loop of the bead frame before closing the loop.

4 Repeat steps 1–3 with the other tassel. ●

Difficulty rating

Materials

purple earrings 2¼ in. (5.7 cm)
- **2** 12 mm pearls or round beads (Swarovski, bronze)
- **2** 18 mm round bead frames (www.jjbeads.com)
- **6 in. (15 cm)** 24-gauge wire (gold-filled)
- **2** 6 mm cord end caps (TierraCast, gold)
- **4** 4–5 mm star-shaped spacer beads (gold)
- **2** 6 mm jump rings (gold)
- **1** pair of earring findings
- S-Lon nylon cord (Tex 70, purple)
- Big Eye needle or tapestry needle (optional)
- E6000 adhesive
- business card or scrap piece of card stock
- candle or lighter (optional)
- toothpicks
- scissors
- **2** pairs of chainnose, flatnose, and/or bentnose pliers

Information for the alternate colorways are listed at facetjewelry.com/resourceguide.

Basics, p. 13
- square knot
- opening and closing jump rings
- wrapped loop

choose your frame

Different bead frames such as the ones here, can alter the look of the design.

e

f

214

Revolutionize how you collect vacation keepsakes by making molds from inspiring settings.

When you travel, you never know what you're going to find — that's the magic of it. Each time you leave your everyday life, you enter into a new space of potential wonder, creativity, and transformation.

In the summer of 2016, I traveled to Tahiti with my family and stayed on a small island called Ninamu. It is one of the most magical places I've ever been. The ocean is a perfect cerulean blue dotted with tiny coral islands. Fresh, salty ocean breezes swirl through the palm trees. Coconut crabs and hermit crabs overrun the island. And the rhythmic lap of waves against the beach is now my favorite musical memory.

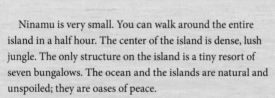

Ninamu is very small. You can walk around the entire island in a half hour. The center of the island is dense, lush jungle. The only structure on the island is a tiny resort of seven bungalows. The ocean and the islands are natural and unspoiled; they are oases of peace.

Even though I usually do not create art while I am traveling, my artist's eye is always open and watching for new inspiration. I never know what to expect, so I always travel with molding compound to create casts of unusual leaves and plants. Since there are many things that can't be taken home, this offers a wonderful way to preserve the unusual textures that I encounter.

In Tahiti, one of my favorite things to do is to explore the islands and the ocean while kayaking. Some isles hold palm trees while others are so small that there is nothing but solid coral that disappears under the sea during high tide. Because these coral islets have never been tumbled by the waves, the coral is pristine with some of the most amazing natural textures I've ever seen.

Equipped with reef shoes, I ventured out during low tide to many small coral atolls. I used my mold compound to capture parts of the coral that were the most striking, careful not to disturb the living creatures.

I treasure these molds because they can be used over and over again to create gorgeous mementos of my sun-soaked days of exploring the ocean.

STEP LIGHTLY
Coral reefs are invaluable to the ecosystem and should never be disturbed. According to the U.S. Fish and Wildlife Service, "Coral species may be protected under international, domestic, or even state environmental laws." It is important to educate yourself on local species acts before interacting with any wild flora and fauna and never remove items from protected locations. Please note that no coral was harmed in the making of this project.

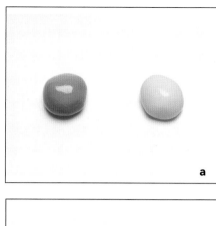
a

b

c

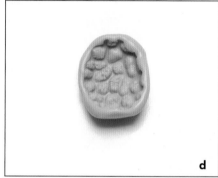
d

materials

silver clay component
½–2⅓ in. (1.3–5.9 cm);
your size may vary

- molding compound, two-part silicone (Mega-Sil)
- **16 g** PMC III clay
- artifact for impression (dead coral shown)
- **10 g** PMC III one-tip syringe, pre-filled with silver clay
- kiln (Paragon SC-2, or other PMC jewelry-making kiln)
- flexible sanding pad and round metal file
- craft scalpel
- water brush
- metal stylus or awl
- metal clay roller, optional
- Pro-polishing Pad or jewelry polishing cloth
- 3 mm cubic zirconia (CZ) stone (spinel blue), optional
- fine tweezers, optional but needed for CZ
- liver of sulfur, optional

Mold

1) Starting with equal parts of the molding compounds **(photo a)**, knead the blue and white compound together until the color is uniform. (Estimate the amount of compound needed by determining the size of your desired finish project and doubling.)

2) Flatten the top of the compound with your fingers or roll it out with the roller **(photo b)**, making it deep enough to accommodate your artifact.

3) Press your artifact into the compound **(photo c)**. If you are using a deep artifact, you may need to press the compound around it with your fingers.

4) You can reposition the artifact while the compound is soft. When pleased with the look, let the artifact and compound dry together, about five minutes. When dry, remove the artifact **(photo d)**.

Component

1) Estimate the amount of PMCIII clay needed to fill the mold (this will be the size of your finished project). Shape the clay with your fingers to resemble the mold's opening **(photo e)**.

2) Press the clay into the mold **(photo f)**. Let the clay dry. You can expedite the drying process by using a hair dryer or food dehydrator.

3) Remove the clay from the mold **(photo g)**.

4) Use a flexible sanding pad and metal files to define and sand the edges of the piece **(photo h)**.

5) Gently, use a scalpel to make a connector hole **(photo i)**, and then use a round metal file to smooth out the hole **(photo j)**.

6) Dip a paint brush in water, and swipe the back to wet a section **(photo k)**. Use a stylus or awl to sign your component **(photo l)**. Let dry five minutes.

7) With a sanding pad, smooth the back of the component. Turn the sanding pad over to the smooth side, and wipe the component's back once more to remove any remaining debris **(photo m)**.

8) Optional: If you choose to set a cubic zirconia stone (CZ), do so using the "blob method": To make a blob, wet the component where the CZ will sit, using a wet brush. With the PMCIII syringe, extract a blob of clay that is 1½ times the size of the CZ **(photo n)**. Use the brush to reshape and flatten the bob slightly. Use tweezers to place the CZ on the blob, and then push down, keeping the stone centered. Reshape the blob's side with the brush, if needed **(photo o)**.

9) Dry the component, then fire for two hours at 1650 degrees F. When cool enough to handle, polish the components with a polishing cloth.

10) If desired, add a patina to the component by dipping in liver of sulfur **(photo p)**. Polish again, and integrate into a finished piece of jewelry as desired. **B&B**

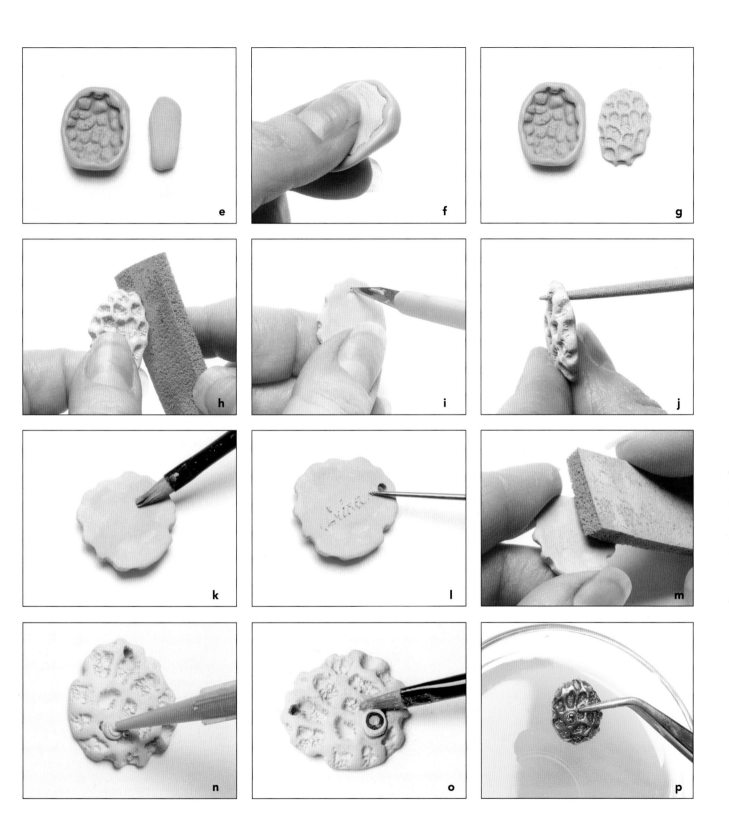

Scarab earrings

I love ancient Egyptian jewelry, with its fascinating symbols, shapes, and colors, and decided to create a pair of "scarab" earrings using faux cloisonné.

designed by Alice Todd

materials
earrings 2 in. (5 cm)

- Nunn Design components and supplies (nunndesign.com)
  - **2** 22 x 12 x 2 mm double-loop mini links, oval (antique gold)
  - **2** 19 x 16.5 x 2.7 mm single-loop mini links, triangle (antique gold)
  - **4** 2-in. (5 cm) head pins (antique gold)
  - **2** 9 mm texture circle jump rings (antique gold)
  - **1** pair of earring findings (antique gold)
  - Nunn Design resin kit
  - Castin'Crafts Opaque Pigment in three colors (white, blue, red)
- microbeads (gold; americancrafts.com)
- 5-minute 2-part epoxy adhesive
- plastic bag to cover work surface
- gloves or barrier cream
- ruler
- flush cutters
- metal file
- tweezers
- mixing cups and sticks
- toothpicks

I chose an oval bezel for the scarab body and a triangle bezel to suggest the pyramids. I glued wires inside the bezels and then added colorized resin and gold microbeads in the enclosed areas to bring the design to life.

PREP THE BEZELS

1) Cover your work surface with a plastic bag.
2) Cut the head pins into 10 pieces as follows: Cut two 6 mm segments, six 8 mm segments, and two 9 mm segments. Adjust and smooth the pieces by lightly filing them with a metal file until they fit into the bezels **(figures 1 and 2)**.
3) Mix up a small amount of 2-part epoxy adhesive per the manufacturer's instructions.
4) Using tweezers, pick up an 8 mm wire segment, dip it into the 2-part epoxy, and place it horizontally inside the oval bezel about one-third of the way from the top of the bezel **(figure 1, segment A)**. Dip a 9 mm segment into the epoxy, and place it about 2 mm below the first one and parallel to it **(figure 1, segment B)**. Dip an 8 mm segment into the epoxy, and place it perpendicular to the previous piece in the center of the oval bezel **(figure 1, segment C)**. Repeat to create the same design in the second oval bezel.

N O T E **You may need to repeat step 3 if your glue starts to dry.**

5) Dip an 8 mm segment into the epoxy, and place it into the triangle bezel, about one-third of the way from the top **(figure 2, segment D)**. Dip a 6 mm segment into the epoxy, and place it about 2 mm below the previous one **(figure 2, segment E)**. Repeat for the second triangle bezel.

ADD RESIN

1) Wearing gloves or barrier cream, mix a small batch of resin and hardener in a plastic cup per the manufacturer's instructions.
2) Blend a small amount of red pigment into your resin. With a toothpick, put a tiny quantity of the red resin into the middle compartments of both the oval and triangle bezels. For best results, let the red resin cure for at least six hours or overnight before preparing the turquoise and blue resins and filling the other compartments. This will prevent the colors from bleeding into the adjacent areas.
3) After the red resin has cured, mix another small batch of resin and hardener and pour it into two different cups. Add small amounts of white and blue pigments to one cup to make a turquoise shade. Add only blue pigment to the other cup.
4) With a toothpick, put a small amount of the turquoise resin inside the "wings" of each scarab and inside the bottom compartment of each triangle bezel. Sprinkle some gold microbeads into the turquoise resin.
5) With a fresh toothpick, put a small amount of blue resin inside the remaining compartments of the bezels.
6) Let the resin cure for 12–24 hours.

ASSEMBLY

1) Open a 9 mm jump ring, and attach it to the bottom loop of an oval bezel and the loop of a triangle bezel. Repeat with another jump ring and the other two bezels.
2) Open the loop of an earwire, and attach the top loop of an oval bezel. Repeat to complete the other earring. **B&B**

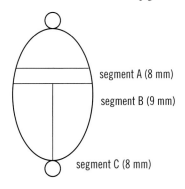

segment A (8 mm)

segment B (9 mm)

segment C (8 mm)

FIGURE 1

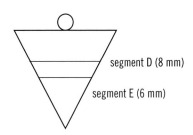

segment D (8 mm)

segment E (6 mm)

FIGURE 2

Contributors

Thomasin Alyxander is a designer living with her two dogs in Windsor, California. When not beading, she enjoys drinking tea and eating chocolate with her nose in a book, and is the author of *26 Quick Stitched Elements: Endless Jewelry Possibilities*. Visit ubeadquitous.com or email her at ubeadquitous@att.net.

Natalija Bekic (La Perla Benatta) is a fine jewelry designer from Switzerland with passion for silver, gold, lace, vintage crystals, and pearls. Contact her at laperlabenatta65@gmail.com, facebook.com/laperla.benatta, or benatta.blogspot.ch.

Jimmie Boatright is a retired public school educator who teaches her original designs at Beadjoux Bead Shop in Braselton, Georgia. Visit beadjoux.com to see more of her designs or to purchase patterns. Contact her at dboatri931@aol.com.

Cary Borelli works full time designing beaded jewelry and writing patterns in Las Vegas, Nevada. Contact her at CreationsbyCary@aol.com or via her Etsy shop, CreationsbyCary.Etsy.Com

Karen Bruns has been beading for 23 years with no plans to stop. She teaches beadweaving and bead embroidery internationally, and at Bead Dreams in Stockton, California. Visit Karen at etsy.com/shop/KarenBrunsDesigns.

Sarah Caligiuri is a Western Shoshone jewelry artist from the Yomba Tribe, merging culture with contemporary design. View her website at wildeelementjewelry.etsy.com. She can be contacted at sarahcreates@yahoo.com.

Alicia Campos is from Spain and started beading about four years ago. She enjoys designing and creating unique jewelry. When not beading, she enjoys reading, listening to music, and going for walks. Contact her at malizzia23@hotmail.com or visit complementosalicia.etsy.com.

Carolyn Cave is the author of two books, *Beautiful Designs with SuperDuos and Twin Beads*, and *Stitching with a Handful of Beads*. She lives in Lacombe, Alberta, and loves creating new designs and textures with beads. E-mail her at ladybeadledesigns@nucleus.com.

Svetlana Chernitsky lives in Israel, has been beading for more than ten years, and loves working with two-hole beads. Email her at lirigal@gmail.com, or visit lirigal.com or etsy.com/shop/lirigal.

Lorraine Coetzee of Cape Town, South Africa, has been beading since 2006. To see more of her work, visit artfire.com/ext/shop/studio/TrinityDesigner-Jewellery. Email her at trinitydj@tiscali.co.za.

Magdalena Dec began beading as a hobby but now teaches and writes a blog called "Ergane Beading." She is inspired by her students. Visit erganebeading.blogspot.com.

Contact **Norma Jean Dell** in care of Kalmbach Books.

Contact **Josane Demuylder** in care of Kalmbach Books.

Patrick Duggan resides in Sydney, Australia. He has been an avid bead weaver since 2007, and his designs are known around the world. His favorite part of beading is designing, engineering, and making new centerpieces, especially with new bead shapes. Purchase more of his tutorials at artfire.com/ext/shop/home/patrickduggandesigns or visit his blog at patrickduggandesigns.blogspot.com.au. Also check out how Patrick works with FireLine: http://patrickduggandesigns.blogspot.com.au/2013/10/the-perfect-connection_18.html.

Diane Fitzgerald is a bead artist, teacher, and writer with 12 published books and more than 100 magazine articles. Please visit her website, dianefitzgerald.com, or contact her at dmfbeads@bitstream.net.

Margherita Fusco lives in Cremona, Italy, and started beading about nine years ago just for fun. Now she knows she has found her true passion in bead weaving. Contact her at fusco_margherita@yahoo.it, or visit 75marghe75.etsy.com or 75marghe75.blogspot.it.

Adrienne Gaskell is passionate about teaching and encouraging innovations in the ancient art form of kumihimo braiding. She can be contacted at agaskell@me.com or via her website, KumihimoResource.com.

Melissa Grakowsky Shippee is a published beadwork designer who teaches workshops internationally, contributes regularly to books and magazines, illustrates diagrams for other instructors, and has won awards for her bead artistry. Her work has been featured in several publications. To view more of Melissa's designs, visit mgsdesigns.net.

Becky Guzman is a full-time bead nerd, designing clay beads, unique kits, and custom jewelry at her lively, full-service bead store and creative studio, Diakonos Designs in Stoughton, Wisconsin. Contact Becky via diakonosdesigns.com or at 608-873-0210.

Olga Haserodt was born in Russia and has been living in Germany for 12 years. She is a self-taught artist who learned how to bead from the internet when she was expecting her third child. She enjoys the creativity of beading and the joy it brings herself and others. Contact Olga at perlenharmonyoase.blogspot.de or visit PerlenHarmonyOase.etsy.com.

Debora Hodoyer was born and raised in Sardinia, a gorgeous island in the middle of the Mediterranean Sea, a land of rich millenary history, culture, and traditions. She's always been involved in various artistic disciplines and loves backpack traveling. Since she discovered the wonderful world of beads, she hasn't looked back. Contact her at crownofstones@outlook.it or visit crownofstones.etsy.com.

Contact **Joanie Jenniges** via email at joanie@beadworkdesigns.com or visit her website, beadworkdesigns.com.

Lisa Kan is an author, bead weaver, jewelry designer, and glass artist. She creates elegant, wearable beadwork that is often modular or reversible, and has been published in many beading magazines. Email her at lisakandesigns@yahoo.com or visit ariadesignstudio.com.

Karen Karon is a chain maille jewelry designer, teacher, and author of two chain maille books. She can be contacted via her website, karenkaron.com.

Cindy Kinerson is a mixed media jewelry artist and full-time owner of the Reno Bead Shop in Reno, Nevada. She can be contacted at cindy@renobeadshop.com or via her web site, renobeadshop.com.

Isabella Lam is the author of *Beautiful Beadweaving*. She is a full-time jewelry artist and instructor who creates original beadwork jewelry with innovative beads. She can be contacted at scarlet@actcom.co.il, or visit her at isabellalam.com oretsy.com/shop/bead4me.

Artists **Lane Landy** and daughter **Cara Landy** work together designing jewelry and creating extremely detailed and easy-to-follow beading tutorials available on their SimpleBeadPatterns.com storefront. Contact Lane at Lane@SimpleBeadPatterns.com.

Visit **Kim Leahy's** website, estherbeadwork.com, or contact her at kimleahy@estherbeadwork.com.

Graziella Malara is a jewelry artist who loves bead weaving and embroidery. Contact Graziella at maegra@alice.it.

Annick Mathieu Puca has always been a creative person, but she finds her greatest joy in beading. She is from France and is the designer of the Kheops par Puca bead and the new Arcos par Puca and Minos par Puca beads. Email Puca at annickmth@gmail.com, and visit perlepuca.canalblog.com and pucashop.etsy.com.

Irina Miech owns Eclectica in Brookfield, Wisconsin, and is the author of many books, including *Wire Jewelry: Beaded and Beautiful*. Contact her via phone at (262) 641-0910 or info@eclecticabeads.com. You can also visit her store website, eclecticabeads.com.

Deb Moffett-Hall is the inventor of the Endless Loom, along with other handy beading tools like the Quick Start Peyote Cards. You can find many more patterns by Deb at patternstobead.com.

Shirley Moore has published several projects and is working on more! Email her at shirleymooredesigns@gmail.com.

Mandi Olaniyi is an aspiring bead designer based in Columbus, Ohio, who likes to experiment with bead stitches by breaking the rules. Her favorite stitch is herringbone. She currently works at her local bead store, 1 Stop Bead Shop. Visit beadwovendreams.etsy.com or email her at beadwovendreams@gmail.com.

Jayashree Paramesh is inspired by fine jewelry and loves to use some gold or silver in her pieces. To see more of her work, please visit Nchantme.com. Many kits and tutorials of her designs are available at etsy.com/shop/Nchantme.

Patricia Parker is a bead artist and board member of the Bead Society of Eastern Pennsylvania. She enjoys sharing her knowledge by teaching bead weaving and can be contacted at roseblubeads@yahoo.com.

Regina Payne is a jewelry designer and teacher who has written several magazine project articles. She can be contacted through her Etsy site, NightOwlStudioJewels, or at regina-payne@hotmail.com.

Szidonia Katalin Petki is a self-taught beader who creates original, elegant, and very easy-to-recreate wearable jewelry designs. Contact her at spetki@gmail.com or visit sidoniasbeads.com and etsy.com/shop/SidoniasBeads.

Cecil Rodriguez dedicates her time designing jewelry that people will enjoy making. These pieces will bring out their individuality, showing the unique qualities that make every person beautiful in their own way. Contact Cecil at cecil.rodriguez33@gmail.com.

Contact **Tamara L. Rubio** in care of Kalmbach Books.

Dana Rudolph is a designer, teacher, and the owner of My Bead Gallery in Englewood, Florida. Contact her at mybeadgallery@gmail.com, or visit mybeadgallery.com or the shop in Florida to see more of Dana's work.

Svetlana Sapegina is a famous Russian bead artist and exhibitor, author, and teacher of bead workshops. Her most extraordinary pieces can be found in art collections belonging to the British Royal Family, First Lady of the USA, Governors of Russian regions, and Russian art museums. Visit superbiser.com or email her at superbiserbysvetlana@gmail.com.

Cassandra Spicer and her husband Chris own Beads To Live By in Jackson, Michigan, where she teaches and spends lots of time communing with the beads. Contact her at cassandra@ beadstoliveby.com or visit beadstoliveby.com.

Justyna Szlezak was a very talented bead artist from Poland. She passed away in 2015 after a battle with cancer. Her "Blooming flower pendant" was published in *Bead&Button* magazine in June, 2015, and several projects have been published since then. Her family is generously allowing us to publish this pattern. Find more of her patterns at inmemoryoferidhan.etsy. com.

Alice Bignami Todd is a self-taught designer whose jewelry is inspired by her fascination with flowers, childhood memories of the seaside, and an interest in ancient history. She enjoys working with resin because it is a very versatile material — you can cast any shape, embed most materials, and even paint with it! Visit resinjewelsbyalice. etsy.com or email her at alicetodd73@ gmail.com.

Jamie Van is a university student from Huntington Beach, California, and an active participant in crafts. She believes in doing what you enjoy. Jamie loves spending time with her family and friends, and loves integrating inspiration found in her surroundings into her designs. Contact Jamie at jamieyoungloving@gmail.com or visit jjbead.com.

Zsuzsanna Veres, also known as Vezsuzsi, is a full-time Hungarian designer who lives in Austria with her husband and two children. She has been designing and teaching since 2008, and has been published in several beading magazines. Contact her at vezsuzsi@ gmail.com, see her blog atvezsuzsi.hu, or visit beadsbyvezsuzsi.etsy.com.

Sharon Wagner is a beadwork designer, and Crystaletts retailer from Sterling Heights, MI. Visit her website, yadasi-beads.com, where you will also find her Etsy shop, or contact her directly at sharonwagner@comcast.net.

Francesca Walton is a hyper-creative polymath residing in Calgary, Alberta. When this amusing, eccentric Scot isn't traveling, she can be contacted at onentxx@aol.com.

Contact **Glynna White** in care of Kalmbach Books.

Marsha L. Wiest-Hines discovered and fell in love with bead weaving in 2007. She has a BFA and MA in Costume Design for Theater, and has made her living for the last 28 years designing for competitive ballroom dancers. Email Marsha at marshawiesthines@gmail. com, visit her Etsy shop at hauteice-beadwork.etsy.com (where she sells kits for this necklace), or read her blog at www.hauteicebeadworks.blogspot.com.

Kristy Zgoda is a full-time jewelry sculptor and pattern designer. Contact her at kristyzgoda@gmail.com and kristyz.zibbet.com.

Gianna Zimmerman is from the Netherlands and has been beading for more than 10 years. She teaches via video on www.etsy.com/shop/b4pbakup, and is the original designer of the AVA bead.

Index

Project Books for Every Bead Stitcher!

Ready, Set, Bead!
25 quick & easy stitching projects
Jane Danley Cruz

Stitching with a Handful of Beads
necklaces • bracelets • earrings • pendants • rings
CAROLYN CAVE

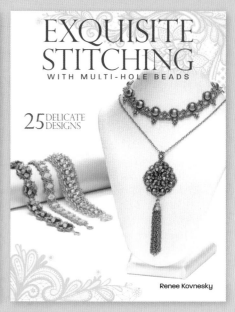

EXQUISITE STITCHING
WITH MULTI-HOLE BEADS
25 DELICATE DESIGNS
Renee Kovnesky

Ready, Set, Bead!

Designer Jane Danley Cruz shares 25+ stitching projects you can create in just one sitting using easy-to-find, affordable beads and materials.

#67895 • $21.99

Stitching with a Handful of Beads

Bust your stash! Each of the 25+ projects in Carolyn Cave's new book only uses 2–5 types of seed beads, crystals, pearls, and shaped beads.

#67898 • $22.99

Exquisite Stitching with Multi-Hole Beads

Renee Kovnesky offers 25 projects for beautiful and delicate necklaces, bracelets, earrings, and pendants that are ideal for stitchers at every level.

#67903 • $21.99

Buy now from your favorite craft or bead shop!
Shop at JewelryandBeadingStore.com

KALMBACH BOOKS

Sales tax where applicable.
P31885